MANAGEMENT AND THE SPECIAL SCHOOL

MANAGEMENT & THE SPECIAL SCHOOL

EDITED BY
TONY BOWERS

CROOM HELM
London • Sydney • Dover, New Hampshire

Croom Helm Ltd, Provident House, Burrell Row,
Beckenham, Kent BR3 1AT

Croom Helm Australia Pty Ltd, Suite 4, 6th Floor,
64-76 Kippax Street, Surry Hills, NSW 2010, Australia

Croom Helm, 51 Washington Street,
Dover, New Hampshire 03820, USA

Reprinted 1985

British Library Cataloguing in Publication Data

Management and the special school.
1. Exceptional children – Education – Great Britain 2. School management and organisation – Great Britain
I. Bowers, Tony
371.9'042'0941 LC 3986.G7

ISBN0-7099-3231-6

Printed and bound in Great Britain by
Biddles Ltd, Guildford and King's Lynn

CONTENTS

Contributors to this Book

Acknowledgements

Figures and Tables

Introduction 1

SECTION 1 - LEADERSHIP IN A CHANGING ENVIRONMENT 5

1. The Future of the Special School 6
by John Fish

2. Curriculum Development in Special Schools: The Role of Management 21
by Mel Ainscow

3. Change in the Special School 40
by Tony Bowers

4. Headship: Aspects of the Role 51
by Peter Turner

5. Shared Leadership in the School - "Primus inter pares" 67
by Ian Galletley

SECTION 2 - LINKING THE SPECIAL SCHOOL WITH OUTSIDE SYSTEMS 82

6. Special Schools and the Mainstream - "The Resource Stretch" 83
by Tony Dessent

7. Governors and the Special School 98
by Terry Bailey

8. **Links with Other Professionals: The Head as a Multidisciplinary Team Member** 116
by Vic Thomson

9. **Parents of Children with Moderate Learning Difficulties** 129
by Mike Marra

10. **Working with Parents of Emotionally Disturbed Children** 148
by Muriel Colley

SECTION 3 - STAFF DEVELOPMENT 164

11. **Power and Conflict: Facts of Life** 165
by Tony Bowers

12. **Special Needs and School-Focused In-Service Education** 180
by Vivien Casteel

13. **Developing Effective Teams** 199
by Richard Knight and Tony Bowers

References 215

Subject Index 224

CONTRIBUTORS TO THIS BOOK

TONY BOWERS (Editor), Tutor in Psychology and Special Education at the Cambridge Institute of Education.

*****

MEL AINSCOW, Adviser for Special Education, Coventry.

TERRY BAILEY, Adviser for Special Education, London Borough of Enfield.

VIVIEN CASTEEL, Head Teacher, Colnbrook School, South Oxhey, Watford, Hertfordshire.

MURIEL COLLEY, Head Teacher, Cavendish School, London Borough of Ealing.

TONY DESSENT, Senior Educational Psychologist, Cambridgeshire.

JOHN FISH, until recently Staff H.M.I. for Special Education.

IAN GALLETLEY, Senior Adviser for Special Education, Newcastle upon Tyne (at the time of writing, Head Teacher, Kirkleatham Hall School, Cleveland).

RICHARD KNIGHT, Principal Officer, Essex Social Services.

MIKE MARRA, Head Teacher, Shawfold School, Stockport.

VIC THOMSON, Head Teacher, Bennett House School, Abingdon, Oxfordshire.

PETER TURNER, Head Teacher, Whitefield School, London Borough of Waltham Forest.

ACKNOWLEDGEMENT

My grateful thanks go to all the contributors to this book and to Barbara Shannon for her untiring assistance in the preparation of the manuscript.

A.J.B.
Cambridge.

FIGURES AND TABLES

Figure 1:	Curriculum Development - Four Levels of Decision-Making	24
Figure 2:	The Stages of Curriculum Development	32
Figure 3:	Roles in Curriculum Evaluation	38
Figure 4:	Typical Special School Structure	79
Figure 5:	Traditional Hierarchy	79
Figure 6:	Alternative Management Strategy	80
Figure 7:	Typical Primary School Power Dependency Model	170
Figure 8:	Special School Power Dependency Model	171
Figure 9:	Example Appraisal Interview Form	187
Table A:	Rank Ordering of Means for Teaching Aims	113

INTRODUCTION

by Tony Bowers

If today we were to be faced with the task of developing, from a baseline of no provision, a service for pupils with special needs, there would no doubt be considerable debate over whether separate institutions, in the form of special schools, were desirable or necessary. As in most educational issues, however, what happens now has to be placed in the context of what has gone before. As Chapter 2 of the Warnock Report (D.E.S., 1978) chronicles, the first special schools were founded nearly two hundred years ago; after the 1944 Education Act, the growth in special school provision was considerable, largely reflecting an attempt - again in the context of thinking at that time - to make some positive discrimination in favour of pupils seen as handicapped. The inclusion of pupils who before the 1970 Education Act would have been seen as "ineducable" meant that at that time we again saw a large increase in the number of special schools as the former junior training centres became administered by local education authorities.

It is now, of course, generally recognised that a substantially larger number of children than can - or should - be provided for in special schools have some form of special educational needs. The 1981 Education Act has placed responsibility upon ordinary schools to make special educational provision available within them and upon L.E.A.s to ensure the education of any child with identified needs within an ordinary school. These requirements, however, are moderated by the conditions in Section 2(3) of the Act. Special schools, at the time of writing, seem likely still to form a part of the continuum of provision for pupils with special needs.

As Tomlinson (1982) has pointed out, those in special schools now face more pressure for accountability than has hitherto been the case. Such demands spring, obviously, from current legislation, in particular the 1981 Education Act, with its insistence that children's needs be identified and appropriate action by the school be evaluated through the annual review procedures. A second and pervasive source of the current demands, however, is the restrictive economic atmosphere which has grown over recent years. Special education, and the differing services under its umbrella, are competing for resources in a period of retrenchment in commitment to educational and social services. Increasingly, however much it may be realistic or fair, "value for money" is likely to become a yardstick by which all are judged. Beyond legislative and economic pressures, though, is that which derives from the internal scrutiny and judgement of colleagues within special education. This third and positive force for accountability, often as uncomfortable as it is valuable, makes it incumbent upon practitioners to incorporate contemporary knowledge and techniques within their work and to be able to articulate their reasons for using or rejecting any of these.

In considering teacher education and training, the Warnock Report (D.E.S., 1978) noted the importance of courses directed towards the development of managerial skills in head teachers and senior staff concerned with children with special needs. In most cases, when such training has been made available for the staff of special schools, it has been as part of other offerings for primary or secondary school staff, such as those currently organised as part of the training initiative set out in D.E.S. Circular 3/83. The works in this book provide an attempt to look at some of the issues which arise for those in managerial positions in special schools. In many cases they may not differ significantly in principle from those encountered in the management of any small or medium-sized organisation; their content and context, however, justify their being given separate consideration. The book has not set out to address itself to concrete administrative issues, since these may differ in substance from one L.E.A. to another, and between maintained, non-maintained and independent schools. Resolving administrative confusions, of course, may in itself call for considerable managerial skills, and it is hoped that aspects of leadership behaviour in relation to these are given sufficient consideration.

Given the diverse backgrounds and approaches of contributors, it is hardly surprising that at times conflicting views are expressed. This is no bad thing: the reader is invited to consider the approaches advocated by each author in the light of his or her own experiences, using them where necessary to shed light upon and modify practice in the workplace. The book is divided into three sections, although some overlap between them is, of course, inevitable.

In the first section, entitled Leadership in a Changing Environment, John Fish examines the future implications for special schools. Having analysed the current strengths and weaknesses of special schools he looks, in the context of non-categorical placement, at possible organisational and curricular structures which may need to be adopted. As a link with the second section, he warns against the special school adopting a rigid and self-isolating role, examining the idea of an area special school and some of the conditions which must be met for a special school to operate as an area resource. The vital place of effective leadership in developing and implementing a curriculum appropriate to pupils' needs is emphasised by Mel Ainscow. Advocating a participative style if staff involvement and commitment are to be fostered, he looks not only at the process which a school needs to adopt but at the ways in which resisters among the staff may be responded to. His concern is with change, and in the third chapter Tony Bowers elaborates on the process of change, the task of management in achieving it and the effects which changes in expectations of them may have upon staff members.

An innovator himself, Peter Turner looks at key aspects of the role of the special school head teacher in relation to delegation, co-ordination and leadership of staff whose professional expectations and skills may differ widely. He examines, too, the varying levels of "community" which the school services, and the head's role in ensuring that parents' needs are adequately met. Like Mel Ainscow, he sees optimum results springing from staff consultation, advocating an appropriate forum within the school for this. This theme is further expanded upon in the final chapter in this section, in which Ian Galletley, who as head of two special schools has encouraged the formation of staff decision-taking bodies, considers the issues involved in sharing leadership rather than attempting to impose it.

The second section directs itself particularly to the special school's interface with outside systems. Elaborating upon the resource role of the special school which John Fish raises in Chapter One, Tony Dessent points out that any developments will be dependent on the quality of the services that mainstream schools within its environment are able to provide for children with special needs. Looking at the nature of the resources which may be provided, he outlines the conditions under which an effective resource delivery may be achieved. Importantly, he sees any such development as a stage in a changing process of special educational provision. As a link with the community and the surrounding educational system, governors have a vital - if seldom realised - role. Terry Bailey reviews recent research into governor effectiveness and provides comprehensive suggestions for ways in which they can play a more involved part in the operation of the school.

In looking at the head's role, Chapter Four discusses relationships with parents and with other professionals. This last topic is explored by Vic Thomson in Chapter Eight: educators in special schools must be prepared and able to work in concert with others whose professional perspectives and primary objectives may differ from their own. Such preparation has implications for the internal organisation of the school and for the way in which responsibilities are allocated. Finally within this section, two head teachers provide their own accounts of the ways in which parents are consulted and involved within their schools. A recent work by Mittler and McConachie (1983) has examined the school's role in relation to parents of pupils with severe learning difficulties; in Chapters Nine and Ten, Mike Marra and Muriel Colley respectively look at their responses to parents in schools for children formerly classified as moderately learning disabled and emotionally disturbed.

Section 3 is entitled Staff Development since it deals with aspects of the personal and professional growth of individuals working within the school. Vivien Casteel, whose school has a long history of school-focused INSET, recounts the process of integrating an in-service system with the school's curriculum and looks at some of the constraints which may impose themselves. In the following chapter, Tony Bowers pays attention to the demands which those in leadership positions inevitably must meet, analysing the influences which can be brought to bear on and by them within special schools. The potential for conflict is heightened within a multidisciplinary setting, and some approaches to dealing with this are considered. Finally, the critical issues of leadership style and team development are addressed by Dick Knight and Tony Bowers. We hear the term "team" used so often, but how can staff be encouraged to work cohesively rather than divisively? In the last chapter, the role of management in achieving this end, so important if special education is to be effective, comes under scrutiny.

It is intended that this book should be read by practitioners; those contributing to it have extensive experience of successful work with children with special educational needs. There is no doubt that many special schools still have much to do to improve their practice: it is hoped that this book, directed at those holding or intending to hold leadership positions, will assist in this.

SECTION 1

– LEADERSHIP IN A CHANGING ENVIRONMENT

Chapter One

THE FUTURE OF THE SPECIAL SCHOOL

by John Fish

Special institutions for those who are handicapped have existed for over two hundred years and the availability of special schools for all who need them has increased markedly in this century. Although the most impassioned advocates of integration wish to see them disappear from the education system, in many countries they are likely to fulfil an important role in the foreseeable future. The question to be answered therefore is not whether special schools should continue to exist but what should be their contribution within a range of special educational arrangements. Pressure to educate more children with disabilities and significant difficulties within ordinary schools will and should continue although primary and secondary schools will continue to set some limits on the nature and degree of difficulties with which they are able to deal.

What have changed significantly are the reasons for the existence of special schools. The assumption that such schools were the right place for all children assessed as handicapped is now questioned. The educational needs of individuals with the same disabilities are now recognised as different. For some, needs may be satisfactorily met in ordinary schools given appropriate special supporting arrangements. Thus the future of special schools now depends more on the limitations of ordinary schools to deal effectively with individual differences. It no longer depends on the belief that there is a separate group of children for whom they provide the only educational answers. This shift in attitudes and in the understanding of individual differences requires that special schools of the future should be much clearer about what they have to offer. Their future development needs to be considered in close collaboration with those responsible for ordinary schools and not as the central component of a separate special education system.

The purpose of this chapter is to look ahead, to

consider trends to which special schools will need to respond and suggest possible lines for future development. Before doing so it may be helpful to look at the recent history of special education and the major ideas developed in the Warnock Report (D.E.S., 1978), and this constitutes the next section devoted to the background to future developments. This is followed by an appraisal of the strengths and weaknesses of special schools as they exist. On this basis a major section deals with the dimensions or parameters which might now determine terms of reference for special schools in the future. The final section poses some questions which might form an agenda for the detailed discussion of the future contribution of individual schools.

THE BACKGROUND

The early history of special education was dominated by the provision of special institutions or schools for categories of handicap. These categories were determined by medical diagnosis. Training and subsequently education in a broader sense was developed to meet the needs of groups supposed to be homogeneous on the basis of their medical classification. The Education Act 1944, although forward looking in many aspects and bringing special educational treatment within the framework of ordinary education, enshrined this approach. Categories of handicap were defined based on a medical examination and there was an implicit assumption at the time that educational methods would be developed in each category.

In the last forty years the basis for assessing special educational needs has broadened with increasing contributions from psychologists, teachers and therapists of all kinds. Experience has shown that children with the same disability vary widely in their response to it depending on such factors as family and social circumstances, intelligence and personality and on the social and educational situations with which they are faced. The handicapping effects of the disability or difficulty can vary widely depending on these factors and on the effectiveness of early intervention programmes and other special arrangements. Similarly, more comprehensive assessment procedures have shown many children to have a mixture of disabilities and difficulties so that many cannot be neatly fitted into mutually exclusive categories.

However, even where individual difficulties are recognised, the need for particular methodologies, such as oral methods of teaching the hearing impaired, or therapies, has continued to determine the grouping of children in special schools, often creating major educational problems. The special schools for children with physical disabilities provide a good example of these difficulties. Children grouped for medical supervision, nursing care and a variety of therapies may range in educational needs from potential 'A' level candidates to children with very severe learning difficulties. In a school of 100–150 pupils from 4+ to 18+, age groups are small and appropriate education for all almost impossible to achieve. If one then starts to place the most able and most successful children in ordinary schools with support, as has been the case, the nature of the learning difficulties and the curriculum, rather than the disability, become the reasons for the school's existence.

These trends, namely the increased recognition of individual differences and combinations of disabilities and difficulties, the decreasing appropriateness of existing categories and increasing education expectations provide the background to current problems. When the Warnock Committee started work it might have moved in one of two directions. One way might have been to change and increase the number of categories. There was pressure in this direction as illustrated by the setting up of schools for autistic children and for those described as dyslexic. The other approach was to do away with categories and this was the conclusion of the Committee. It, in a sense, returned to the basic approach of the 1944 Act, namely that each child should be educated according to his age, aptitude and ability.

The Warnock Committee considered the distinction made between handicapped children and ordinary children as damaging and irrelevant. They endorsed the notion of a continuum of special educational needs and saw no further use for categories. A child's special educational needs and the means to meet them should be assessed individually and a range of provision to meet them in ordinary schools and elsewhere should be developed. The Committee considered that special schools would continue to be important elements in that range of provision. These ideas have now been incorporated in the 1981 Education Act.

Although the Warnock Report (D.E.S., 1978) had much to say about the role of special schools as resource centres, it did not comment in detail about the range and kinds of special school which might be needed in the future. This topic has been discussed at courses and conferences but as yet little has been written about the future structure and functions of special schools in the light of new legislation. Economic restrictions and falling rolls have resulted in a defence of the status quo rather than new thinking. Research and development work on the future contribution of special schools in a range of special educational provision is now urgent.

The new legislation, which specifies procedures for multiprofessional assessment and for making statements of special educational needs and the provision to meet them, requires special schools to be clear about what they offer. They will need to be more precise about their curriculum and organisation, the services and therapies available and the limits of what they can provide. Before the 1981 Act placement in a special school could be likened to a parent signing a blank cheque. Now the statement is a form of contract between the local education authority and the parents, and special schools will be required to provide the educational services defined in the statement.

It will take some time for the new approaches to be widely understood. Old ideas and attitudes will persist for some time. It is therefore important to recognise the background and context against which new developments are taking place when considering the future of special schools.

CURRENT STRENGTHS AND WEAKNESSES OF SPECIAL SCHOOLS

As has been said, many of the problems of special schools stem from outmoded ideas such as the belief in homogeneous categories and in the implicit value of special schooling. Those recommending such placements seldom specified their expectations in any detail. Those responsible for their administration seldom set them clear terms of reference. Those running them are only now being required to describe their curriculum in any detail. The challenge of new legislation and in particular the recent emphasis on integration has tended to polarise views. It is a fact of life that people who emphasise the value of special schools stress their strengths while those who wish to see them disappear emphasise their weaknesses. Perhaps one way forward is to consider the current balance of strengths and weaknesses and see how the former can be maintained and the latter overcome in the future.

One of the most commonly accepted strengths of the special school is the concentration of knowledge and experience which can be built up by a team working with children with a specific disability or with complex learning difficulties. This specialist knowledge, together with the insights and skills necessary to enable children considered handicapped to learn, is an important aspect of special education. It is difficult for the single teacher in charge of a unit in an ordinary school to acquire. In the special school good leadership can ensure that the staff share experience and collaborate with each other in solving common problems. As a result, the good special school is a source of information about the effects of disabilities, about the associated educational, social and personal learning problems that result from them and about the best methods to overcome these problems.

Secondly, it is possible to develop appropriate variations of the curriculum, materials and methods for the population for which the school caters. The effectiveness of the curriculum can be evaluated over a reasonable time span, particularly in the all-age school. Individual programmes can be planned within the school's curriculum framework. Because most schools are small, the staff can know each other's work and together develop a programme which is both consistent and coherent.

A further strength in many schools is the opportunity to develop multiprofessional approaches to problems. Teachers and therapists can develop collaborative patterns of working. Visiting and peripatetic specialists can concentrate some of their efforts in such schools and develop cooperative approaches.

Finally, but by no means of least importance, is the care and concern for the individual which it is possible to develop. Children who might fail to thrive in the ordinary school may receive understanding help and develop confidence in an environment sensitive to their needs.

In summary, the active, thoughtful, well-run special school can be a major resource centre for the group of special educational needs it is set up to meet. It can develop and promote specialist teaching competencies and develop methods and materials. Above all it can provide a setting in which an individual's special educational needs can be assessed, understood and met.

The major weaknesses are also well known. Schools originally set up for one category of handicap now recognise that their pupils have a wide range of other disabilities and associated learning difficulties. A small school for one disability group may have an ability and achievement range as wide as a comprehensive school ten times its size covering half its age range. Such schools have few children in each age group. It is difficult to provide educational programmes at many different levels which challenge both the able and the least able.

By concentrating on the special characteristics of their population, many special schools have become remote from the standards and expectations of ordinary schools for children of the same age. Their curriculum has been developed in isolation, and a preoccupation with overcoming learning difficulties, particularly in language and literacy, has narrowed the range of educational experience offered. A broader approach might itself stimulate communication. However, a small staff often limits the curriculum offered, particularly at the secondary stage.

Children being taught with others with similar

disabilities and difficulties over a long period have few opportunities to interact with their contemporaries in ordinary schools. They may be sheltered from many situations which they will eventually have to face as young adults in the community. Social confidence and competence may be limited as a consequence. Without regular opportunities to live and learn with others who do not have their difficulties, the transition to adult life in the community can be more difficult.

In summary, the special school provides an artificial social situation and limited opportunities to learn to live in an ordinary community. Educational opportunities may, in many instances be restricted, particularly for older and abler pupils. Few schools as yet maintain a close and regular educational association with ordinary schools which might overcome some of these limitations.

TERMS OF REFERENCE FOR SPECIAL SCHOOLS IN THE FUTURE

It may be relatively easy to agree on criteria to determine which children with special educational needs should be the subject of statements and which should be placed in special schools. It is much more difficult to decide what kind of special schools are needed for them. Categories are now abolished. Grouping children for the effective delivery of health services and therapies, while attractive in times of limited resources, does not often provide a school population appropriately grouped for educational purposes. How should children be grouped in special schools in the future? What should be the main factors determining the terms of reference of special schools?

These questions are difficult to answer and there are a number of factors which influence the kind of answer which might be given. These include the incidence of different disabilities and difficulties, the geographical nature of the area or region to be served and whether individuals require day or boarding special schools. We now know that the incidence of special educational needs requiring special school provision will be determined to a large extent by the degree to which primary and secondary schools are able to cater for individual differences and meet special educational needs. The nature and incidence of disabilities has in the previous era of categories had a strong influence on the grouping of children and on whether day or boarding provision is needed. It is the main contention of this contribution that in future the major determinant of a special school's contribution should be the nature of its educational programme and that other factors should be considered in this light.

Before developing this statement in more detail it is necessary to consider another dimension, namely the time which a child might spend in a special school. There are perhaps four different types of attendance at a special school in terms of time, two common and two less common. The first might be described as "full-time long term" where an individual is expected to receive all his primary and/or secondary education in a special school. An example of this time scale might be the education of children with severe learning difficulties (E.S.N.(S) in the previous terminology). A second common type of attendance may be described as "full-time short term" where a child may attend a special school for a few years either to solve problems or to acquire special techniques for education in ordinary schools. Such placements might be made in the case of maladjusted behaviour or specific learning difficulties. The two less common types might be described as "part-time" and "regular intermittent short term" placements. In the case of the former, a child remains on the roll of the ordinary school and attends the special school for a number of sessions each week. Children with behaviour difficulties have been provided for in this way. Finally, the regular intermittent short term arrangement, although not used in the U.K. as a matter of policy, is used in some countries for children with visual or hearing disabilities. The residential special school in this instance provides a series of special courses each year for pupils and their teachers in ordinary schools to back up integration by providing special teaching, counselling and recreational activities while at the same time acting as a resource for the ordinary school and peripatetic services.

If the educational programme is to be the major determinant of the work of a special school then the four time dimensions outlined will influence the kind of programme. In the first instance the school will need to be the base for all the educational experiences of the child. The curriculum will need to be broad, covering all areas of study and all skills and competences. The second type of placement provides perhaps the most difficult education problems since there will be a natural tendency to concentrate on the learning difficulties. At the same time the educational programme will need to be broad enough to enable the individual to make a reasonable adjustment to the ordinary school programme at the end of his placement. The third and fourth types do allow the special schools to collaborate closely with ordinary schools. They can concentrate on the individual's special needs and learning difficulties while he is having access to the ordinary school curriculum.

One decision therefore that needs to be taken is the

time scale or phase of the child's education on which the special school should concentrate. If this is to be full-time long term then a division into primary and secondary schools is recommended by the Warnock Committee. There will be the additional question of how many of the time scales should be expected as part of a single school's terms of reference.

The next major question is what is meant by the educational programme. In this context it is the planned and taught curriculum of the special school. This cannot be derived from the sum of the individual programmes required by pupils in the school. On the contrary, individual programmes can only be adequately planned within the curriculum framework and resources of the school. As has already been mentioned, it is virtually impossible for a small special school to provide both the range of the ordinary school curriculum and appropriate variations for a range of achievements from public examination levels to severe degrees of intellectual impairment. What then might define a special school's educational programme?

The Warnock Report argued that the aims of education should be the same for all children, but that the goals for those with severe learning difficulties would be more limited. It also stated that the special education curriculum should be as broad in scope as that for ordinary schools and educational expectations should be as high as possible. Similarly, Wilson (1981) argued for a close association with the ordinary school curriculum. Hence what is suggested is not a series of special school curricula developed in isolation from mainstream developments, but a series of variations of the curriculum for all children. As a start it may be helpful to consider three kinds of variation:

(1) A curriculum similar in range and level to that taught to the majority in ordinary schools, modified by the means by which it is taught and perhaps the pace. The modifications would include special techniques and equipment in the case of sensory or physical disabilities and attention to the setting and relationships in the case of those who are maladjusted.

(2) A curriculum similar in range to that taught in ordinary schools, but modified in terms of objectives and pace. Such a curriculum designed for children who are slow to learn, or with moderate learning difficulties, should be realistic in what can be accomplished in the time available. It should, however, have relatively

high levels of expectation and be much less dependent on literacy skills for access to the normal range of subjects or areas of study.

(3) A curriculum for children with severe learning difficulties which places major emphasis on the development of social skills and personal autonomy. The choice of experiences and objectives should reflect those encountered by the majority of children.

One further point should be made about the ordinary school curriculum. It is recognised that the curriculum and methodology for slow learning and less successful pupils in ordinary schools is not always well thought out or appropriate. The future development of a curriculum variation for them in ordinary schools should go hand in hand with the development of (2) above. In suggesting this variant for a group of special schools, the intention is that a useful amalgamation of good practice in both ordinary and special schools might be effected in future.

How might this approach affect the future pattern of special schools? At present it is difficult to answer this question as there have been few analyses of the special school population in terms of curriculum needs. However, as special schools develop curriculum statements, and as new assessment procedures specify educational needs more precisely, progress may be possible. It will however require a radical shift from thinking of the population in terms of categories. This should not mean abandoning specialist teaching skills such as those required to teach the visual and hearing handicapped, children with severe learning difficulties or those who are maladjusted. It may mean new groupings of these skills on the staff of individual special schools.

To make this point clearer it may be helpful to consider the group of schools previously described as catering for the E.S.N.(S) group. Firstly, these schools have been active in developing a curriculum similar to that specified in (3) above. Secondly, as well as severe learning difficulties, many children in these schools have physical and sensory disabilities and behaviour difficulties. Thirdly, cooperative work has developed between teachers of the blind and deaf and the staff of these schools to produce appropriate individual programmes and materials. In summary, the main reason for placement has been a curricular one. In any new pattern of provision these schools would continue to be an important element.

If the same approach is adopted to the former E.S.N.(M) schools developing the curriculum variant (2) above, then they may be expected to include a wider range of disabilities and difficulties, always provided that the curriculum is appropriate for the individual. Provided the staff included some specialists or that they were regularly available to the school, less severe physical and sensory disabilities might be appropriately placed in these schools. Pupils with behaviour difficulties already are.

It is with variant (1) that most difficulties might arise for two reasons. Firstly, it is children in this group who may be most likely over time to have their needs met in ordinary schools, so that it may become a smaller group. Secondly, in small special schools it is difficult to provide specialist teaching to the level required for the whole curriculum. Nevertheless, a small group of special schools catering for severe degrees of specific disabilities or of maladjustment will be necessary.

What seems relatively clear is that no special school can currently provide all three variants of the curriculum and attempts to provide two have not been notably successful. If the primary purpose of the special school is educational, and if social welfare and health considerations are secondary, then the next generation of special schools must have a defensible educational role. This role must be practicable and they must be staffed to enable them to carry it out. It is likely that they will only be able to provide one variant successfully.

SOME OTHER CONSIDERATIONS

Many of the problems of special schools have resulted from a fixed concept of the self-sufficient school doing its own thing. The care and concern for individuals has resulted in a fortress mentality where children are protected from the harsh realities of ordinary life as exemplified by their unrewarding experiences in primary and secondary schools, or that such experiences would be unrewarding if they had them. Although this is changing, other forms of special school organisation may be worth considering. One has already been mentioned, namely the school providing regular intermittent short term help, which is highly specialised and supports children in ordinary schools.

Another form which may be worth considering is the dispersed area special school. In the Swedish Mental Handicap Service, each county has a number of special schools with a headmaster, staff and support service. But the classes of the school are often dispersed in groups of two or three in ordinary schools with the appropriate age range. There is a coherent special school policy and a staff working on the agreed curriculum but this is supplemented by social interaction in ordinary schools and some curriculum input from the ordinary school staff in specialist areas. Could this be one approach in rural areas or where travelling to a central school is costly and time consuming?

Another consideration is the question of boarding education. It has come into being to collect together enough children with the same disability, to provide social care where homes are under stress and to avoid travelling long distances daily. It has been seen as important in dealing with some kinds of maladjustment. However, its educational justification is less certain. When social service departments are turning from residential provision to a more widespread use of fostering, what are the educational grounds for continuing to provide boarding special education? This question will need to be tackled when planning the future of special schools.

THE SPECIAL SCHOOL AS A RESOURCE CENTRE

No discussion of the future of the special school would be complete without looking at this topic. The Warnock Report (D.E.S., 1978) made the suggestion that many special schools should be able to help ordinary schools assess and provide for children with special educational needs. As a result, to become a resource centre has come to be seen by many as a passport to survival in the age of integration. There are a number of different ideas as to what this means in practice and it may be helpful to consider two related aspects, namely, what are the necessary preconditions in a special school to becoming a resource centre and what sort of a centre might it become?.

It is generally agreed that not all special schools are capable of becoming resource centres. One precondition is that they should be effective well run schools which provide effectively for the children who attend them. This can be made more specific in a number of ways. The school needs to know its own limits and not attempt to be too omniscient. In terms of the new Act it should know the range of disabilities or difficulties for which it can provide, it should have a well devised and documented educational programme, and it should know and work well with the appropriate supporting and peripatetic services it needs. In addition it should know, use and develop the specialist skills of members of staff.

Among these skills, four may be particularly important. These are the educational assessment of individuals which together with the skills of task analysis and programme planning result in work appropriately adapted for individuals. Secondly, the school will need to have curriculum development skills and an imaginative curriculum framework and educational programme. Thirdly, it should have the capacity to adapt and develop appropriate materials and to use appropriate technology. Finally, and by no means least important, members of staff should be skilled in collaborative and co-teaching so that they can work with colleagues in ordinary schools.

There is one other precondition which may be summed up as a detailed knowledge of how ordinary schools function. The staff of the special school should know the constraints under which ordinary schools work. They should know their local schools and have built up working relationships with them over time. Special schools need to study the special educational problems which arise in primary and secondary schools and the kinds of provision for them which they make.

All this implies that there is a necessary period of preparation before a school can offer assistance and resources. This preparation will also include estimating the teacher time necessary for work with ordinary schools and if possible obtaining additional staffing to enable work outside the school to be done without serious interference with the school's own programme.

These last considerations cannot be discussed in any detail unless decisions are taken about the kind of resource centre the school aims to be. Before outlining possible activities there will be differences resulting from the nature of the school's main task. For example, schools for moderate learning difficulties and for children who are maladjusted may have something to offer to all ordinary schools in their area. Schools catering for physical and sensory disabilities may have wider catchment areas and only work with some schools. Each special school may have general skills and expertise, for example in assessment and programme planning, and special skills related to one aspect of special education.

What kind of resource centre should a special school attempt to be? Again there are at least four different possibilities:

(1) The school can be on call. Having made its work and resources known to ordinary schools, it can wait to be asked to help with an individual problem or with a general problem in its field. This may not be very different from current practice where schools are open and welcoming, and teachers in primary and secondary schools find it useful to call in for advice and help. Visitors may also borrow materials.

(2) Teachers from the special school may undertake

regular advisory and teaching activities in ordinary schools. Working with regular teachers, they may assess and prepare programmes and material and work with small groups of children drawing on the resources of the special school.

(3) The school can provide teaching sessions for groups of children from primary and secondary schools. These regular sessions may provide specialised teaching not available in ordinary schools.

(4) The school can act as a centre for in-service training for teachers in primary and secondary schools.

It is not suggested that these functions are mutually exclusive or that special schools can only offer one of them. What is suggested is that each involves a different use of the school's resources and each needs to be planned differently.

In summary there is considerable scope for schools to act as resource centres in the future, but to do so many of the points discussed earlier in this chapter have to be considered. A role as a resource centre will depend on the kind of special school which emerges in the next few years.

THE WAY FORWARD

There are some important traditions in special schools which should not be lost in future changes. But there are also long-standing special interests which separate existing types of special schools and specialist teachers, and a history of isolation from mainstream education. The way forward will depend on questioning many accepted ideas and practices.

The nature of the special school population has changed both in the type and degree of disability and significant difficulty. More children with a single disability are being educated with special help in ordinary schools. The population of many special schools is becoming more severely and multiply handicapped. Now that categories have been discontinued there is a need for a new look at the special school population, new ways to describe educational needs and new ways to group children in schools. This chapter has set out some of the dimensions which may need consideration in future.

It is recognised that the pattern of special school

provision may need to be different in urban and rural areas and in highly populated and sparsely populated regions. The balance between special school and unit provision in ordinary schools may continue to shift towards the latter. What is argued is that a new rationale for the existence of special schools is needed. Because in future, placements will be based on individually assessed needs and not allocation to categories, the needs to be met by special schools, which cannot be met in ordinary schools, will need to be more precisely stated. The functions of an individual school and the services it offers will have to be clearly specified.

A central feature of this specification should now be the nature of the educational programme offered and the variant of the general curriculum for schools being taught. This should normally cover in its own way the range of experiences and fields of knowledge offered to other children so as to minimise isolation from the mainstream of education. At the same time, this close association may help to modify what is on offer to less successful learners in ordinary schools.

The tradition of assuming that most special schools provide day or boarding full-time education over a primary and/or secondary phase needs to be questioned. There may be other forms of special school and other forms of organisation which need to be explored. As special educational provision for the individual is adjusted over the compulsory school period to meet changing needs, there is likely to be an increase in the number of children moving in and out of different elements in the range. More schools may have a short-term or part-time role. More time may need to be devoted to backing up and reinforcing attendance in ordinary schools.

Finally, the place of boarding education will have to be reviewed to establish the educational grounds for its continued existence. Many placements are now made for social reasons at a time when social services are actively providing alternatives.

This attempt to discuss the future of special schools poses more questions than it answers. It is by no means exhaustive and only touches on a selection of major issues. Planning the future pattern of special schools and determining the functions of individual schools needs more attention. The recent past has seen an increasing knowledge of individual difficulties, more sophisticated assessment procedures and better plans for individuals. The range of provision to meet individual needs has during the same period increased in an ad hoc way with little fundamental research into what elements in that range can and should contribute. Special schools as vital constituents have lacked a clear brief from those who administer and use them. It is hoped that the next decade will see these issues tackled.

Chapter Two

CURRICULUM DEVELOPMENT IN SPECIAL SCHOOLS: THE ROLE OF MANAGEMENT

by Mel Ainscow

This chapter makes the case that a concern with curriculum development is an essential feature of an effective special school and that it is a head teacher's responsibility to establish a working atmosphere in which such developments can occur. It goes on to examine how this can be accomplished, examining theory and practice of innovation and implications for management roles.

Whilst the chapter is written from the point of view of the head teacher, other aspects of leadership are discussed, particularly the work of post holders. To illustrate the points I wish to make I have drawn from my own experience and my observations of other heads in a variety of special schools.

IMPORTANCE OF CURRICULUM DEVELOPMENT

Recent years have seen an increased interest in the idea of curriculum planning in special education (Wilson, 1981). Not so many years ago, for example, little or no reference was made to the theory of curriculum on advanced courses for special education teachers. Furthermore, the curriculum in many special schools tended to emphasise the need for care and enrichment, and consisted of a range of largely unrelated experiences derived from the interests of individual members of staff.

Why then this change of emphasis? Why is there now so much concern with curriculum planning in special education?

In part this new trend reflects the changes in thinking about how children with special needs should be educated. The traditional approach, with its emphasis on labelling, segregation and care was based on the assumption that a child's educational progress was largely a function of his personal abilities and attributes. More recently we have come to recognise that the situation is far more complex and that a child's special needs result from the interaction of his individual aptitudes and the environment in which he exists (Wedell, 1981). This has led to a greater sense of optimism that environmental factors can be manipulated in order to ameliorate individual difficulties (Ainscow and Tweddle, 1979). Within school a key variable is the curriculum in terms of both its planning and implementation.

Many educationalists recognise that successful schools share certain attributes (e.g. Rhine, 1981; Rutter et al, 1979). So, for example, the Warnock Report states that whenever high quality special education is evident two features emerge:

> First, well defined guidelines for each area of the curriculum have been drawn up, which enable teachers to plan their own work and relate it to that of colleagues and other professionals. Secondly, programmes have been planned for individual children with clearly defined short-term goals within the general plan. (D.E.S. 1978, 11.15)

The first part of this quotation is equally applicable to any form of educational programme, whether it be a nursery class or a university course. Teachers at all levels do seem to operate more successfully within a context in which they share a common sense of purpose and where they can relate what they are doing to the work of their colleagues.

It is the second part of the Warnock quotation that is more specifically related to special education. A key responsibility of the special educator is to take an existing curriculum framework and match it to the needs, aptitudes and interests of the individual pupil, taking account of any disability that may exist. Thus the important focus is on the individual, necessitating a much closer working relationship between teacher and pupil. There is also a need to focus on short-term objectives as a means of clarifying intentions and monitoring progress.

Recognising the importance of this type of thinking, many special schools are now giving considerable attention to the planning of curriculum in such a way as to facilitate its adaptation to meet the needs of individual pupils. In so doing they are responding to the limitations of segregated provision (e.g. isolation, limited curriculum) by maximising its greatest asset: the consistency and continuity of teaching that results from close team work.

Unless a special school has a cooperative working atmosphere in which mutual support, professional debate and group problem-solving are part of everyday life, the case for the existence of such a school is a limited one. Clearly, therefore, it is one of the key tasks of management within a school to facilitate such an atmosphere.

Management is often defined as: "Getting things done through people." This definition suggests three important management questions:

(1) What things need to be done? (i.e. PRIORITIES)

(2) How are they to be done? (i.e METHODS)

(3) How are the results to be assessed? (i.e. EVALUATION)

Some heads argue that management is largely a matter of intuition and that the key components of success are personality and charisma. Without denying the benefits of these it seems reasonable to assume that there are principles and strategies that can be acquired and which help in the task of management, particularly as they apply to the development of curriculum.

CURRICULUM DEVELOPMENT

Before going on to consider management principles and strategies as they relate to bringing about changes in school practice and policy, we need to be clear about what we mean by curriculum development. Essentially it is to do with the notion of "common sense of purpose" referred to earlier. Our assumption is that schools are more likely to be successful when there exists a common philosophy and agreed practices within which individual teachers can plan their work. Curriculum development is the process through which these philosophies and practices are clarified.

The term curriculum is used to mean different things by different people. It can refer to any activity that takes place in a school, whether planned or unplanned. I wish to argue, however, that the era of unplanned curriculum in special education is now dead and that there is a recognition that planning can provide a range of important benefits. For purposes of discussion, therefore, I intend to use the term curriculum to describe the "what" of education, i.e. what it is the children are expected to achieve as a result of the experiences in which they participate. Following on from this, the "how" of education refers to the methods and organisation used and experiences provided by the school in order to bring about these achievements.

This distinction between the curriculum and the methods is a useful one. In particular, it emphasises the point that whilst a school must have a common curriculum, reflecting agreed aims and philosophies, the methods used by individual teachers to implement that curriculum can and should be varied.

There are a number of ways in which schools can translate their beliefs and purposes into a written format and it is only fair to point out that proponents of the various orientations to curriculum planning remain in dispute (Stenhouse, 1975). Without getting into such arguments, however, it will be helpful to agree a general model of curriculum planning out of which a definition of terminology can be provided.

The diagram below presents curriculum development as a series of four levels of decision-making that need to be undertaken.

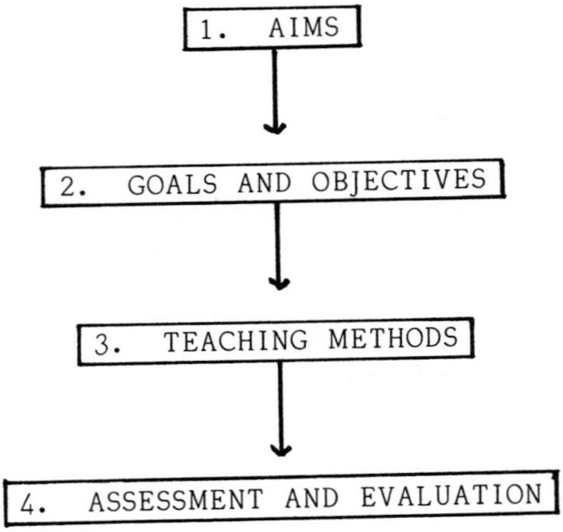

Figure 1: Curriculum Development - Four Levels of Decision-Making

Aims are usually defined as the long-term philosophical purposes of an educational programme. It is often said that British schools are successful in stating their aims but not so good at defining what these aims mean in terms of day-to-day practice (Brennan, 1979). In terms of special education, it is interesting to consider whether the aims of education should be in any way different from those agreed for all children.

Having said that, it does make sense for the staff of a school to agree their overall aims based on an assessment of the needs of the youngsters and the demands of the community in which they live. This came to life for me recently when discussing curriculum philosophy with teachers in a special school for children with physical disabilities. Whilst their aims had to be the same as for all children they felt it necessary to emphasise certain aspects related to their pupils' disabilities. So, for example, their knowledge of the difficulties these pupils experience after school led to a particular concern with personal development work in connection with relationships.

A school staff can translate their agreed aims into a more specific form through the definition of goals and objectives. Goals refer to priorities for teaching within a particular area of the curriculum. An example would be: To increase the pupils' skills in taking part in conversations. Out of such a goal more specific objectives would be derived.

The idea of stating objectives in curriculum planning is one of those areas of disagreement to which I referred (Macdonald-Ross, 1975). Questions about how specific objectives should be, and whether the stating of objectives is helpful or inhibiting are still matters of debate. In the field of special education, however, there is considerable research evidence to suggest that planning by objectives does facilitate childrens' learning (Ainscow and Tweddle, 1981, includes a summary of this research). Recognising possible limitations, however, it is necessary to keep the idea of planning by objectives in perspective.

In order to maintain a sense of balance in the curriculum, objectives should attempt to define different types of outcomes, i.e. skills, knowledge, attitudes, values and interests. To facilitate this, use can be made of three different forms:

(1) Behavioural objectives. Learning outcomes written in terms of pupil behaviour that can be observed and measured.
Example: Given a 15 cm square of paper held by an adult, the pupil cuts it in two with scissors, in 5 trials without error.

(2) Expressive objectives. Situations designed to engage children in a problem, experience or task, without specifying in advance what the particular learning outcome will be.
Example: Following a visit to the zoo the pupil will take part in a classroom discussion about wild animals.

(3) Affective objectives. Interests, values and attitudes to be developed.
Example: The pupil undertakes new tasks with a positive attitude.

As was stated earlier, the specification of a curriculum plan in terms of aims, goals and objectives need not limit the teacher's choice of methods, apparatus and organisation. Indeed, I would argue that where teachers are working within an agreed framework their practices are likely to be more effective.

Built into any good curriculum plan must be methods of assessing pupil progress. In the past assessment has been seen as being outside of the curriculum, based on rather narrow forms of testing. The limitations of this are now widely accepted in special education (Duffey and Fedner, 1978; Salvia and Ysseldyke, 1978) and the move is towards curriculum-based assessment approaches. Criterion-referenced tests can, of course, be bought, but it is preferable for assessment items to be built into the curriculum based on some form of on-going record keeping.

To sum up so far, curriculum development is a process by which the philosophies of a school are defined in terms of aims, goals and objectives. These provide the "what" of education from which individual teachers can devise the "how". Strategies must also be incorporated in order to monitor pupil progress.

CHANGE

All of this sounds fine. Few would argue that a special school which works to a common philosophy and agreed curriculum guidelines is likely to be more successful, but the big question is how do we do it? How are such curriculum plans developed? How can groups of staff be persuaded to work along agreed lines?

First of all it has to be recognised that changing schools is difficult. It has been estimated, in fact, that major changes in any large organisation may take up to five years to be fully implemented. Therefore, anyone attempting to introduce something new into a school has to be prepared to allow time for its adoption. In some schools, particularly those in which there are already difficulties within the organisation, the mere suggestion of change can create stress, tension and conflict.

The traditional approach to bringing about new developments in schools has been to identify key individuals who can be given extra training and then used as "change agents" (Havelock, 1970). This model is subject to a number of possible difficulties which can limit its chances of success (Henderson, 1978). Teachers who have been on one-year advanced courses, for example, are often disappointed to find that their colleagues seem uninterested in their new ideas when they return to the schools.

Georgiades and Phillimore (1975) have drawn attention to the limitations of this traditional approach to organisational change. They describe it as the myth of the hero-innovator:

> ... the idea that you can produce, by training, a knight in shining armour who, loins girded with new technology and beliefs, will assault his organizational fortress and institute changes both in himself and others at a stroke. Such a view is ingenuous. The fact of the matter is that organizations such as schools and hospitals will, like dragons, eat hero-innovators for breakfast. (p. 315)

What, then, are the barriers that hero-innovators meet when they propose changes in a school's curriculum? A number of writers have attempted to provide the answers to this question. Following a detailed examination of one attempted innovation, for example, Gross et al (1971) suggested that the difficulties arose because of:

(1) The teachers' lack of clarity about the proposal.

(2) Their lack of skills and knowledge to carry it out.

(3) The unavailability of necessary materials and equipment.

(4) The existence of organisational arrangements which were incompatible with the project.

(5) The lack of staff motivation.

An American writer, Havelock (1970), has attempted to explain the complex interactions that may occur amongst a group of teachers in relation to a proposal for change. His approach was to define the roles that certain individuals may choose to play. For example:

The Resisters

These may be people who will argue against any kind of change as a matter of policy. Often they will use one of the "standard list of excuses", e.g. "We haven't got the time", "We already do it", "We've tried it before and it doesn't work", "Where is the money coming from?", "These keen types are always trying something new - it won't last", "I would rather see how it goes before I get involved."

It has to be remembered, of course, that schools (particularly special schools) are rather subject to "band wagons" and, therefore, resisters may at times be positive influences providing appropriate professional barriers against ill-thought-out proposals. This point is expanded upon by Tony Bowers in Chapter Three, in considering the role of resisters in the change process.

<u>The Innovators</u>

To the person wishing to introduce something new into a school those who might be characterised as being innovators may seem very attractive in that they are keen to participate. If, however, they are individuals who are "always looking for something different" and, perhaps as a result, lack credibility with other staff, they may not be as helpful as it seems.

<u>The Gatekeepers</u>

The capacity of a school to actually implement a new curriculum approach may depend upon the decision of one individual. It may be somebody within the school. For example, a plan to introduce pottery into the art department may be rapidly halted by the school caretaker. On the other hand, somebody from outside may be the critical person, as in the case of a project which requires extra funding which may or may not be provided by a L.E.A. adviser.

<u>The Leaders</u>

Within the staff of a school certain individuals may have a strong influence on the opinions of their colleagues. These people may not always be initially obvious and are certainly not necessarily members of the management team. In terms of any innovation, therefore, their views will be crucial and, of course, they may choose to adopt the roles of resister, innovator or gatekeeper.

MANAGEMENT STYLES

It is clear that introducing changes of any sort into schools is a complex matter and that the traditional approach to curriculum innovation of using individuals to "change the system" has a number of weaknesses.

How then should head teachers of special schools approach the area of curriculum development? Inevitably the answer to this question will depend upon the individual's overall orientation to management.

McGregor (1960) has suggested that management style may be based on two opposing beliefs about the nature of human behaviour, which he refers to as "Theory X" and "Theory Y".

Theory X

Those who base their style on this theory believe:

- The average human being has an inherent dislike of work and will avoid it if he can.

- Because of this characteristic of disliking work, most people must be coerced, controlled, directed, threatened with punishment, to get them to put forth adequate effort toward the achievement of organisational objectives.

- The average human being prefers to be directed, wishes to avoid responsibility, has relatively little ambition, wants security above all.

Theory Y

Management styles derived from this position consider that:

- The expenditure of physical and mental effort in work is as natural as play or rest.

- External control and the threat of punishment are not the only means for bringing about effort towards organisational objectives. Commitment to objectives is a function of the rewards associated with their achievement.

- The average human being learns under appropriate conditions not only to accept, but to settle responsibility.

Stenhouse (1975) refers to four styles of decision-making along a continuum:

TELL — SELL — CONSULT — SHARE

Those who are committed to Theory X would presumably be expected to adopt a largely "tell" style of leadership, whereas Theory Y people tend to favour more consultative approaches.

Certainly there is evidence that people are usually able to describe their managers in terms of their style of management (Sadler, 1975; Nias, 1980). Furthermore, research suggests that:

(1) The consultative style of leadership is most often preferred.

(2) Managers who exhibit a distinctive style of leadership are more effective in promoting confidence and satisfaction among employees.

(3) High job satisfaction is associated with being led in the way one prefers to be led.

(4) Among those who feel they are not receiving the type of leadership they prefer, the lowest level of job satisfaction is among those who perceive their manager displays no particular style.

(5) Positive leadership is characterised by explicit school aims subject, within limits, to negotiation, high standards of personal commitment and professional competence, support and encouragement for individuals, and a capacity to create a sense of cohesion within a school.

Heads will argue that they vary their decision making style dependent upon the situation and issue to be resolved. This seems a reasonable position but it needs to be noted that dramatic inconsistency can create tension. So, for example, the teacher who wishes to make a proposal about some aspect of school policy is going to be reluctant to do so if he or she knows that previous approaches have sometimes been met with a glass of sherry and on other occasions received a cold reception.

CURRICULUM PROCESSES

Given the complexities of introducing new ideas into schools and the research evidence we have examined, consultative leadership approaches which attempt to nurture full staff participation seem to make sense, particularly as far as curriculum development is concerned. My own experience as a head of a special school suggested that the establishment of an atmosphere in which all aspects of the curriculum could be reviewed and developed through regular staff discussion meetings led to a range of benefits. In particular:

(1) Curriculum guidelines that are formulated with full staff involvement are more likely to be implemented in the classroom. I have known schools that have had impressive curriculum documents which appear to have little or no influence upon the work of individual teachers. This may well have been because members of staff, having not participated in its production, feel no commitment to it or, indeed, have only a superficial understanding of the ideas upon which it is based.

(2) Where staff meet regularly to discuss curriculum matters, this provides an excellent forum for in-service training. Whilst courses and workshops that take place in teachers' centres and colleges can be a valuable means of gaining new ideas, the essence of professional development is what occurs within the school. Questions that are debated by the whole staff can be answered in forms that are specific and meaningful to the particular group of teachers, taking account of the constraints that exist within the school.

(3) Curriculum discussions can provide a useful context within which support agencies can operate (e.g. advisers; educational psychologists; speech therapists). Often such visitors to a school are frustrated by their inability to influence practice, not least in that it is difficult to find opportunities to talk with individual members of staff. In curriculum meetings, groups of staff can negotiate with outside professionals as to how best they can contribute to the work of the school.

These arguments illustrate the importance of the process of curriculum development. It is tempting for enthusiasts within a school to want to produce finished material at a fast pace but in so doing they miss out the benefits that can result from full staff participation.

In order to examine the process of curriculum development in greater detail and make suggestions as to how this can be facilitated, in the rest of this chapter I examine the four aspects illustrated in the diagram below. The diagram indicates that curriculum development within a school is a cyclical process by which staff review the needs of the school, establish priorities for develop-

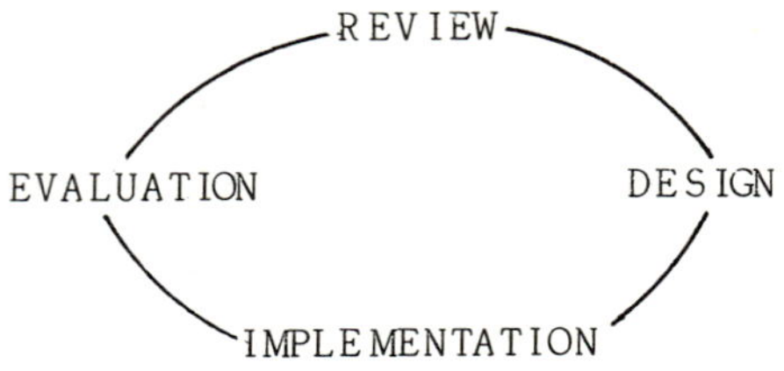

Figure 2: The Stages of Curriculum Development

ment, design a response and then evaluate it by implementation. This leads to a further review to set new priorities.

REVIEW

The importance of carrying out a review of some form in order to set priorities for curriculum development cannot be overemphasised. The process by which this is undertaken is an essential means by which staff participation can be encouraged. It is also important that priorities for development are based on "real" needs. As Coulson (1980) says, "there is a danger that the actual innovation chosen may be determined as much by the head's own interest, and by whatever is currently fashionable, as by careful analysis of the needs of the school and its pupils" (p. 281).

The methods used to carry out the review will, of course, reflect the overall management of the school. Some heads may tend to rely on their own observations, assisted by their colleagues and, perhaps, supplemented by the views of the school adviser. Given what I have said about the advantages of staff participation, however, more consultative methods are advisable.

One approach that is worth considering is to produce a checklist which includes all the curriculum areas normally dealt with in the school, leaving space where others can be added. Each member of staff is asked to indicate areas in which they feel their teaching is satisfactory and those with which they would welcome support. From an analysis of all the completed forms, areas that need further consideration can be pinpointed and used as the agenda for discussion at a full staff meeting.

Where a head takes over a school, a thorough review

of the existing curriculum is particularly important. This must be handled sensitively in that it may appear that the newcomer is questioning the practices of the previous regime. As a new head I found this a very difficult period. Many meetings over a period of months were necessary before I felt we were at a stage where my colleagues were confident enough to openly question the approaches being used. It seems to me that until such a stage has been reached any major innovation is unlikely to succeed. Stenhouse (1975) summed up the issues when he wrote: "I am inclined to believe that the key quality needed in a school, if development is to take place, is reflexiveness: a capacity to review critically and reflectively its own processes and practices."

As part of the curriculum review process a head may feel it necessary to reconsider the role of postholders in the school. Until recently such posts, particularly those at Scale 2S level, tended to be awarded to successful teachers on the basis of some nominal area of responsibility. The capacity of such individuals to provide leadership and co-ordination within the curriculum is now increasingly recognised. So, for example, in their survey of primary schools published in 1978, H.M. Inspectors stated that:

> Where a teacher with special responsibility is knowledgeable and able to give a strong lead in planning and carrying out a programme of work, this is effective in influencing the work of other teachers in the school. This in turn would appear to raise the levels of expectations of what children are capable of doing ... (D.E.S., 1978a, p. 17)

One special school carried out a very interesting exercise in which the staff reviewed the whole curriculum and through discussion established areas that needed further development. From this analysis the head, in conjunction with the school adviser, renegotiated each post holder's area of responsibility in order to co-ordinate efforts to meet the stated priorities. The negotiations included discussion about aims, procedures and forms of evaluation. Once agreed, the outcomes were written down as a form of job description. It was also agreed that each person's duties would be reviewed annually with a view to seeing how much progress had been made and whether new priorities should be set. All of these discussions were carried out in an atmosphere of cooperation and openness.

It is important that priorities for curriculum development are seen within the context of an overall framework (Wilson, 1981, provides some interesting examples that schools should consider). As I have said, changing schools is difficult and it has to be accepted that any innovation will take time. If they are to give their commitment to some new curriculum initiative, members of staff will want to be reassured that their efforts represent a response to a realistic need, related to an overall plan for the development of the school.

DESIGN

It is inevitable that staff participation in curriculum development will result in more meetings. When I run workshops for heads and teachers about this topic somebody usually asks, "How do we get everybody to join in?"

There is no easy answer. As a group, teachers represent a diverse range of individuals and as a profession we have been concerned to maintain the individual's right to classroom privacy. Nevertheless most teachers, particularly those who elect to work with children who have special needs, are keen to do their best for their pupils. It is necessary, therefore, to convince colleagues that meetings to discuss curriculum issues will in the long run benefit the school.

The head and senior staff have an important role to play in this respect. They must show that they are firmly committed to the enterprise by their attendance and contribution. They must also be sensitive to their colleagues' view and provide encouragement for all who participate.

It is important to remember that one of the main purposes is to promote team work and cohesion amongst the staff. Where a head teacher is keen to introduce some new approach it is tempting to work with those colleagues who seem particularly keen (i.e. "the innovators"), but in so doing he or she may give unintended messages to others that may lead them to adopt the role of "resisters". The management task is to get all members to participate and at times this may mean holding back the enthusiasts in order to get the staff working as a whole.

I well recall one teacher who attended regular after school curriculum discussion meetings each week because his head had made it clear that this was required. He showed his objections to this by reading the newspaper throughout. This caused great annoyance amongst a number of his colleagues, one of whom had to be dissuaded from setting the newspaper alight. Gradually, however, as the teacher realised over a period of weeks that his newspaper reading was having no effect he began to listen to the discussion and, eventually, participate. Following sound behavioural principles, at this stage he was given suitable reinforcement.

If meetings are to be regarded as purposeful by members of staff they should be arranged and conducted in a business-like fashion. Experience has shown that the following steps can help:

(1) Staff should be provided with a programme of meetings for the term outlining dates and times in order that they can make arrangements to attend, particularly if they are held after school. Times of meetings should be stuck to rigidly.

(2) Before a meeting, participants should be provided with information about what is to be discussed in order that they can prepare their ideas. If an actual section of curriculum is to be developed, a rough draft can be a useful way of facilitating discussion.

(3) Meetings should be concerned with making decisions. Teachers tend to enjoy talking and if discussions are not structured they become aimless. At the end of a meeting it is helpful if decisions are summarised.

(4) Where appropriate, after a meeting decisions should be written up and each member of staff issued with a copy.

When a meeting is concerned with a particular subject area, the head needs to consider the role of the relevant post holder. In some schools they are asked to act as chairperson for the meeting, whilst in others they take responsibility for providing pre-meeting notes and recording the decisions that are made. It is important to recognise that some teachers may find it difficult to respond to this type of responsibility, particularly if they have not had a lot of experience of this form of decision-making. The head must see to it that appropriate professional support is available, perhaps through a senior colleague or an adviser.

The head of one special school for children with severe learning difficulties which has carried out some exciting curriculum development, outlined for me the procedure used in his school in order to get full staff participation in decision-making. It consists of the following steps:

(1) Initial meeting of the full staff discusses the

priorities within a given curriculum area.

(2) Sub-group of the staff work out the target objectives and their arrangement.

(3) Second full staff meeting considers the proposed target objectives and types of task analysis to be used to generate learning steps.

(4) Individual members of staff analyse the target objectives into suitable programmes of learning steps.

(5) Final staff meeting agrees the completed curriculum plan prior to field-testing.

This procedure has been shaped over a period of years and has proved to be very successful. Indeed, the head explained that he is occasionally tempted to push through some minor decision in order to speed up the process but his staff are so used to participating in decision-making about the structure of the curriculum that he finds this impossible to do.

A further important feature of this particular school's approach is the emphasis on field-testing. Curriculum design should be seen as a process of hypothesis formulation which is followed by action research in the classrooms. Plans and materials that are developed through discussion must be tried out with the children and then modified in the light of this experience. This type of experimental teaching should be a feature of any special school and is a further important aspect of staff development.

IMPLEMENTATION

In the special school of which I was head we spent a period of years dealing with curriculum development, and curriculum discussion became an integral part of school life. During the early stages, much of the time was spent on agreeing priorities, working out goals and objectives, and learning about task analysis as a means of individualising our approaches (Ainscow and Tweddle, 1979). What I had not realised at that stage was that the review and design aspects were only the first stages of the process. Once individual teachers attempt to implement a curriculum plan other problems arise.

For example, I found that for a long time some colleagues found it difficult to modify their teaching approaches and organisation to fit in with the agreed plans. In some cases they continued to teach in exactly the same way as they had always done and then, almost as an afterthought, attempted to relate this back to the goals and objectives we had developed. As time went on their struggles became even more of a worry since most of the younger teachers did not seem to have these difficulties and they became somewhat frustrated by their more experienced colleagues.

At the stage of implementation of any curriculum innovation, therefore, it is important that the head identifies possible difficulties and tensions with a view to providing appropriate help and support.

One special school introduced a new language scheme that included a very detailed assessment procedure. Anticipating that some of his colleagues might have problems with this, the head arranged to spend time in each class assessing one pupil. He explained to the staff that he wanted to learn the techniques involved for himself. By this means he was able to demonstrate good practice to individual teachers within their classrooms. Eventually he got to a stage where he could observe their attempts at assessment and provide them with appropriate feedback. All of this required careful negotiation and sensitivity since the presence of the head in the classroom can be a very threatening experience for some teachers.

A further way of providing support to individuals is to organise workshop sessions at which groups of staff meet to devise new materials and collate existing resources related to the curriculum plan that is being implemented. This is a useful means of facilitating greater teacher cooperation as well as providing a forum in which members of staff can offer one another mutual support.

EVALUATION

The assessment and record-keeping procedures built into a curriculum provide one means of gathering data for evaluation purposes. As a head I made it my responsibility to collect in groups of records to get an overall picture of what was going on in each classroom. Review meetings about individual pupils also throw up information which is relevant to curriculum evaluation.

In terms of curriculum development, however, wider aspects of evaluation have to be considered in addition to the monitoring of pupil progress. The types of questions that need to be considered are:

- Does the curriculum relate to the long-term needs of the pupils?

- Do pupils understand the purposes of the curriculum?

- Do the parents understand and agree with the purposes of the curriculum?

- Are all teachers implementing the curriculum as it is defined?

- Are there any areas of the curriculum in which groups of children are failing?

The presence of a written curriculum statement provides a basis for considering this type of issue.

Once again the task of management must be to encourage staff participation. With this in mind it is worth considering the roles that various individuals within a school might adopt. The proposal outlined in the following diagram (adapted from Maund et al, 1982) makes suggestions for such roles related to the four levels of decision-making referred to earlier.

Levels of Decision-making	Class-Teachers	Post Holders	Senior Management
1. AIMS			X
2. GOALS AND OBJECTIVES		X	X
3. TEACHING METHODS	X	X	X
4. ASSESSMENT AND EVALUATION	X	X	X

Figure 3: Roles in Curriculum Evaluation

The role implications of this are:

(1) Class teachers. They are responsible for evaluating the effectiveness of their own teaching and matching the curriculum guidelines to the attainments and interests of individual pupils.

(2) Post holders. Having been responsible for the development and co-ordination of a particular aspect of the curriculum, they must work with colleagues to ensure that the specified goals and objectives are being achieved using methods which are in line with the overall aims of the school.

(3) Senior management. The head and his senior colleagues must check that the two other evaluation phases are being satisfactorily accomplished, including the incorporation of any necessary modifications and provision of support as required. They must also ensure that individual initiatives fit into the overall pattern and are consistent with the school's aims.

FINAL THOUGHTS

The most important point that I have attempted to make in this chapter is that a key management role is to encourage all members of staff to participate fully in the process of curriculum development. Visits to various kinds of special school in different parts of the country have convinced me that such participation can be enormously influential in improving the quality of education for children.

Chapter Three

CHANGE IN THE SPECIAL SCHOOL

by Tony Bowers

It is axiomatic in education that change is inevitable. Schools, if they are to remain effective, must be prepared and able to adapt to the demands of the system in which they operate. That the system is changing is apparent to anyone as we see, for example, changing patterns of employment: a higher level of unemployment, less unskilled employment, traditional industries no longer being seen as viable or inviolate, and a premium placed upon technological aptitudes or skills. Robert Oppenheimer's observation in 1955 that "the world alters as we walk, so that the years of a man's life measure not some small growth or rearrangement or moderation of what he learned in childhood, but a great upheaval" (p. 10) applies even more today than when he made it.

For special schools, perhaps even more than mainstream schools, the pressures for change are now intense. Bowers's (1980) alternative to flexibility - entropy - could now more realistically be replaced by the prospect of atrophy. Indeed, despite provision in the 1981 Education Act which entails D.E.S. involvement in the closure of any special school, it is clear that schools which are unable both to adapt and to remain flexible in their response to the demands which are made of them may not be with us for long. Brennan's (1982) confident prediction that there will be less special schools echoes Peter (1981); such a realisation, no doubt, was in Turner's (1979) mind when, as a special school head, he produced his defiant prediction "whichever way you throw us we shall stand" (p. 19).

THE DEMANDS OF CHANGE

The nature of the changes which it may be desirable for a special school to make will, of course, depend upon such factors as its present state of development, the forms of provision for children with special needs which exist within the community which it serves, and the expectations of such outside agents as educational psychologists and advisers, and on the needs of mainstream schools. Mel Ainscow, an innovator within his own special school, has delineated (Ainscow et al, 1978) the conditions which must exist in a school for it to encompass one major area of change - the development of a resource role in relation to mainstream schools. There should be specialist knowledge in the special school which is not seen in mainstream schools; this knowledge should be evidenced, the special school demonstrating good practice in assessment, curriculum content and method, and the monitoring of progress; and finally, the school staff should have the abilities necessary to disseminate their expertise. Here, then, to achieve one diversification of its traditional role, is the demand that a number of preconditions should be met, each one of which may involve the school in radical change.

Brennan (1982) has asserted that special schools will require more specialised curricula and teaching methods; this is undoubtedly an area for major change if special schools are to have a significant role to play in the future. Cameron (1983), himself a head teacher of a special school, has presented a scathing critique of many special schools' curricular priorities; recently, though, special schools' curricula have come under fire from other quarters. Tomlinson (1982) offers an over-generalisation which nevertheless provides pause for thought for some schools when she says that the special curriculum "offers 'non-knowledge' in that children who are offered a special curriculum have already been defined as not able to benefit from even the low-status knowledge of a normal curriculum" (pp. 135-136).

Change, then, in terms of staff roles within the school and the wider community, their knowledge and their methods of working, is something which either is happening or may well have to happen to ensure a school's viability. How, though, can changes most effectively be achieved?

LEVELS OF CHANGE

Mayo (1945) has suggested that there are four levels of change in people. In ascending order of difficulty these fall into the categories of knowledge, attitudes, individual behaviour and group behaviour. Changing what people know is very different from endeavouring to change what they actually do, as anyone who has been concerned with in-service work or with the organisation of school-based workshops will be aware. Individual behaviour is difficult enough to change, but it becomes even more complicated when we try to change behaviour within a group of staff, since the existing norms and expectations of that group, which may have been built up over many years, must be altered. For a head to attempt to adjust the views of school staff concerning the importance of parents in the educational process, for instance, may demand some intensive discussion both in private and in staff meetings. Acceptance of the notion, however, may fall some way short of staff accepting parents in the classroom to work alongside them, accepting that parents often know many things about their child's ways of learning and behaviour which are significant to its development and useful to the teacher, and visiting homes at times which are inconvenient to them but critical to the child and its family.

LEADERSHIP APPROACHES

Hersey and Blanchard (1977) have distinguished between two cycles of change, each profoundly influenced by the prevailing leadership style within the school; issues of such style are discussed more fully in Chapter Thirteen. The first cycle of change, the directive, is probably one with which many of us are familiar. It is usually exemplified by a head or other member of staff with specific responsibility for some activity, telling colleagues what is expected of them. "I've decided that our record-keeping isn't systematic enough, so in future we'll be using the check-lists which I've brought back from my last course", or "Now that you've got a scale 2(S) post, I'd like you to take responsibility for Maths and get something written down that the whole school can use" provide examples of the directive change approach. The alternative, Hersey and Blanchard (1977) term the participative change cycle. Here knowledge is made available to the group of individuals concerned, and they are asked to participate in problem-solving. The record-keeping issue, within this approach, would be put to the individuals concerned in the hope that they would acknowledge the need to change and get together with one another to develop an improved procedure.

The terms directive and participative change merely provide polar categories, and it is possible to put most change efforts at some point along a continuum between them. The participative cycle is one frequently attempted in curriculum development efforts within special schools, though often the introduction of such a cycle has a strongly directive ring about it. Hersey and Blanchard (1977) devote some considerable space to the advantages and disadvantages of both change cycles. A critical consideration for anyone embarking on change is the nature of those with whom they are working. For those who are achievement-orientated, and want to take on responsibility and have a degree of knowledge and expertise, a directive style is likely to be highly inappropriate, leading to conflict and opposition to change. Where staff members are less ambitious, tend to be dependent and are generally unwilling to take on new responsibilities, direction and structure may well prove effective strategies.

Another important aspect of leadership is the tendency of individuals in positions of responsibility to be more or less innovative. Morrish (1976) has observed that innovators are rarely popular people, and many head teachers will contend that they prefer gradual change, based on systematic small steps and the observation of others' experience, to the risks inherent in radical alterations within their schools. Stringent definitions of innovation, such as that of Schon (1967), who sees an act as innovative only if it adds to the sum of known inventions, are perhaps, though, too exclusive for the purposes of this chapter. An innovator is seen as somebody who attempts considerably to speed up the process of change within the school in a planned and deliberate manner.

Kirton (1977) has usefully distinguished between innovators and adaptors, and has devised an instrument to measure innovative tendencies in managers. Whereas the innovator will often be irreverent to the views of established groups, acting as a catalyst to stimulate them to change existing practices, the adaptor will tend to minimise conflict, seeking to modify existing structures only when absolutely necessary. The innovator is usually low in self-doubt, not needing a consensus from others to maintain his or her views; the adaptor, on the other hand, tends to be higher in self-doubt and to be vulnerable to pressures from others. The adaptor would be unlikely to take risks in such areas as staff appointment, the adoption of curricular methods or materials, or the redefinition of individual and institutional roles; to the innovator, the risks would be worth the potential benefits.

One characteristic of Kirton's adaptor which is not shared by the innovator is the ability to tolerate routine tasks and to be impervious to boredom. Relatively short bursts of detailed routine work are all that the innovator can manage. Since much of the work of a special school (for example, the administration and co-ordination of review procedures) is fairly routine, it is therefore tempting to speculate on whether the ideal head/deputy head partnership might not best be created by only one or other being highly innovative. So far, though, there is no firm evidence that such a relationship would be particularly productive.

POINTERS TO SUCCESS

In his book devoted to educational change, Morrish (1976) has paid considerable attention to the characteristics of innovative schools. Among them are staff members' agreement upon and acceptance of what they are trying to achieve, openness in communication, cohesiveness, the ability of those low in the formal hierarchy to influence policy, and high morale. These are issues of team development and the mechanisms of this are elaborated upon more fully in Chapter Thirteen of this book. Some of Morrish's specified qualities are quite easy to recognise, but as behaviourally achievable objectives they may well present problems.

Of perhaps more direct use are some of Warren Bennis's (1972) experiences in educational innovation. Of the points which he makes, the following may be of particular use to those concerned with managing change within special schools:

(1) <u>Build support among like-minded people, whether or not you recruit them</u>. For some who are new to a school, there may be a tendency to fall prey to the notion that the school came into being on the day they arrived. Often, new management appointments are made in the expectation by representatives of the L.E.A. that changes in policy or direction will occur. However, talk of "new starts" will almost invariably create anxiety in those who have been used to seeing themselves as competent professionals. It is therefore vital to look to the strengths and potential of existing staff members.

(2) <u>Guard against the crazies</u>. Beware that the original plans for development do not become distorted. There is then the danger that you will become identified with that distortion. Some years ago, the author was involved in establishing a programme of teacher performance evaluation within a large special school.

Using an approach termed "critical incident technique", its purpose was to help teachers to identify both the strengths in their performance and those areas which an individually-designed in-service programme might assist. Inevitably, a development such as this was potentially threatening and it had therefore to be introduced within a context of trust and confidentiality if it was to be successful. This was done, and all went well until other senior members of staff saw the information generated as a means of identifying people for promotion and for using in writing references. Suddenly the participants didn't want to know!

Even if staff members are apparently co-innovators, ensure at all times that they go about things in a responsible and amenable way. Watch out, in any clash of interests which apparently involve the changes that are being implemented, for old scores being settled or old antagonisms rekindled.

(3) Have a clear-cut understanding of how to change as well as what to change. So often, changes are embarked upon with the knowledge of what should be done, but not how it may be achieved. Probably one of the most widespread examples of this at present is the adoption of microcomputers within special schools. The purpose can often be made quite explicit; for example, to assist in the implementation of individual programmes; to aid communication; to provide pupils and teachers with immediate feedback on performance; to familiarise pupils with computer usage. However, the means of change are often inadequately thought out, particularly in terms of developing staff expertise, providing time for the preparation of appropriate software, ensuring that all staff familiarise themselves with available materials, linking computerised material with the class's or school's curriculum, ensuring the individual relevance of materials, providing appropriate space for hardware use, and so on.

(4) Remember that change is most successful when those who are affected are involved in the planning. Bennis (1972), of course, was working within an academic setting with individuals who had a high sense of self-worth and a need for some autonomy. For him, this

platitude of planning theory is as true as it is trite: the highly directive approach with competent professionals will simply make people resistant to changes and new approaches.

(5) Allow time to consolidate gains. We may be familiar with individuals who jump on to every bandwagon as it comes along - and jump off the last one. Ensure that when developments are made, they are given a chance to work and to become a part of established practice.

(6) Don't settle for rhetorical change. Often the innovations which we may hear about or read about in specialist journals or the press do not bear close inspection. A mythology may grow up around certain schools or certain teachers which is not necessarily matched by reality; Barton and Moody (1981), criticising special schools' relationships with parents, have pointed clearly to this. Indeed, it may be cynically suggested at times that the best way to gain a reputation is not to spend time consolidating or perfecting some area of change, whether it is, say, a leavers' preparation scheme, computer-assisted learning facilities or staff in-service workshops, but to use that time in telling other people about it. Make sure that the actuality matches, or exceeds, the words that are used to describe it. Thoroughly butter your parsnips.

THE PHASES OF CHANGE

At first glance, it is easy to think that where the above conditions are met then problems involved in change will be minimised. In particular, where everyone is agreed on the advantages of whatever changes are proposed, then it would seem that only positive changes can occur. However, anyone who has been involved in innovatory activities will know that the extent of co-workers' - and perhaps their own - enthusiasm varies at different stages of the process.

Kelley and Conner (1979) have proposed a useful model of change which involves five stages in the experiences of those who are committed to change in organisations:

(1) Uninformed optimism. This is the time of greatest certainty. Feelings run high, morale

is at a peak; without such optimism, it is unlikely that changes would be embarked on. However, such initial certainty is usually based on a lack of knowledge of the problems and difficulties that will make the task more complex than it appears at this early stage.

(2) Informed pessimism. Now the problems start to surface: unplanned occurrences, resistance from others, lack of time, money, and so on. While this is clearly a dangerous phase for the success of any attempted change, it is important to remember that it is natural and even desirable for negative feelings to be generated at this stage. However, if pessimism extends beyond individuals' tolerance levels, a withdrawal of personal investment will occur. This can take one of two forms. The first, public withdrawal, is just that - a refusal to take part that all can see. It may be accompanied by such overt rationalisations as "I really can't keep wasting my time in this way" or "I always had my doubts about this". Private withdrawal, on the other hand, is probably more threatening to the success of any project. Here the staff members will continue to pay lip-service to the project, but quietly go their own way. This can happen in such things as group-co-ordinated curriculum development activities. Documents are prepared, content, method and sequence arrived at; but an individual teacher, while publicly subscribing to the changes, will still quietly continue to function in the time-honoured ways.

(3) Hopeful realism. If the previous stage is overcome, and areas of difficulty confronted, then participants' perceptions of the project will be different from those that they held at the beginning, but will be positive. Not only have past problems been survived, but a new confidence has been developed in members' capability to handle whatever new problems may surface.

(4) Informed optimism. This is marked by growing confidence in both self and project. It tends to be accompanied by a fresh burst of energy linked to overcoming problems.

For Kelley and Conner (1979) there is a fifth phase,

which they term "rewarding completion" (p. 121). For so much that is newly started within the special school, however, this stage will often be inappropriate, the stage of informed optimism being the successful managerial goal.

RESISTERS

In gatherings of head teachers, the author has frequently found the response, "Yes, that's all very well, but what do I do about so-and-so who will block anything that I introduce? If you had some of my staff ..." While this section cannot provide easy answers, it should be made clear that just in the same way that Freud, in the context of psychotherapy, has emphasised that without resistance patients might be overwhelmed by the interventions of the therapist, and therefore will need it, so in more complex social systems resistance is natural and even desirable. In Chapter Two of this book Mel Ainscow has pointed to some of the characteristics of the resistant staff member, and argues that he or she may in fact have a positive role to play.

Few changes can be made within the school without impairing the existing situations of some individuals or groups. Either time will be used, with its consequences for other areas of life, or physical resources, such as space or materials, may no longer be as accessible to some people, or satisfaction derived from a particular way of working may be threatened by a change to another mode. The teacher who has traditionally taught stable groups within their own space, for instance, may have to cope with a re-evaluation of his or her competency and to seek different rewards from a more diffuse role in relation to groups of children.

Klein (1976) refers to the needs of all individuals to maintain integrity and to feel that their power and resources are adequate to meet the challenges which they face. Such integrity may, though, be based on a view of reality that is no longer tenable, thus leading to dissonance between past experience and the current situation. For him, resistance to change, however irrational, has as its objective the defence of self-esteem, competence and autonomy.

The tendency is often for the proponents of change to ignore, override or dismiss as irrational anyone who emerges as an opponent. The cost of such a policy will often be to transform the process of change into a conflict in which energy is devoted to winning rather than achieving the initially desired outcome. However time-consuming, irritating or frustrating early collaborative planning with individuals who are potentially the strongest resisters is probably more likely to be fruitful than engaging in a win-lose struggle. It is sad to find, even in the school with a reputation for innovation, disaffected staff who are "boxed-in" with a futile but determined opposition to each new influence.

STAFF STRESS

All change requires energy both from individuals and from the system of which those individuals are a part. Where excessive demands are made on the energy and resources of individuals, then extreme responses may be manifested. The results of occupational pressure are generically referred to as stress responses or, more recently and more colloquially, the "burnout syndrome" (e.g. Cunningham, 1982; Mattingly, 1979).

While much research and literature has been devoted to stress and burnout in teachers in general, some recent work has looked at aspects of these phenomena in the context of special educational provision. Mattingly (1981) has addressed herself to the problems encountered by residential child care staff, while Shaw et al (1981) have looked at the specific issues confronting special educators in the U.S.A., particularly in the context of recent legislation there. These last authors have identified as potential stressors the changes in demand caused by such new administrative requirements as annual and other periodic reviews, by shifting teacher roles from a class base to a resource orientation, and by the increasing ambiguity of expectation which results from decategorisation of pupils. It is not difficult to envisage similar problems within our own context; indeed, in this volume Tony Dessent draws attention to the reduction in job satisfaction which many teachers may experience in the future.

Signs of stress are not always easy to see. Often the individual experiences uneasiness; the pleasure derived from their job begins to slip away. Symptoms include being constantly tired, being dissatisfied, depressed and physically run down. Physical maladies such as insomnia, frequent colds, headaches, and loss of appetite are common. Mattingly (1977) has suggested, though, that there are no health problems specific to burnout but that under conditions of stress, medical problems begin or become intensified. In a British study, Kyriacou and Sutcliffe (1978) have reported the symptoms of teacher stress, in order of frequency, to be exhaustion, frustration, anger, tenseness, anxiety, depression, nervousness, headaches, rapid heartbeat, inability to cope, loss of voice, increased blood pressure, panic, acid stomach, tearfulness and cold sweat.

It may be relevant in the context of this chapter to note that a number of authors (e.g. Cook and Leffingwell, 1982; Spanoil and Caputo, 1979) view the lack of opportunity to participate in school decision making as a major contributor to teacher stress. Of interest, too, is Mattingly's suggestion that excessive involvement in work is a sign of burnout. She draws attention to the residential worker who fails to take allocated breaks and chooses to work on rest days; such "commitment" may signal that the individual lacks the additional energy to develop and sustain a personal life separate from his or her work.

In response to signs of stress in a staff member, there is unfortunately all too often a tendency for colleagues and senior staff to employ a traditional inner psychic view. Personal problems or weaknesses are seen to be the source of their difficulties, presenting an easier organisational option than the acknowledgement that working conditions within the school may have had a major part to play. It is all too easy to be irritated by someone who isn't pulling their weight and to see them as needing to "sort themselves out", rather than acknowledging that all colleagues have a responsibility for providing support. Maslach (1976) has found that burnout rates are lowered for those professionals who actively express, analyse and share personal feelings about their work with their colleagues, rather than keeping things to themselves. It is arguable that a major benefit of effective team development is the staff group's ability to provide support for members who are potentially under stress through the creation of norms which encourage problem-sharing and constructive feedback (see Chapter Thirteen).

Quite clearly, the function of leadership in the school, in addition to encouraging and modelling supportive behaviour, is to ensure that staff have developed sufficient skills to meet the increasingly varied demands of their jobs. It is here that the co-ordination of in-service training, both outside the school in the form of long-term and short-term courses, and within it (see Chapter Twelve) become vital leadership responsibilities. In addition, those in senior positions should have sufficient sensitivity to recognise and understand signs of staff stress which may subtly show themselves. It is often easy to become engrossed in the processes and outcomes of change efforts within the school and to fail to recognise the effects which they may have upon colleagues. Ultimately, the success of a school will rest upon the effectiveness of its most vital resource: its staff.

Chapter Four

HEADSHIP: ASPECTS OF THE ROLE

by Peter Turner

"Uneasy lies the head that wears a crown" may be thought an overstatement of the anxieties of many special school head teachers. On the other hand, the numerous conflicting demands facing the head can result in the quotation being somewhat less than totally misplaced. The effects of recent legislation, both real and imaginary, have done little to reduce the sense of anxiety. Under these circumstances, the fact that some schools appear to have a reduced sense of purpose should not have been totally unexpected.

If special schools are not to suffer a further deterioration of spirit, strategies must be adopted which can counter the less supportive influence of the past. My intention in this chapter is to examine some of the more significant elements of the head teacher's role and to consider ways in which he or she can create structures to facilitate the development of the school's operational practices in the face of these pressures.

DELEGATION IN MANAGEMENT

Of the leadership and administrative skills which are taught as part of school management training courses, perhaps the most significant is that of delegation. It can be argued that delegation is a key to successful management as a consequence of careful rank-ordering of the head teacher's time allocations. To that end the advantages of delegation need to be examined in some depth.

A significant number of special school deputy head teachers achieve promotion and are then quite obviously inexperienced in decision making. This leads one to the conclusion that they have not had tasks delegated to them which would have more effectively prepared them for accepting future responsibilities, though Bowers and Mayes

(1982) have speculated that special school deputies are better prepared for leadership than their primary school counterparts. Given that a major responsibility for any head teacher is to prepare deputies for future promotion (Burnham, 1968) it follows that the deputy head must be given experience of all aspects of institutional leadership. To achieve this the head will need to list the responsibilities one normally would expect to retain within one's own control and then allow the deputy gradually to gain experience of all aspects of leadership decision-taking. The head cannot of course abdicate his or her ultimate responsibility but the deputy will have had as appropriate a preparation as possible if the process is conducted in this way.

Beyond the responsibility for training deputy heads, the advantages of delegation to both the school and the head can be seen in terms of ensuring the latter's time is used to the maximum efficiency level. The head who spends his or her time beset by the minor domestic issues of caring for the building, keeping the books and issuing stock is unlikely to gain credibility with the staff or have sufficient time to cope with planning more major developments. If the head is prepared to delegate a majority of the decisions he or she might otherwise expect to take single-handedly, the reaction of the staff is likely to be very positive. There will follow not only an enhanced recognition of what is involved in maintaining and developing the school organisation, but also a greater degree of staff motivation and commitment towards achieving the institution's goals.

The key decisions to be delegated are undoubtedly those concerned with major policy changes. If such decisions are taken on a basis of equal involvement, rather than a purely consultative one, it is far more likely that the staff will exert themselves to ensure the policies actively function.

The methods and systems to be employed in delegating responsibility will vary according to the school. A first task for the head will be to establish, in conjunction with the staff, what are the major institutional goals and which resources are at the disposal of the school in order to meet these goals. Only at this juncture will emerge the tasks that can be delegated and those which will have to be retained by the head.

The areas of decision-taking most frequently retained by head teachers seem to be in connection with the budget, contact with outside agencies, staff recruitment and innovation. Given a suitable forum, which can act as an alternative to single-handed decision taking, it would appear that the majority of the tasks connected with the first three of these functions can be carried out by staff members, other than the head teacher, without detriment to the service.

Clearly the head will have to retain responsibility for some functions within the school. Amongst those will be negotiations with senior officers of the L.E.A., elements of his or her role as an innovator and perhaps the final stage of staff selection. What emerges from this conclusion is that a significant part of many decision-taking processes can be carried out by members of the staff.

An introduction of certain decision-taking structures into the school organisation will be a necessary pre-requisite of any major delegation of the head's responsibilities. The creation of planning groups which report to a central forum will facilitate the development of this process. Ian Galletley elaborates further on this in Chapter 5, and in my own experience, the head who is prepared to delegate responsibility for all policy matters to a forum made up of all employees in the school is likely to reap considerable benefit on a personal basis whilst the advantages to the institution are considerable. In law the head cannot surrender responsibility for the consequences of such a move but that is not necessarily an argument to retain power on an exclusive and personal basis.

THE MULTIPLICITY OF STAFF DISCIPLINES

The second half of the twentieth century has witnessed a change in school leadership styles from the head being the sole decision-taker to the adoption of an ever-widening consultative process. The special school head has not escaped this role-transformation, although the pressures to make changes have in some instances come from a different source compared with that of main-stream institutions. At the beginning of the 1950s, a greater proportion of special schools catered for children with physical and sensory handicaps. The heads of these schools were well used to the demands of leading a multidisciplinary staff. However, the frequency with which the schools appeared to divide into two, three or even more communities would indicate that not all heads were able to come to terms with the subtleties of the role required of them.

The rapid increase in the number of special school places which took place in the second decade of this half-century was almost totally accounted for by the establishment of schools for intellectually retarded children. These schools were originally more narrowly based in their staffing structures. Although there was a gradual expansion of the range of professional and semi-professional disciplines represented in the schools, the conflicts which occurred both between the staffing groups and between these groups and the head all too often underlined the latter's difficulties in coping with the co-ordination of multidisciplinary staff. The great preponderance of head teachers of the new special schools had acquired some, if not all, of their teaching experience in mainstream schools. This resulted in their being less well equipped than their colleagues in the longer established institutions to cope with this new demand. The implementation of the 1970 Education Act resulted in a further sudden increase in the number of new headships. Again a significant number of these head teachers were recruited from the ranks of teachers in the ESN(M) schools and as such had little opportunity to gain experience of the difficulties of leading a multi-disciplinary staff. Many of these new schools - the previously named junior training centres - began with almost equal numbers of teachers and ancillary staff, often the latter groups having had the greater experience of the severely retarded children who made up the school population. The last ten years have seen special school leaders seeking to develop the necessary skills to create a team approach to achieve the goals of their institutions; a move towards which might more properly be defined as interdisciplinary working. It is in this respect that the special school head's role as a team leader differs most significantly from that of his or her mainstream colleagues. Specifically, the special school head's "right" to direct the staff of the school is lessened in the case of those members who are not employed as teachers: therapists, nurses and social workers etc. This situation necessarily has an effect upon the head's relationship with the non-teaching ancillary staff and to some degree with the teachers themselves.

The increase in the number of ancillary staff in special schools heightens the possibility of conflict and may create many new and delicate role-definition problems for the head. Where the head has shared managerial responsibility for therapeutic staff, that same tradition has little carry-over in relation to his or her responsibility for the classroom aides. Nevertheless, if the corporate identity of the institution is to be maintained, these workers must also be involved in group decision-taking.

The establishment of a group forum such as the Staff Council described by Ian Galletley, in order to examine publicly the implications of any proposed development, lends itself to the promotion of group decision-taking. In turn the taking of group decisions motivates task behaviour. In my view, an awareness of the need to create a sense of corporate identity and to avoid actions which suggest an inclination to return to an autocratic style of leadership, are essential first steps on the road to co-ordinating team effort. Beyond this the head will have to employ a wide range of strategies to achieve the goal of interdisciplinary working.

It must not be assumed that all the problems of co-ordination arise from the existence of a number of staff, drawn from differing professional backgrounds, having to work together. Special school organisational structures have most closely followed the model of primary schools where the staff consists of a number of teachers working independently within a set of guidelines which have not always appeared in a written form. The special school teachers may well need to be persuaded of the desirability of carefully defining teaching goals, let alone assisting with identifying objectives to be achieved by the whole staff.

Not all head teachers feel it necessary or even desirable to create immediately a decision-taking body with equal membership for all. However, at the very least, a regular forum at which all staff are entitled to be present and to raise issues will need to be established. Using the forum as a problem-solving body is unlikely initially to threaten any but the most insecure leader's peace of mind.

Once the members feel the forum has real value and status, it should be possible to develop its function to the point where it also acts as a planning group. Where the size of the school justifies it, a further step could be to delegate the preparation of some aspects of planning to sub-committees which report their findings to the main forum. The sense of security developed by the continuing existence of such a group is also likely to lend itself to the promotion and acceptance of greater demands upon the individual members and a consequent extension of the school's activities. Whether the head retains the office of chairman will depend upon his or her own sense of security, but it is likely that, should they relinquish the office, their standing in the eyes of colleagues will be enhanced rather than diminished. This will in turn allow the head more time to devote to the social/emotional aspects of the role of co-ordinator.

THE HEAD AS CO-ORDINATOR

Where there exists a professionally disparate group of adults faced with the common goal of educating and treating special needs children, the traditional role of head teacher as the fount of all professional wisdom must be eschewed or group conflict will develop. On the other hand, if the institutional goals are to be achieved it is clearly the responsibility of the head to ensure that the contributions of all staff are suitably harmonised.

As co-ordinator of the team's efforts the head is likely to succeed in fulfilling both the main aspects of his or her role, that of task leader and that of social/ emotional leader. The dialogue to be conducted between the head and any one of the professional groups within the school community not only assists the development of relationships but also contributes to the identification of that sub-group's reaction to the other groups' methods of achieving goals. The head is then in the unique position of being able to draw out, in any common forum, the relevant contributions to a specific project.

The need for the head teacher to exercise his or her skills as a co-ordinator of the efforts of colleagues is unlikely to be diminished in the future. To underline this point, two developments arising out of implementation of the 1981 Education Act are likely to add new elements to the responsibilities of the special school and consequently create further opportunities for the head to act as a co-ordinator. The assessment procedures, to be carried out by the school as part of placement requirements (D.E.S. Circular 1/83, para. 16), involve the head bringing together the views of a wide range of contributing professionals in addition to those of the parents. Also, with the school cast in the role of supporter of handicapped children in mainstream schools, the task of co-ordinating the activities of the host and the supporting staffs may well fall upon the special school head.

THE HEAD AND PARENTS

Whilst head teachers differ in many ways in their interpretation of what are the key elements of their role, it is doubtful if any would deny the significance of that aspect which is concerned with parent guidance. It is also one of the few aspects of the work with which heads are familiar when they are first appointed. The special school head has had as long an experience as any of his or her mainstream colleagues in fulfilling this role. Indeed not only is that experience extensive, it is also intensive. Allowing that a special school is populated entirely with children who have difficulties, it is not surprising that the head teacher has ample opportunities to develop this aspect of his or her skills.

Apart from the difficulty of resisting the demand for advice and support from parents, it is doubtful if many heads would wish to divest themselves of this responsibility. It is an activity, in the positive sense, which provides a head teacher with a sense of purpose and achievement. The two chapters by heads on this theme within this book serve to emphasise this. The feeling of usefulness which stems from supporting parents helps to counterbalance the sense of frustration which results from having to perform the constant round of routine administrative tasks demanded by the L.E.A.

It may well be that the last point is the most significant when heads are faced with establishing priorities in relation to their workload. It is, however, unlikely to be considered so. Indeed it would be inappropriate to ignore the other quite legitimate demands upon the head to sustain this facet of his or her responsibilities. Most parents, it must be allowed, expect to be able to discuss their child's difficulties with the head teacher and it is no rare occurrence for such a discussion to turn into a wider consideration of the family's problems. As a consequence of this, the head may well end up by having a wider knowledge of the family's problems at home than he or she has of the child in school.

From a more positive viewpoint, many heads will seek to accept the burden of parental counselling in order to relieve pressure on the rest of the staff. It is quite understandable that heads will seek to deal with complaints received from parents and from that it is but a short step to funnel many more issues through their hands. Indeed it is traditional that, where a parent approaches a school, the head teacher should deal with the issue personally. This is particularly appropriate if all the rest of the staff are committed to the children when the parent arrives unannounced.

Schools are quick to appreciate that despite the increases in social work provision, many parents of handicapped children have no one else to turn to for assistance. The school represents a haven of comparative stability in a world where many workers in the supportive professions appear to change post with what must seem to their clients to be a distressing frequency. The head teacher is perceived as being synonymous with the existence of the school and is likely to be sought out by parents on that basis alone.

Although the barriers between home and school have been greatly reduced in the last twenty years, there are still schools where the head will not permit direct contact between staff and parents. Somewhat surprisingly, where this occurs parents still seem prepared to accept a counselling role from the head teacher. The majority of teachers in special schools, however, do have well-established contacts with the parents of children in their classes. Smith (1983) has provided an excellent A to Z of the mechanisms involved in such relationships. Of those who are appointed to head teacher posts, probably the great majority would wish to retain that kind of contact. Involvement with parents is seen as a means of retaining contact with the child.

Despite this lengthy catalogue of apparently logical reasons for the head to maintain his or her role as the school's parent counsellor, there are other considerations to be taken into account. This issue is undoubtedly one where the head's ability to delegate is brought into focus. Before the issue can be considered, however, two other questions must be answered. Firstly, what needs to be done? and secondly, by whom should it be done? Whilst each case must necessarily be treated on its own merits, it is clearly desirable for the school to have some agreed policy on advising parents. This policy must be one easily understood by parents and agreed to by the staff if it is to succeed.

Some broad guidelines are needed so that parents will not seek to take up the time of the head, or indeed the teaching staff, with minor queries. Staff, in turn, must recognise that their wish to be helpful can prove to be counter-productive if they have not the necessary resources to meet the parents' needs. The head might be best advised to devote time to negotiating an element of staff resources to cope with this demand. A sense of purpose and usefulness may equally be achieved by the successful outcome of such negotiations. The head must also be prepared to place the meeting of his personal needs in a secondary position to that of ensuring the needs of the school are met. A procedure by which parents can be made aware of the school's view of their child's progress, and in which they can contribute to the staff's knowledge of the child, is a developing feature of many special schools. The annual review required by the 1981 Education Act will also provide an opportunity for the head to delegate parent advisory tasks to class teachers.

Delegation of specific tasks is easy to institute, but if the head is to view the transfer of responsibility with equanimity, then certain precautions must be taken. The most obvious of these is to equip the staff, or at the very least those key members through whom the counselling service is to be delivered, with the necessary skills to perform the task. Ideally the school might choose to direct some resources in order to create a separate staff responsibility for parental advisory work. The outcome of such a move would be a more appreciative and supportive group of parents and a reduction in the time which has to be taken from other priorities to meet parental needs. The economies of having to employ sophisticated training schemes with only one or two staff are obvious.

With regard to the conduct of counselling sessions, schools have recently employed the group approach (Rose and Marshall, 1976). The time saving, coupled with the development of relationships between parents, are obvious advantages to be gained from such an approach.

THE HEAD AND THE COMMUNITY

The pressures upon special schools to move from the isolationist policies of the past have frequently been coupled with the desire of the head and staff to become part of the surrounding community. This has resulted in many institutions having strong local connections. Contacts with the local community have now come to be the norm as far as the majority of special schools are concerned. The qualitative and quantitative aspects of the relationship may vary from school to school, but the general principle is firmly established. In many cases the change has been born of a wish to seek the community's support. The fact that other advantages have accrued to both partners has occurred almost incidentally.

The local community has, of course, many facets. The local education community is quite a separate concept from that referring to the immediate geographical environs of the school. Beyond this there is the wider community from which the children are drawn. To integrate with one or more of these communities has come to be thought of as a desirable goal in its own right. It is equally true that a significant number of practical advantages are to be gained by pursuing such an objective. With regard to the immediate environs of the school, concerns tend to centre upon the domestic issues of good neighbourliness, parking, minor damage etc. Better relationships between the school and its neighbours bring about more positive manifestations of support than a mere reduction in the scale of complaint. Children in distress are likely to be offered assistance, and sympathetic consideration extended to parents whose children may be displaying the less acceptable manifestations of their handicap.

Involvement with the local community, from which the children are drawn, may result in increased acceptance and recognition of the children as community members in their own right. Once effective links have been established, the education community will be inclined to recognise the legitimacy of the special school claim upon shared resources when conflicts of interest arise. Following increased liaison, some advantages occur which are common to all forms of community. Building the school's image as part of the local community and for which that community has responsibility may well result in increased investment in the school. This may occur not only by way of gifts of equipment but also from influence upon the members of the local authority when more major developments are being considered.

The community may also contribute by way of its members acting as volunteers in the school. There can be few schools who could not make use of voluntary aides. There is undoubtedly a largely untapped volunteer labour force awaiting recruitment in most areas.

If use is to be made of the advantages of integration with the local community, a plan must be developed to foster that development. The responsibility, in the first instance, must be the head teacher's. But in this he or she should seek to act as a co-ordinator of the school's efforts rather than as the sole link with the outside world. If there is to be joint action then there must be a clear definition of the goals to be achieved. Equally the staff must be willing to accept these goals. The staff, the parents and the children are all agents of the school and as such need to be adequately prepared to meet that responsibility.

The head teacher will need to define with which elements in the local community he or she is going to establish contact, and then seek to rationalise the avenues of approach in relation to the time allocated for completing this task. These avenues of approach will include the development of good relations with the local press, the production of adequate publicity material and the acceptance of as many invitations as possible to speak to local organisations on the work of the school.

It is of equal importance to ensure that the communication channel operates in both directions. The community needs to have the opportunity to view the school in operation and to see its strengths as well as being aware, at first hand, of its specific needs.

Whilst the head teacher is in a privileged position to act as the main community liaison officer, he or she is by no means the only worker in this field. The staff, by their individual membership of local organisations, by their contribution to in-service training programmes operating on an L.E.A. basis, and above all by their individual and personal contacts will play a major role in this work. The head must therefore consider how to bring about a consensus view of the kind of briefing each representative of the school should have before attempting to carry out this task.

THE HEAD AND STAFF DEVELOPMENT

The development of teachers' centres as a focus for local initiatives in teacher in-service education serves to underline the difficulties that beset many special schools. Whilst it remained economic for even moderately funded L.E.A.s to promote staff development within their teachers' centres, the incidence of children with specific difficulties was assumed so low that in-service training provision for special schools' staffs was only provided on a token basis. The problem at that point was clear enough. However, the publication of the Warnock Report (D.E.S., 1978) highlighted the falseness of the premise that the incidence of learning difficulty is synonymous with placement in a special school. Although a rapid increase in the amount of in-service training provision, made available to both special and mainstream school staff, might have been expected, that has not generally proved to have been the case. Special schools have often, therefore, been thrown back on their own resources in order to solve this problem.

It is tempting to suggest that where a L.E.A. is not in a position to provide the resources necessary for in-service training, schools may make a rod for their own backs if they act unilaterally. However, it can also be argued that having conducted in-service training, schools are in a better position to present a case for further resources. The case for in-school self-financed training of staff does not rest on the immediate absence of L.E.A. funding alone. The ever-increasing sophistication of training needed by teachers working with special needs children would suggest that the economies of scale will always militate against adequate provision being made outside the school. Coupled with this is the point that other staff working with the children, and who need further development, are even less likely to have their training needs met externally.

As more clearly defined goals and strategies for their achievement are developed, it will be necessary to equip the staff, and in particular new members, with knowledge of the methods of achieving these objectives. In this case the school will almost always have to use its own more experienced staff to provide assistance. The need to familiarise staff, of differing professional expertise, with newly developed teaching programmes, underlines the necessity for a system of defining training requirements on an individual basis. In-school training of staff, particularly that of an interdisciplinary nature, also allows the institution greater control of the qualitative aspects of the work. Increasingly, practical training in the acquisition of skills offers opportunities to conduct an objective evaluation of teaching ability as well as allowing staff members to gain feedback in a supportive setting. Staff motivation in relation to personal development is also likely to be positively affected by appropriately planned and executed in-school training.

The role of the head teacher in this aspect of the school's activities is most advantageously centred upon acting as a stimulator rather than a conductor. It can be argued that, except in the case of those schools fortunate enough to have a full-time member of staff organising in-service training, no one individual should conduct the staff development programme. The main substance of the argument would be that an individual who is committed to teaching a specific group of children cannot at the same time have a sufficient breadth of vision to train colleagues who are drawn from a wide professional base. Apart from that point, the time factor alone would almost certainly result in impossible demands being placed on the individual concerned.

The task of organising the staff development programme is more likely to fall directly upon the head in smaller schools. Whether the head is responsible for the organisation of in-service training or not, he or she will need to play a major part in promoting staff involvement in such work.

The methods by which the head can perform this part of his or her role are numerous. In the early stages of the work it will be necessary for the head to make a positive and direct contribution to training sessions. As staff perceive the worth of the work, the talents of others can be increasingly employed and eventually contributions can be sought from those outside the school. However, it will be necessary for the head to ensure that any such external contributions are relevant to staff perceptions of their own needs.

Allowing that this will not always be the case, the occasion of a contribution which is not recognised by the staff to be appropriate to their needs can itself be turned to some advantage. Such an occasion may well present an opportunity to raise the issue of developing a satisfactory system of determining the training needs of staff on an individual basis. With an ultimate goal of establishing a system of annual training needs interviews it should be possible for the head, intent on capitalising on this opportunity, to persuade colleagues of the desirability of creating a formalised consultative process.

Clearly the head's role as a stimulator of staff training cannot be viewed in isolation from other aspects of his or her work. The methods of promoting staff interest in this, as in other areas of the school's function, must depend on the progress made towards staff involvement at all levels of decision-taking. For a period of time the eliciting of staff views on the worth of particular elements of the training programme may have to be gained from informal discussions. However, total dependence on such an approach is unlikely to produce totally valid and reliable responses.

The use of post-session questionnaires, the results of which are published without the contributor's identity being established, is more likely to provide an exact view of staff reaction. Given that the results of such surveys are acted upon, the interest of staff is likely to be sustained. Staff motivation in training, as in other aspects of the school's operation, is likely to be positively affected by the style of individual contact adopted by the head teacher. This will, of course, in turn be affected by the degree of credibility awarded to the head by the staff. A further opportunity for motivating the staff arises from the head's perception of the need to persuade colleagues of the desirability of sharing their skills with mainstream teachers. It is hoped that this perception will extend to incorporating the need to acquire new skills to perform more demanding tasks. In particular, responsibility for the work of others has come to be recognised in both financial and promotional terms. Motivation to acquire managerial and other relevant skills is likely to be enhanced if the relationship between acquisition, performance and appointment to senior positions is clear.

The view has been expressed (Warwick, 1975) that the best in-service training is that which takes place as close to the job as possible. If this holds true it follows that the head should seek to persuade colleagues of the desirability of contributing to the development of others.

THE HEAD AS INNOVATOR

Special schools are frequently thrown back on their own resources in terms of development as a result of appearing within local authority provision as a minority interest. It is unreasonable to expect many L.E.A.s to provide in-depth professional support to schools whose role is assumed to be highly specialised. If there is cause, therefore, for the special school head to pay particular attention to any one aspect of his or her role, it is almost certainly that concerned with innovation. Given that situation, coupled with the expectation placed upon the schools to offer an ever-widening range of family support services, the innovatory aspect of the special school head's role is one of major significance.

These particular considerations aside, the special

school is open to the pressures to develop, and consequently to those on the head to innovate, which are common to all schools. Awareness of the educational process as a dynamic concept, recognition that schools cannot isolate themselves from the influence of external agencies and above all acknowledgement that many new developments are likely to have their origins outside the service, are all factors requiring careful consideration by managers of educational institutions.

In the future, the need for the special school head to act as an innovator is likely to be increased as a direct result of a growing number of children with learning difficulties being educated in mainstream settings. The fostering and developing of ideas, both in relation to teaching techniques and to the provision of counselling and support services for special needs children, are unlikely to take a premier position in mainstream schools heads' ranking-ordering of priorities.

On the basis of an assumed reduction in the total number of special schools (Brennan, 1982), the remaining heads must of necessity devote a greater part of their energies to the promotion of new developments. At the same time these activities will need to be conducted bearing in mind the needs of a population wider than is likely to be contained in the special school of the future. The stage is set, therefore, for the special school head to pay further attention to the innovatory aspects of his or her role.

If he or she is to be successful as an innovator, then clearly the head teacher must give some thought to what is involved in the process of innovation. It would appear that in preparing for change, there are two principal areas for consideration. The first is concerned with the background against which any development must take place and the second is focused on the skills which the head must acquire as a prerequisite of any successful programme development.

In a significant number of instances, innovatory projects will involve the acceptance of a central idea by external agencies; furthermore, additional resources may have to be found in order to make the project work. Allowing that in the majority of cases development funds are found by the L.E.A., it will be obvious that an appropriate presentation will have to be made and that the L.E.A.'s normal channels of communication are employed.

The ability to present a well argued case which is clear, succinct and comprehensive is an essential prerequisite of any written submission. It is doubtful if a prepared paper alone will suffice in a majority of cases and therefore preparation of supplementary material, which may need to be presented orally, is of equal importance. To perform both these tasks the head will need to have researched all possible information relevant to the case and in particular be prepared to meet all potential counter-arguments.

One of the benefits arising from the development of teaching programmes which are focused on the achievement of specific goals is that schools are in a position to employ the same planning principles when seeking to create change. The number of L.E.A. officers who report that it is difficult to establish the true worth of many innovatory developments is sufficient to give cause for concern. It follows that a clear definition of the specific goals of the project is an essential first step in the process.

In recognition of the fact that much of local authority operational planning is based upon the rule of precedent, time spent investigating parallel projects would appear rarely to be wasted. However, not all innovatory projects lend themselves to being supported by objective arguments whose validity is easily evaluated. In such a situation, the personal credibility of the presenter, and his or her commitment to the ideas fundamental to the project, become of even greater importance to the case.

Whilst case presentation is of major relevance to any new project, clearly it is not the only matter for consideration. Any appropriately planned development is manifested as a multi-faceted process covering the aspects outlined below.

Beyond the initial case presentation it is arguable that the four most significant aspects of all innovatory developments are the resource locations, the target audience, the implementation methodology and the progress monitoring system. Where financial or material resources are concerned, it is comparatively simple to quantify the demand and list the potential supplying agencies. However, few developments can take place without ideas and time availability being taken into account. If they are viewed as resources, the head teacher will need to consider from where these two important commodities are to be found.

However carefully a case is presented or resource needs and locations identified, if the target audience preparation is given less than adequate attention then the project itself, if not guaranteed to fail, will certainly require an additional investment to make good the deficiencies of that preparation. The total cost of the project will therefore have increased and caused the ultimate worth of the idea to be questioned. In recent times a number of potentially valuable curriculum developments have failed to live up to their early promise despite substantial financial and manpower investments. In many cases it is apparent that this has occurred as a direct result of less than adequate preparation of the target clientele: the implementing teachers and the children they are required to teach.

Closely linked to the adequate preparation of those who are required to deliver or receive the new service is the manner in which the methodology of implementation is to be determined. The benefits of involving the deliverers of the service in the planning of implementation methodology might appear obvious, but again there is evidence to suggest that sufficient attention to this point is not always demonstrated. In his chapter in this volume, Mel Ainscow further elaborates on the importance of adequate staff participation in any curriculum innovation.

Finally, before any major development is put into operation, it is of obvious value to define a system of progress monitoring. Goal achievement may be the most apparent symbol of success, but if lessons are to be learned for future developments then the establishment of a process of evaluating the sub-elements of the plan and its implementation are likely to prove of considerable worth.

Despite all the planning which it is argued here is imperative for success, it should not be forgotten that the English education system has made major steps forward via an apparent process of makeshifts. The quality of planning is perhaps not what is questioned but the occasion of implementation. The possibilities of opportunity should not, perhaps, be totally discounted.

Chapter Five

SHARED LEADERSHIP IN THE SCHOOL - "Primus inter pares"

by Ian Galletley

The means of decision-making has traditionally been less available to schoolteachers than decision direction or content. It is the intention of this chapter to demonstrate that an alternative leadership strategy is not only a desirable objective for educational management in its own right, but also that it is more likely to attain most stated objectives. Exceptional objectives which democratic decision-making cannot attain are those clustered around anti-democratic thought.

This writer bases the chapter on nine years' experience of collective decision-making in special schools, six of these as a head teacher. It is worth noting at this stage that Poster (1976) claims that there are very few instances of successful democratic processes in schools; he may, though, be confusing different models of "democracy".

The two major genres may be termed "romantic" or "parliamentary/bureaucratic". Although perhaps similarly intentioned, the differences between the two are very great. The writer favours the latter, regarding the former as unsupportable within the rule-governed confines of a state education system.

Special schools are similar managerially to those older industries which have suffered worst in the economic recession. Both groups attempt to face the future with a largely unchanged product, both have failed to retrain and reequip for new circumstances and both have failed to see the possibility of new circumstances until they arrived. The failure for many years of special school management to develop the curriculum led to chronic insecurity prior to the publication of the Warnock Report (D.E.S., 1978) and to enforced change via the 1981 Education Act. At both times schools employing a traditional, hierarchical pattern of management could not demonstrate sufficient flexibility to cope creatively with new stimuli or demands. The nature of élitist management tends towards equilibrium and stagnation, since these states maintain the status and salaries of senior post holders. It thus reflects the conservatism common in many senior staff of special schools. This group is unique in education in having a heavy vested interest in learning failure. Their schools may be seen as seeking success equally with other schools, but depending on prior failure to supply a raison d'être. They also have a ready-made reason for any subsequent failure: that of the child's apparent inability. At times when children were referred in abundance, this attitude was self-evidently successful; however, as referral patterns change, it can be seen as a symptom of the deeper educational malaise of low expectations - of both children and professionals.

It is possible to object to predominant management values on ethical grounds, quite apart from their quantifiable ineffectiveness. The industrial analogy does not, of course, fully apply to educational criteria; in most states industry exists, unfortunately, merely to produce and create wealth, and it does not perceive a role concerned with human growth. Schools are intended to "develop" rather than "make" the children with whom they are concerned. It is then reasonable to ask if this should not apply equally to adults working within them. Educational managers, through their systems of ordinance, too frequently contradict their stated aims for the children (e.g. "independence", "maturity") in their dealings with subordinate adults.

One can therefore embark on a process of democratisation from either an evaluative, "cost-effective" stance, or from the impetus of a superordinate philosophy, or from a combination of both. The more the impetus comes from the first source, the more likely the method chosen is to be parliamentary-bureaucratic, the more from the latter source, the greater the chance of its being romantic in design and implementation.

MANAGEMENT AND EMOTION

Hierarchies do not exist to consider the feelings of participants other than those in the greatest authority. The élite are constantly reassured by the insulation of power, but subordinates have no "upward" channel for unhappiness other than through highly mechanistic means such as the withdrawal of labour. In special schools, where industrial action is very rare, those who cannot liberate feeling because of apprehension or anxiety are left powerless and alienated; this is particularly galling when its ethos is supposedly the strongest element of a special school's approach. Authority uses the good will of professionals towards disadvantaged children to ensure that autocracy remains unchallenged.

Democratic decision-making procedures are not necessarily "happier" than their counterparts, but they are more healthy because of their comparative openness and susceptibility to the input of the individual. It is therefore difficult to prophesy accurately the outcomes of an individual set of interactions. Some may feel acutely threatened and seek either to leave the system or sabotage it; others may unexpectedly flourish and develop. Such differences will not fit neatly into previously distributed salary scales, and an early challenge for an infant democracy will be the management of the disparity between institutionalised and individualised roles. This applies in all human groups where wider social values are at variance with in-group values.

The speed at which a given school environment will "feel" more mentally healthy will depend significantly on the disposition of neuroticism in the adults concerned, the extent to which democratic processes are permitted to penetrate the school's activities, the career mobility of disenchanted staff, the tenacity of the head teacher as an initiator and so on. One can generalise, however, to say that given procedures, particularly of the parliamentary variety, combined with the traditionally accepted view of the head as an authority figure, will, if sensitively handled, produce a more cooperative and recognisably pro-active atmosphere. These procedures will be discussed in detail subsequently.

WHAT IS A "GOOD" SCHOOL?

A head teacher may initiate collective decision-making in an undemocratic way, by merely announcing that the school will henceforth be administered in that fashion. This would be the last autocratic decision he or she would make, but it would never alter the fact that in doing so, he or she would be constantly exercising his/her prerogative. To democratize is not to relinquish responsibility; rather, it is to make available the reality of power whilst seeking to be acknowledged through merit, and circumstances external to the school, as the chief executive. This executive would be putting into practice policies agreed as acceptable by as large a majority of adult opinion as possible.

An early value judgement is thus imposed. Consensus rule gains some status by its being chosen as the means of government. Those who subsequently oppose it are either those who feel former status threatened, or those who enjoy attacking authority because of emotional inadequacy or minor personality disorder.

A "healthy" school is seen inevitably, therefore, by democrats, as being democratic. However, in Dalin's (1978) terms, "goodness" should not be confused with "health", since a democratic school could be used to make "bad" decisions. A group of adults might collectively decide to introduce cannibalism at school lunchtimes; it is quite unlikely that the L.E.A. would regard this as symptomatic of a "good" school. "Goodness" is defined by <u>all</u> the participants.

> A "good" school is more than a "healthy" school. A "healthy" school might live within its own norms and values; it is healthy in the terms set out above, but it is not necessarily good for everyone. A "good" school is first a "healthy" school but it goes beyond that. The question of what is a good school is primarily a question of values. Do we agree with the objectives and the values guiding the school? A very traditional subject-oriented school might very well be a "healthy" school, but not necessarily a "good" school. A "good" school then is one that is healthy with values with which we can identify. A "good" school is a school that is good for "me". (Dalin, 1978, p. 54)

It is considered perfectly rational for teachers to discuss the "quality" of a school. Dalin's point is that this is a consensus activity in itself. Standards for "quality" cannot be arbitrarily imposed in areas such as the interaction between the school and the environment, human relations and strategies for responsibility, and yet maintain a veneer of consensus. The nature of "quality" in these areas is <u>negotiated</u> between the participants, albeit unequally.

Traditionally, values have remained fairly static, allowing complex organisational structures to develop for the maintenance of the status quo. At a time of plentiful referrals to special education this is understandable even if not, in this writer's view, desirable. Dalin (1978) proposes a systematic learning organisation, "... whereby political control over educational development can be maintained, and at the same time create a system whereby each individual has a genuine possibility of choice among alternatives and has influence over his or her own development" (p. 55). He proposes an open structure, which becomes creative for all, in the hope that the widest possible variety of input will lead to a more informed response to agreed difficulties and decisions. Agreeing what the problem is, is in fact part of the solution to the problem.

Burns and Stalker (1966) discriminate between mechanistic and organic forms of organisation. Mechanistic organisations are hierarchical, with specialised tasks; control of objectives is centred on a few individuals, initiatives come only from above, and interaction tends to be "vertical".

Organic structures are more responsive to change, and are constantly redefining their tasks and how the tasks are to be completed. Problems are "owned" collectively and communication is circular or horizontal, since authority is earned and status is justified and acknowledged, without the debilitating psychological disorder of a hierarchy.

This writer has always assumed that organic structures are not only more effective in an industrialised society in a state of readjustment, but also that they are more inherently just. Let us therefore proceed to a discussion of how collective decision-making might be implemented.

STRUCTURES FOR COLLECTIVE DECISION-MAKING

Some organisations which are fundamentally undemocratic regularly claim that decisions are made collectively within themselves: the board of directors who "speak for" the shareholders, the autocratic trade union which "represents" its members and so on. It might be possible to define a democratic body as any body within a democracy, but this would obviously be a deliberate obfuscation. No, a democracy only exists when all its participants are granted an equal right to an opinion, to voice that opinion, and an equal right to vote for it. If these essentials are to be maintained once established, ordinances must be effected which resist anti-democratic procedures. This is not likely to be achieved through a romantic, loosely-knit group approach. State schools are too influenced by external forces to enable them to exist in opposition to predominant values. Success and progress are only achieved by offering attractive gradualist policies. Salary scales and community expectations ensure that answerability will continue to be applied differentially. The psychological enterprise of open group dynamics has never been successfully undertaken in an L.E.A. school, but an understanding of human interaction in groups is essential to the formulation of rules for a democratic body. Such rules may be kept to a minimum, not only remaining within the law, but encouraging initiative.

A satisfactory set of standing orders for a democratic

special school decision-making body would be as follows:

(1) The Staff Council may discuss and make proposals on any aspect of school life susceptible to change.

(2) All adults working full-time in the school are eligible for full membership.

(3) A simple majority of votes will carry a proposal into action.

(4) The officers will be a chairman and a secretary, elected annually.

(5) All ballots will be secret unless designated otherwise by the Council.

(6) All meetings will end by -- o'clock.

(7) The head teacher retains the right of veto.

(8) The Council will not discuss matters of a confidential nature relating to any member's personal or professional life.

(9) More than 60% of all members must be present at any meeting.

(10) The staff shall not meet unless a seconded proposal is placed on the agenda.

(11) Members may/may not smoke during meetings.

(12) Typed copies of minutes will be available to all members before meetings take place.

(13) The Council meets on ---days.

(14) The management team retains the right to make decisions outside the Council, but all decisions are answerable within it.

On first examination, these standing orders may seem bland, almost non-committal, since they do not seek to describe in detail the specific nature of decisions to be made inside the body itself. It is this writer's opinion, however, that this is not significant, since the institutional nature of schools will ensure that it operates within decision-making parameters similar to those of a more traditionally managed school.

The first and major ordinance of a Staff Council, allied with the fourteenth, often takes staff some time to assimilate; that all aspects of the school's life are available for review. This does not, of course, mean that no decision can be made without a meeting; some decisions are more effectively made individually or in smaller groups. Examples of this might be the review of a child's progress, or curriculum decisions for a very particular area of understanding. However, major decisions concerning the overall development of any "thinking" school must by definition be made openly, since the majority of the participants otherwise become implementers only, rather than thinkers. It might be seen as rash to open so many fundamentals to all, but if the head has intellectual stature, experience shows that staff follow a combination of who he or she is and what he or she says. If the head has no intellect, staff merely follow the former determinant. It is this writer's belief that unless staff are convinced that an innovation is rational and likely to achieve its stated objectives, they are unlikely to permit it to do so, even though they may be obliged to by force majeure. Thus the only true lesson they learn in an autocracy is the truth of power and how it is operated. The objectives actually being attained may be very different from those imagined by the initiator. For example, children may make more gains in reading scores, but at the cost of hating books for the rest of their lives.

The inclusion of all adults in the decision-making body, rather than making it the exclusive preserve of teachers, may prove contentious, but only initially. Considerations of status amongst teachers, and of inferiority amongst non-teaching staff, are rapidly dispelled, destined to remain only in that minority who object to democratisation in all its aspects. Non-teaching staff tend not to vote or participate in those matters which they do not fully understand, but they are vital in bringing a commonsense appraisal to the often presumptuous schemes of schoolteachers. They also tend to supply from amongst their ranks excellently unbiased officers for the Council, and are usually its staunchest defenders at times of difficulty or stress, for they appreciate better than teachers how it feels to have low status and no real influence over their working lives. In special schools the distinctions between teaching and non-teaching staff often become blurred, in terms of job definitions, control of classes and significance in the eyes of the children. It is therefore a simpler matter to propose their admission to a Council than it might be in some mainstream schools, where they might be regarded as members of an inferior caste, doing a job very different from that of a teacher.

The use of a simple majority rule is only a starting

point for a negotiation about change. It is possible that such a rule could alienate sizeable minorities of opinion, constantly being overruled. Differential arrangements can therefore be made for decisions of varied significance. For instance, it might be decided that a restructuring of job descriptions would call for a seventy-five per cent majority, whereas an amendment to the day and time of meeting would require eighty-five or ninety per cent. A decision on the date of an occasional meeting might require only a simple majority, the allocation of school fund monies sixty-six per cent and so on. Arrangements become satisfactory when they are "legal" in the eyes of participants.

Experience under both secret and open ballots seems to suggest that the former are more suitable for groups new to the idea of collective decisions. When the group becomes more self-aware, and individuals realise that there is no need for fear when all votes are of equal significance, the open ballot comes quite naturally into use. People who have worked in hierarchical systems often have wounds and antipathies which can take years to heal; they are, in such cases, incapable of accommodating immediately the trauma of complete openness. Open ballots are not more valid per se than secret ones; they merely demonstrate a healthy openness amongst individuals. On a personal note, this writer objects to secret ballots on the grounds that the marking of small pieces of paper by large people around a table in total silence always seems little short of farce. However, if the net result is a decision more readily abided by, then a farce is worthwhile.

No local authority would permit a head teacher to give up the right of veto, for this would symbolise an abdication from the responsibilities of the post. However, having a right does not necessarily mean exercising it; the mere possession of the right ensures that the discussion must remain within certain parameters, as the head teacher of William Tyndale School found to his cost! British head teachers are granted freedom of manoeuvre unparalleled in other countries, but they are ultimately contained within a powerful net. State-governed institutions must be the servants of whatever spoken or unspoken norms prevail within a society at a given time, much as teachers might care to see themselves as creative social engineers. Democratic decision-making in special schools will only ever be capable of achieving objectives within the conservative confines which state institutions, by definition, are permitted to inhabit. Once he or she strays outside these confines, the head's position becomes untenable. Thus, as long as the head remains within a tenable position, the school will not drift into anarchy; it may make a series of decisions which are a collective nonsense, but it will be a legal nonsense. This writer has never used his right of veto.

All this writer's experience shows that openness increases the head's opportunities to create new initiatives, and that those in senior management positions remain responsible for proposing most innovation. This state exists since the people who introduce collective decision-making are also likely to be those with new ideas for all areas of the school's functioning. In this respect, the deputy heads (the school is sufficiently large for two people to be paid as deputies) assume great creative power, for of all staff they tend to flourish most. Many staff prefer to see the Staff Council as a means of stopping events rather than starting them, content to have a safeguard against "injustice".

To include a caveat about the personal lives of Council members is usually unnecessary, since staff almost instinctively steer away from embarrassing situations. However, the few occasions when indiscretions may arise (usually when tempers flare) mean that standing order number eight must remain. Its implementation rests with the Chairman, and should the holder of this post show signs of weakness, other members must remind him/her of his/her responsibility.

It is essential that Council meetings attract sufficient members for their decisions to stick. If attendance falls below two-thirds, decisions tend to degenerate either through apathy or through a lack of preparedness to accept decisions made in one's absence. Enthusiasm can always be generated by way of the agenda, which the head can fill with items of interest to all. On the other hand, meetings should not take place if there is a genuine absence of matters to discuss. Too many school meetings are, as all readers will know, occasions of stultifying boredom.

Standing order number eleven has twice proved an interesting first decision for an infant Council to make. The issue of smoking in meetings is an excellent example of interests in conflict. The way in which the issue is resolved becomes a fascinating exemplar for the Council members; what at first seems a perfectly straightforward issue can quietly be guided into a theoretical consideration of the subordination of the individual's choice to the wishes of the majority.

The choice of a committee procedure for the making of decisions can be criticised as bourgeois, not necessarily appropriate for creative change. This criticism may have some validity, but committee structure does at least guarantee a certain level of democratic expression. Less formal systems, although more creative when totally successful, are slower to implement, more prone to instability when staff changes occur, and more potentially dangerous for the head teacher should his or her concentration fail as overseer to the process. The meeting's formality does, moreover, serve a psychological purpose; its studied composure adds to an air, if not a reality, of detachment and, one hopes, rationality. Most staff greatly enjoy this compliment to their intelligence. Non-teaching staff in particular are initially flattered by being involved, then increasingly interested. Their contributions are often very significant, even though rare, and these members make excellent officers, through pride in their office and wider social experience than can be claimed by many teachers.

Readjustments have to be made when collective decision-making is introduced. Regardless of salary, some members hold disproportionate influence and favouritism under élitist systems. On taking up a new headship, the author recalls a man who himself had no career ambitions but enjoyed manipulating the lives of others; he had been encouraged to divide whilst the head ruled in a previous setting. He found the acceptance of equal significance virtually impossible, believing the majority of humanity to be infinitely more stupid than himself. His position became virtually untenable, as he sought to rebuild identically a shattered role. Other personalities, formerly of depressed status, feel the move towards equality as highly significant, changing the way they perceive their working days.

The head teacher's role might be seen as losing status; this is not the case when democratic decision-making has a part to play in a school. A politician once cynically remarked that a camel was a horse designed by a committee. Many decisions must still be made by the head, and staff are content that it should be so. The Council then exists as a reactive body, commenting on decisions or overturning them.

The Council's greatest strength exists in formulating future policy and achieving a consensus on the means of achieving this. Curriculum development does not take place when it is imposed; it is mere curriculum change. This is a theme strongly emphasised by Mel Ainscow elsewhere in this book. Similarly, individual professional growth can only take place in a cooperative atmosphere. This implies an intellectual and spiritual process quite apart from salary and title, arising solely from a higher estimation of personal worth. Within a hierarchy, this can only be achieved at the expense of another person.

The head teacher's status actually grows when openness is achieved, for the person is measured on two important criteria: the decision to be democratic at all, and the clarity of ideas seeking approval and votes. If a head presents ideas and has them voted into action, how much more likely they are to be successful than if they were arbitrarily imposed.

In such a setting the head relies greatly on the deputy head to explain and prepare the way for a new initiative. The deputy sows seeds, gives information, explains before and after meetings and, very importantly, informs the head of the likelihood of certain reactions. Thus the embarrassment of total rejection of an idea can be avoided. This function of the deputy head depends upon a close working relationship with the head, and frankness of interaction between the management team as a group.

The very different personalities in a school staff gain in various ways from the loosening of former ties. Articulate, extrovert characters seize an early psychological advantage by enhanced freedom of speech. However, this advantage remains psychological only, since quiet introverts have the same voting rights. It is important that talkative people talk, as it is important for reflective people to listen; the latter cannot exist without the former. Indeed, the mechanics and events of Council are of vital importance to the school's functioning, since they are not only cathartic but also act as a barometer of opinion and belief. Head teachers can easily be ignorant of, or misled about, the true events of the school or the climate of opinion within it. Only by guaranteeing freedom of speech will the head be more likely to acquire a reliable reflection of affairs.

MAKING A DECISION

Let us examine the process through which a decision of major significance may be made in a school using collective decision-making techniques. (The following example is hypothetical.)

The head wishes to reconsider the means by which the children are grouped within the school. He wishes to change from chronological to ability groupings. Firstly, he initiates an assessment procedure for all children, saying in Council that it is for the purpose of grouping of children; no one objects. The assessment, a lengthy process, is finally completed, and the head discovers that attainments are sufficiently evenly spread to justify, in his view, an even spread of ability groups. He presents the new groups to the Council, a particular meeting which happens to be sparsely attended. The groups are approved without a vote, but the majority of teachers most affected are not present. The head teacher goes home, pleased that he has "democratically" introduced ability groupings to the school. The summer holidays follow, and the agreed time for the implementation of change arrives. Suddenly, or so it seems to the head teacher, a proposal appears on the agenda that grouping by ability be abandoned. The head teacher realises that he is being played at his own game, and prepares a detailed case to justify ability grouping in general, and ability grouping in that school in particular. The meeting arrives, and the debate is heated. The head wins convincingly on a secret ballot, but is left to wonder whether it is he or his ideas which are being followed. The defeated antagonist retreats to almost perpetual opposition, and ability groups are instituted immediately. What did the head do wrong? He sought to subvert democracy by "back door" diplomacy, and hurled staff into an innovation they did not feel consulted about. As it happened, ability groupings were indeed successful in raising attainments, so the head's judgement was vindicated. However, a lasting impression existed that involvement of the staff from the outset would have been preferable.

Here is a dilemma of the parliamentary-bureaucratic process; the head (prime minister) retains the right to make decisions of a major or minor nature in private, yet can be in trouble for them later. Does this mean that the decisions should not be made, or that this particular sort of conflict is inevitable within an L.E.A. school operating "democratically"? Perhaps the latter is the case, since heads would not wish to give up the capacity to launch major new initiatives.

There is, perhaps, no alternative within a graded salary structure to "inner" and "outer" or "upper" and "lower" levels of accountable responsibility. This certainly has been blurred over years because teachers were formerly in short supply, students plentiful, and promotion often dangerously rapid. Times have changed, and decisions made (and indeed the means by which they were made) have been brought into sharper focus. Much of the blame for the decline in the quality of the special school curriculum, which Philip Williams, in his 1980 address to the N.C.S.E. National Conference, described as the "deserted garden", must lie in complacent leadership; such complacency is inappropriate to a world in which virtually no special school leavers will get a "real" job.

The important decisions facing special education are too significant at this nodal point of the service's history to be made alone; the head should be actively disseminating all appropriate information, promoting new ideas and leading a collective progress towards agreed new directions. Special schools are alone at this time in having the potential to move organisationally in different ways. If they rely on their staffing structure, as reflected in salary scales, to provide the springboard for

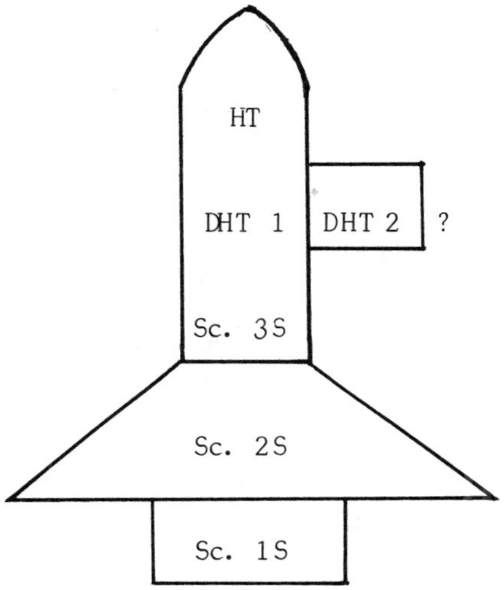

Figure 4: Typical Special School Structure

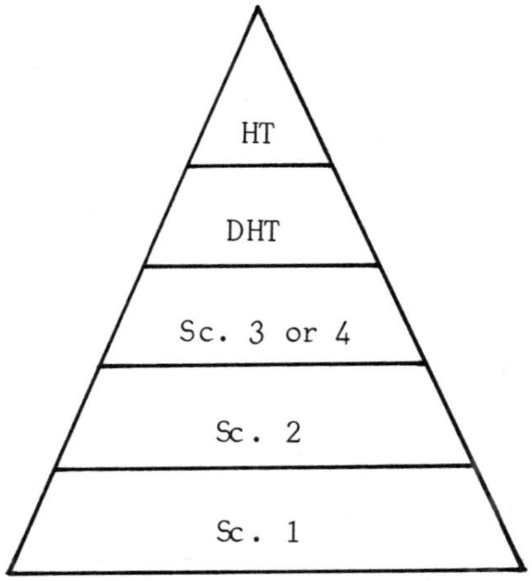

Figure 5: Traditional Hierarchy

Stage 1: Numbers 1-4 (or 1-3) form the management team

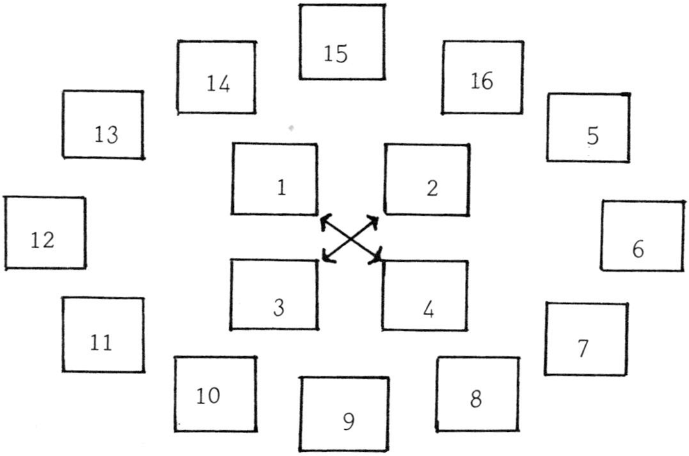

Stage 2: Management team resume their equal status for the discussion of their proposals

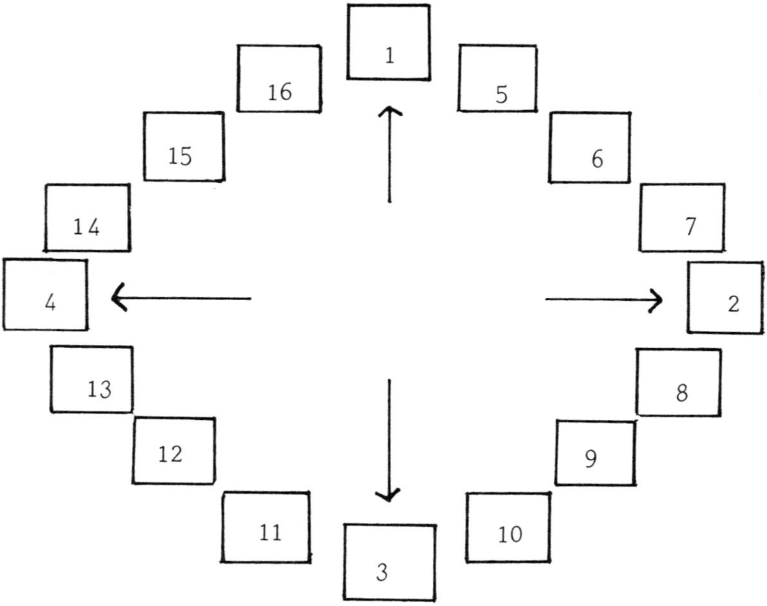

Figure 6: Alternative Management Strategy

change, it is unlikely that they will be successful; what we have (Figure 4) is a curious "aeroplane" creation, unlike larger schools, which are far more pyramidal (see Figure 5). Neither of these configurations, if reflected in attitudes, leads to healthy change. An alternative strategy, as promulgated in this chapter might be demonstrated as shown in Figure 6.

IN CONCLUSIOM

Rée (1968) has defined the head's role as encompassing "listener, encourager, dissuader, reporter, watcher, judge, critic, decision-taker and on occasions commander". This writer would not dispute that all these roles need to be acknowledged and carried out in a modern special school, but as Poster (1968) rightly points out, an overstressing of the charismatic qualities of leadership undervalues the merits of collective responsibility.

Adults in school do need to be led, but with skill, goodwill, honesty and a large slice of good luck, a head does not have to lead alone. Schools administered collectively are not always happier places, since one form of stress can replace another, but they are more just, and justice is a more elegant imperative than force majeure.

SECTION 2

– LINKING THE SPECIAL SCHOOL WITH OUTSIDE SYSTEMS

Chapter Six

SPECIAL SCHOOLS AND THE MAINSTREAM - "THE RESOURCE STRETCH"

by Tony Dessent

INTRODUCTION

"When all is said and done, there is a great deal more said than done." This cynical observation would seem to provide a reasonable description of the state of affairs which exists when considering the whole area of work involving links between special and mainstream schools. The direction for special schools to become "resource centres" and "centres of expertise" was given by Warnock (D.E.S., 1978) and reinforced by the Government White Paper on Special Educational Needs. It has been seen by many heads and teachers in special schools, advisers and psychologists as the most likely future role to be played by special schools, and has featured regularly as an issue at many a special educational conference over the past few years. However, there is a notable absence of any clearly articulated case for such a development, or of any description of what exactly special schools would be doing in this new role. The published literature on the topic is far from prolific and what does exist is either largely speculative (Thompson and Jones, 1974) or of a pilot project/exploratory nature (Ainscow et al, 1978). Published descriptions of special/mainstream services actually operating in Great Britain are few and far between and tend to focus on one well known example (Booth, 1982; Hegarty and Pocklington, 1982; Hallmark and Dessent, 1982; Hallmark, 1983).

Is there a viable role for special schools as resource centres for mainstream schools? Or is the idea no more than a reassuring sop for heads and staff, as in the wake of the new legislation governing special education, special schools are slowly dismantled by L.E.A.s.? There is a need to consider a number of questions. What could be meant by the concept of a resource centre and why has the idea developed? What are the resources which special schools will provide? For whom are they provided and for what purpose? What are the difficulties which exist and what might the future hold?

BACKGROUND - THE ECONOMY OF SURVIVAL

Changes in the nature and role of educational institutions and provisions are rarely instigated by those working from within the educational system. Economic and more general social changes in society's value system usually provide the motivation for change. Thus, the changes that are now being seen in the field of special education result largely from changes in society's view of the place of handicapped individuals, and of minority groups in general, which have led to greater emphasis on issues such as integration and "normalisation".

The position of special schools is an interesting one in this changing climate. As school rolls have fallen, so special schools have developed new orientations. A broader range of client groups is now accepted into any one special school and we have seen the development in some areas of "multicap" schools and centres. Post-16 courses are now common currency and several schools and local education authorities have moved towards the inclusion of pupils in special schools who are placed on a "quick return" ticket to mainstream. The development of the idea of special schools working as resource centres for children with special needs in mainstream schools also has its roots in this "economy of survival". Often individuals involved in this area of development have been acutely aware of the fact that there is rarely any sharp distinction between those children placed in special schools and those children with special needs who remain in mainstream schools. Thus, rather than the special school organising itself to accommodate more of the latter group (as in the "quick return" model), the view is taken that the special school should use its resources to maintain children within the ordinary school in order that the continuum of special need which exists is better matched by a continuum of provision (cf. Hallmark and Dessent, 1982).

Each of the various directions which special schools could take attracts its own advocates. However, the point which they have in common is that each represents an attempt on the part of special schools to survive and to retain, as far as possible, the status quo in a rapidly changing system of providing for children with special needs. Moreover, each of the possible avenues for future development is <u>totally dependent on what is happening outside of the special school and more particularly on the way in which provision is being made, or not being made,</u>

in mainstream schools for children with special needs. It is worth noting at this point that developing a special school as a resource centre should not automatically be regarded as a worthwhile enterprise. The wisdom of such a development depends totally and crucially upon what else is happening within special and mainstream education in the area served by the school. While some special schools may initially look in the direction of developing as a resource centre because of a natural wish to secure a viable role for the school, the future of such a development will eventually be determined by the part played by the school in the overall pattern of special educational and mainstream provision. This interdependence is of course critical in the case of special schools whose client group significantly overlaps with the children with special needs who remain in mainstream classes, in particular E.S.N.(M) and maladjusted schools. What is clear is that in whatever directions such schools move in the future, they cannot afford to remain as they were.

THE RESOURCE CENTRE CONCEPT

Fish (see Chapter One in this volume) has provided a useful breakdown of the kind of resource centre a special school could become and has analysed some of the necessary pre-conditions for their successful operation. A further analysis of what the resource centre concept could mean comes from looking at what has been done by schools actually engaged in this kind of work.

What Resources?

Probably the biggest single problem for many special schools wishing to develop a resource centre role hinges around the identification of resources relevant to mainstream schools and/or parents which are "transportable". The central resource will almost invariably involve teacher/personnel time of members of staff at the special school who have the requisite skills and expertise, in conjunction with either learning and curricula materials or an in-service training function. One of the best known and most frequently described examples of a special school operating as a resource or "service" centre is Heltwate School in Peterborough (described in Hegarty and Pocklington, 1982; Booth and Statham, 1982; Hallmark and Dessent, 1982; and Hallmark, 1983). This school has evolved two major support services for children with special needs in the community which it serves. These are: a Pre-school Portage Home Teaching Service and a Primary School Liaison Service. In addition, the school supports and resources schools and teachers in a number of more informal ways outside of these two services. The central resources utilised by Heltwate in both the Portage Service and the Primary School Liaison Work are staff time (in order to carry out weekly visits to homes and schools and in attending co-ordination and planning meetings) and learning resources and materials. The latter includes toys, language programmes and Portage materials in the case of the pre-school service. The Primary School Service, in supporting up to 100 pupils with special needs in local schools, utilises large quantities of learning resources - early reading, number, language and fine motor materials - as well as supporting games, etc. Much of this material is in worksheet and card format. The work described at Longford School, Gloucester (Last, 1983) appears to have a number of similar elements. Again the principal resources utilised in their experimental "special needs service" is the time of four teachers to visit a number of local primary and secondary schools. Staff are described as utilising a "foundation skills assessment schedule" in their support work with schools which is followed up by the introduction of learning materials produced at the special school in: early language, number, reading, spelling, number and visual perceptual skills.

Thus the major resource requirement for a special school wishing to develop a resource centre approach along these lines would be the availability of sufficient teacher time, from staff with the necessary experience/ expertise, coupled with an adequate supply of transportable learning resources relevant to the needs of children outside their school. The latter requirement is an important one and the difficulties involved in producing and reproducing such materials are not to be underestimated. Few special schools have in the past managed to develop curriculum and learning materials in sufficient quantity and of sufficient quality for their own internal use, let alone for the use of others.

A number of special schools will have attempted to utilise their potential to provide in-service courses for teachers working in mainstream schools. One published report is that of a pilot project based at the Castle School in Walsall (Ainscow et al, 1978). As the authors note in this case, the major resource which is being drawn upon revolves around specialist knowledge which has been put into practice in the special school and which is not evident in normal schools. A course aimed at teachers working in infant schools in the locality and based upon a behavioural approach to learning difficulties and behaviour problems in the classroom was set up. As a result of this pilot project, the authors raise a number of sensible issues and reservations relating to the development of the special school as a resource of advice for teachers in mainstream education. Some of these will be returned to later.

While learning materials and in-service courses have been the principal resources utilised in these recorded projects, a number of other possibilities exist. These might include: special schools acting as a physical resource base for the storage, maintenance and development of specialised equipment used by children within mainstream schools (e.g. special schools for physically and sensory handicapped children); teachers from a special school providing a teaching input for individuals or groups of children with special needs in ordinary schools. An example of the latter, albeit not from a special school base, for disruptive children in secondary schools is documented in the journal Special Education: Forward Trends (Barnsley Special Education Team, 1981). Another option would be for the special school to provide the base for teachers in mainstream schools to gain experience of working with children with special needs, via perhaps a teacher/exchange model.

Whatever the principal resource utilised by the special school in its role as a resource centre, the central questions to be answered are:

(1) Is the resource available in a transportable form? For instance, does the school have a well-thought-out curriculum which has been translated into tangible teaching resources? Do the teachers in the school possess knowledge, skills and expertise which they are able to transmit effectively to other personnel?

and

(2) Is it relevant to the needs of the world outside the special school?

Resources - for whom?

Teachers of children with special needs in ordinary schools are usually the main focus for special schools developing a role as an area resource centre. The Heltwate School example includes a service aimed at parents of pre-school children with special needs and a fruitful area of development for some special schools might be to focus on parents as the target clients. This is more likely to be the case, in fact, where the overlap in terms of needs of the children placed in a special school and those of children with special needs in mainstream classes, is slight or indeed non-existent. For example, in the case of the school catering for severely and profoundly mentally handicapped children, the overlap of needs is likely to be minimal unless the local authority has a policy of mainstream placement for some mentally handicapped children. Here we are likely to see some extensive developments in the role of special schools acting as a resource for parents (either via a home visiting scheme or via the parent workshop model (Cunningham and Jeffree, 1975). Extensions of this approach could also include a special school catering for the mentally handicapped acting as a valuable resource to care staff in a variety of settings and to foster parents/parent substitutes.

For those special schools where the overlap of the needs of children served with those in mainstream is great, then the provision made for children with special needs in mainstream schools could, in the future, form the major focus for a special school operating as a resource centre. As provision in ordinary schools develops, the need for co-ordination, resourcing and support for the teachers and other staff involved is likely to become increasingly apparent. Thus special needs staff working in normal schools could, in the future, be linked in various ways to existing special school provision.

THE "RESOURCE STRETCH"

Regardless of (a) which resources a special school employs and (b) for whom it employs them, the development of a special school as a resource centre usually originates from a need to extend or stretch resources from one location (special school) to another, or several other, locations. This is not to be confused with "over-stretching" the resources of a special school (although this too can easily happen). The point is that the need for teachers from a special school to support teachers from a mainstream school, whether by the provision of learning resources, in-service education, or any other means, is based upon the lack of such resources in the mainstream school. The real need is usually for new or different resources to be made available in those schools. The desirability or otherwise of a special school operating as a resource centre is a secondary issue that may or may not relate to these resource needs. Thus, while it may make a great deal more administrative or economic sense to use special schools to bridge the resource gap than, say, to increase the staffing of mainstream schools or make specific appointments of teachers to work with children with special needs, it may, on its own, prove to have limited educational value in terms of meeting the needs of children in mainstream schools. One thing is certain and that is that new resources or redeployed "old resources" will be required, either in mainstream schools, special schools or perhaps in both, in order to fill the resource gaps.

WHAT IS REQUIRED TO MAKE IT WORK?

There is as yet too little practical experience of developing special schools as resource centres, and a complete absence of any organised evaluation, to answer this question with any certainty. However, a tentative listing of some of the prerequisites for successful development would be as follows:

(1) A commitment from head teacher and staff of a special school towards meeting the needs of children outside the special school. What is required here is more than positive attitudes towards such an approach. Teaching staff will need to feel as committed and responsible for children in homes or other schools as they do for children directly in their charge. For many staff, this will not be an easy task. Many teachers who work in special schools have gravitated towards them from a desire to work directly with children who have failed in mainstream schools. Their interests are in the individual child with special needs, their approach child-centred, and their rewards come from seeing progress being made by the individual child in their class or school. The resource centre approach requires a commitment from such staff to individual pupils with special needs outside their immediate working context; pupils who they may rarely, if ever, see and who are the direct responsibility of another teacher, professional or parent. This kind of work might be regarded by staff as "advisory" rather than teaching, as "teaching teachers" rather than teaching children, and as far too nebulous in terms of reward and feedback compared to that received directly in the confines of the teacher's own classroom or school.

Clearly many special school staff who have been long in the business of traditional special school work will not feel able to take on this role, and are therefore unlikely to have the kind of commitment required. It is also patently unrealistic and unfair to expect such staff to change their attitudes overnight. Nor does it seem likely that any unilateral move on the part of a head teacher to operate a school as a resource centre which does not take account of staff competences and philosophies will succeed in the long term. For the head teacher and individual staff involved in support work of this kind, commitment to such a service needs to be viewed in exactly the same way - and with equal priority - as work with children placed in the special school itself. The day-to-day happenings, incidents and emergencies which occur in a school of any kind cannot be allowed to detract from the responsibilities assumed by the special school staff in their resource centre role. If support work of this kind is regarded as a secondary function of the school, something which happens when time and energy allows, then it is unlikely that any credible well-maintained service will develop. New special schools which begin with this kind of role writ large at the outset, and where staff are appointed to operate a resource centre service, have of course fewer problems to overcome. Their difficulties may in fact have more to do with the attitudes of personnel and services external to the school than with the attitudes and commitment of teachers within the special school.

(2) <u>The role developed by the special school should "fit" with the overall special/remedial provision of the area which it serves.</u> Clear and unequivocal L.E.A. policy on its provision for children with special needs is a rarity. Existing provision in most authorities can usually only be made sense of via a long historical perspective which has more to do with personalities and local politics than a rationally developed policy. It is usually within this context that new developments in the role played by a special school will occur. The development of a resource centre model which is motivated only by the whim and fancy of the special school head teacher or staff, and which has no external backing, is probably doomed to failure in the long term. Such developments need to take account of the role played by a number of other support services, e.g. peripatetic remedial staff, advisory teachers, psychologists and advisers.

Territorial disputes between such groups can all too easily arise. Within an area which has a well-organised, well-resourced remedial service (a comparative rarity!), it might be maintained that there is little need for a support service from a special school for children with learning difficulties in mainstream schools. In some areas problems can arise between the role played by "support" teachers working from a special school base, and the L.E.A. Psychological Service. This might be the case particularly when the "support" service includes an assessment, diagnosis, and advice service to mainstream schools. The level of involvement of the Schools Psychological Service with the development and role of special educational facilities in the area concerned is crucial in this respect. The attitudes of heads and teachers in local mainstream schools is another important contextual factor. A support service offered to schools at a time when their own remedial/special provision is being cut, when overall resources are being reduced and where a strong lobby exists for securing "in-school" provision, may be regarded as a less than helpful sop by mainstream staff.

These cautionary notes do not imply that special schools should play a passive role in the policy and provision for children with special needs in their area, nor that the development of a resource centre approach needs to wait upon L.E.A. policy or initiatives from outside the special school. The very essence of the concept of the special school offering support services itself is to effect change and initiative <u>outside</u> the school. However, developments of this nature will ultimately need backing and resourcing. To secure this, special schools will need to be in the business of convincing agencies outside the school that they have something to offer which is needed in the area which they serve. Head teachers and schools wishing to develop such a role will do well to involve relevant administrative, advisory and psychological service staff at the outset to secure agreements and backing which will avoid, as far as possible, the conflict of interests which can arise.

(3) <u>Adequate staffing and resourcing</u>. If all new developments which occurred in education waited upon the availability of adequate resources, there would be no new developments. Most projects and innovations depend for their success upon the energy, commitment and initiatives of individuals and groups of individuals who

"stretch the resources" available to them, often beyond reasonable limits, to secure the developments they desire. In many situations such "unresourced" developments pay off. The positive results obtained lead to acknowledgement of the development and the necessary resources to maintain the initiative follow. Special schools which are concerned to redefine and redevelop their roles are almost certain, to a greater or lesser extent, to be in the situation of having initially to "stretch their resources" in this way. The positive involvement of L.E.A. administrative, advisory and psychological service staff from the outset is of crucial importance in this respect. Ultimately, of course, the energy, commitment and enthusiasm of individuals is not sufficient to maintain developments of this nature. What might initially be a "shoe-string" initiative will eventually need to be put on a firmer financial footing.

Staffing will, as always, be probably the most important resource upon which to gain some leeway. At times of falling rolls or initial build-up of numbers of children admitted to a special school, a more favourable staffing ratio might be negotiated. This would enable the flexibility of teacher time which is required to provide support services from the special school. As important as the availability of teacher time is the calibre of staff available to offer the services envisaged. Ainscow et al (1978), discussing the results of their in-service education approach from a special school to mainstream schools, note "many special school teachers are skilful classroom operators, knowledgeable in the theoretical and practical issues. Passing on such expertise to other teachers is completely different, requiring new skills and techniques not necessarily found amongst teachers whose experience is solely with children" (p. 16).

Whether the approach adopted is in-service education or follows the model of the "visiting teacher/learning resources based" approach previously described, new and different skills are required from special school teachers.

Adequate staffing for a resource centre based service is, of course, only the tip of the resources iceberg. The level of consumption which can be reached in terms of learning materials (paper, card, printing etc.), not to mention hardware (language masters, tape recorders, storage facilities), can be considerable. Whatever the starting point in terms of an acceptable level of resourcing for such a service, its successful future development will entail a whole host of additional financing which ultimately the L.E.A. will need to take on board.

(4) An organisational structure which will ensure maintenance of the service over time. There are two vital aspects which relate to organisation. The first is that of the internal organisation required within a special school to enable external resource support to occur. An example of the way one special school has organised itself and deployed staff in this respect is detailed elsewhere (Hallmark and Dessent, 1982). The essential requirements are that staff involved in any external support work can be readily and easily freed from their internal work in the special school, and that material resources required can be constructed, prepared, monitored and made readily accessible for external use. The point to be made is that a special school is unlikely to be able to offer services to the world outside that special school and itself remain unchanged. Support services cannot easily be something tagged on to the day-to-day operation of the school. Their operation will have important implications for the internal organisation and work of staff in the special school base itself.

Secondly, and certainly of equal importance, is the need to develop an organisational structure which will ensure effective management, monitoring and evaluation of any support service. It is as well to sort out this aspect of the service right at the outset. The involvement of as many individuals as possible within the L.E.A. administrative and advisory services in a management/monitoring role is vital. This might involve periodic meetings of "managers" at which regular feedback and progress reports on the work being undertaken are provided by the special school staff concerned. The day-to-day supervision of the work is an additional concern. There is a need to ensure that a format exists which enables sharing of information, problem solving and mutual support to occur amongst the members of staff concerned. This may take the form of regular staff meetings with the special school staff involved, which again need to be planned into the internal organisation of the school's work.

These organisational aspects are crucial because of their bearing on the maintenance and long-term development of a resource centre service. As anyone who has been involved in some kind of innovatory work will know only too well, beginning the work is relatively easy; maintaining developments over time when the first waves of enthusiasm have passed is the most difficult part.

THE ADVANTAGES

The extension of a special school service into the mainstream can involve a number of advantages for the special school itself. If a useful and viable role is developed, this may increase the survival value of the school - if this is in question or likely to be so in the future. At a less cynical level, enormous professional benefits can accrue simply as a result of the increased level of contact between special school staff and mainstream staff and children. The special school staff concerned can obtain a new, fresh and realistic view of the extent and nature of children's difficulties within and outside the special school, of the curriculum and expectations for children which are held in mainstream schools, and of the problems and perspectives of mainstream staff. The personal and professional links forged can also create a useful vehicle for the return of special school children to mainstream schools. Thus the resource centre model can confer as many advantages on the special school as the services from the special school provide for mainstream schools.

What advantages are there for an L.E.A. to utilise the resources of a special school to bridge the "resource gap", rather than to develop alternative forms of provision such as peripatetic/advisory services? A number of points can be made in this respect. Support services, including L.E.A. peripatetic remedial and advisory teachers and educational psychologists, have traditionally experienced extreme difficulties in offering a satisfactory service to mainstream schools. Representatives of external agencies such as these are dogged by the fact that schools often perceive them as "experts" who will solve the problems of special needs children. Their contacts with schools are at best irregular and usually only crisis-orientated. In contrast, special school staff have the advantage of being practising classroom teachers rather than "advisers". They are perhaps more able to avoid the "expert consultant" image which usually entails a transfer of responsibility for the child's difficulties from the classroom teacher to an outside agency (Dessent, 1983). Curriculum materials and teaching approaches utilised by special school staff in their work and contact with mainstream schools have the advantage of having been used practically within the special school base, and are therefore well known by the special school practitioners. This has great advantages over approaches where materials are deposited within the schools by advisory staff who have no working knowledge of the resources concerned. Special schools also have the potential advantage of being accessible work bases where staff from mainstream schools can readily make contact, and obtain help and advice. Support can thus be provided at an early stage rather than awaiting the outcome of a lengthy referral process which so often leads to problems being seen as crises. Further, special schools consist of a pool of staff committed to work in the field of special needs, with an inbuilt leadership and management structure which can be adapted to provide a support service to mainstream schools.

THE SNAGS - "INSIDE/OUTSIDE"

All movements towards change bring with them inevitable difficulties and problems which require resolution. Special schools which move towards a system of liaison and support with mainstream schools will not be immune from this process. In the initial stages, the main problems likely to require resolution might relate to conflicts and territorial disputes with agencies external to the school: difficulties which will arise in clarifying the nature of the support available to mainstream schools and in the inevitable struggle to achieve appropriate resourcing of the service. However, if these initial problems are successfully resolved then the major difficulties are likely to centre upon aspects internal to the special school.

Inherent in the concept of a special school operating as a resource centre is the inevitable tension between the priority given to providing for children with special needs inside and outside the school. This tension will always be apparent and requires managing if not resolving. Firstly, there is the problem of involving all special school staff equally in the dual functions of the school. Inevitably, this will not occur in most instances because of practical organisational factors. It is likely that responsibility for and a commitment to the support/liaison work will rest with only some of the special school staff. Head teachers will need to give attention to how other staff can develop commitment to, and involvement in, the work, and to ensure that status and posts of responsibility are not solely linked to key personnel involved in the process.

Secondly, and relatedly, there is the problem of maintaining a commitment to "outside" involvement when it will be clear to teaching staff that, in certain situations, children "inside" the school will get a less favourable educational deal. Providing for children's special needs in an absolute sense, whether inside or outside the special school, is in fact an unattainable goal. There is always more that could be done for children "given better resources, more manpower etc.". The provision of a liaison service to mainstream schools, with all the changes in internal organisation this requires, could be seen as disruptive to the way in which special education is provided for children placed within the special school.

If difficulties of this kind arise and are to be resolved, the commitment of head teacher, staff and all concerned with the resource centre concept will be critical. Although initial "uninformed optimism" will sometimes carry such a new development a long way, its maintenance over time is likely to depend more on the nuts and bolts of internal organisation, staff deployment and responsibilities and timetabling.

THE FUTURE

What then does the future hold for the idea of developing links between special and mainstream schools? Is it to be a growth area for special schools, or are the initiatives taken by the few special schools involved in these developments merely a last ditch attempt to revive an ailing special school system? The largest determining factor in the future role to be played by special schools will be the extent to, and ways in which, special educational needs are or are not met within mainstream schools. Thus, in the wake of the current legislation governing special education, the major concern of L.E.A. policy makers and administrators is likely to be the development of adequate special educational provision in mainstream schools. Special schools operating a resource centre model may or may not have a part to play in this process.

There are a number of factors, external to the special school itself, which could limit the future development of links with mainstream schools. The first relates to the overlap of needs between those children with special needs placed in special schools, and those educated in mainstream schools. Provision could develop in mainstream schools such that there emerges a wide discrepancy between the needs of the children placed in separate special schools and those who remain in the mainstream.

If this occurs then links between special and mainstream schools are likely to be minimal, temporary and only of a token nature. This will occur as the curriculum and methods required for children placed within the special school begin to differ significantly from those required for children with special needs in the mainstream. The second point relates to the development of L.E.A. support services. In the wake of the 1981 legislation, a number of authorities are reorganising old services and introducing new ones aimed at providing support to children with special needs in mainstream schools. If these developments occur without the involvement of special schools then the possibility of special schools being involved in the future resourcing of, and liaison with, mainstream schools will be lost.

My own feeling is that the attempts we are seeing on the part of special schools to develop links and to support mainstream schools is perhaps a stage in the development of provision rather than an end in itself. It may be that such attempts are more important for what else they initiate in a given area (e.g. new responses from mainstream schools towards children with special needs, the development of new resource materials and support strategies) and most importantly in the recognition they give to the current huge overlap between children with special needs in mainstream schools and those who happen to be placed in some special schools.

For these reasons alone the developments we have seen so far are healthy ones and merit encouragement and further development. Perhaps they represent the beginnings of a more radical process in which senior staff from special schools will play an increasing part in the management and direction of the educational facilities which develop in mainstream schools. The co-ordination of these facilities, their structure and management, and the all important career structure for special needs teachers which is required are likely to become a central concern for L.E.A.s in the future. The formal linking of special needs provisions and resources in mainstream schools to the management structure within a special school may provide the mechanism in the future whereby the continuum of needs - which exists - can be better matched by a continuum of provision - which does not.

Chapter Seven

GOVERNORS AND THE SPECIAL SCHOOL

by Terry Bailey

> Governors and Managers are an important part of the educational system. They should represent different elements in the immediate community and act together as a link with the community and a support to the school. They are also the local body to whom the head and staff are accountable for the conduct and curriculum of the school, and are required to participate in many important decisions in the school life. (Burgess and Sofer, 1978)

> Governing bodies provide a link between the school and the local authority and act as a useful forum for discussion about the work and well being of the school. (N.U.T., 1982)

HISTORICAL CONTEXT

The 1944 Education Act laid down that every county secondary school should have a board of governors. The Government published model instruments which dealt with the membership of the governing body - election of officers, rules of conduct of meetings and model Articles which dealt specifically with the functions and responsibilities of governors, in a formal legal way. In many L.E.A.s, sub-committees of the Education Committee acted as governing bodies for primary and special schools.

With the clamour for increased public accountability in the 1960s and 1970s, and the demand for schools to be more fully integrated into the community, many county secondary schools subsequently appointed parent and teacher representatives on to their governing bodies, although the 1944 Education Act did not compel them to do so. A survey carried out by the National Association of Governors and Managers (N.A.G.M., 1975) found that of the 91 L.E.A.s who replied to their questionnaire, 60 had appointed parents to serve as governors and 51 had appointed teachers.

A survey carried out by Sallis (1979) for the Advisory Council for Education found that fifty-two per cent of the L.E.A.s had individual governing bodies for all schools. In other words, some L.E.A.s went on to provide separate or shared governing bodies for primary and special schools.

The Warnock Report (D.E.S., 1978) reaffirmed that many of the roles and functions defined for governors in ordinary schools were equally applicable to special schools and recommended that every special school should have its own governing body.

Section 1 of the 1980 Education Act, which was the Government's response to the Taylor Report (D.E.S., 1977), made it mandatory for all schools to have their own governing bodies, which would include parent and teacher members and representatives from groups other than the L.E.A., such as local industry.

In short, although special schools were excluded from the terms of reference of the Taylor Committee, the governing bodies of maintained special schools now have the same form of instrument and articles of government as the rest of the maintained schools within a L.E.A. In law the roles and responsibilities of governors are broadly similar as for those of ordinary schools. Sallis (1981) felt that the 1980 Act and the new regulations (Statutory Instrument 1981 No. 809) promised a system of school government more participatory and open than previously. Unfortunately, the Secretary of State for Education has yet to name the day when compliance with the 1980 Act will be required. Until that time, some L.E.A.s may do little to change their existing arrangements.

COMPOSITION OF GOVERNING BODIES

Although each L.E.A. sets out the instruments and articles of government, and practices will differ between authorities and between maintained and independent schools, governing bodies must consist of elected members, teaching staff and head teacher, L.E.A. representatives and co-opted members.

The political nominees are chosen by the political parties to serve as L.E.A. nominees. As Burgess and Sofer (1978) point out, the way the L.E.A. appoints governors is not obvious. Usually the political parties represented on the authority agree to divide the places among themselves in proportion to their strength in the authority. Thus, the majority party will have a majority of places appointed in this way on each governing body.

Parents are elected by the body of parents of the school by secret ballot, and teachers, who are elected by the school teaching staff, represent those interests, and on occasions the feelings and views of the pupils.

The head teacher attends as principal education officer to the governors and is a full governor unless he or she elects otherwise, while co-opted governors are recruited for the special role they play in the community and for a specific expertise that they can bring to the school. All governors have equal rights and duties and it is the governing body as a whole which has power to do things, not individual governors acting unilaterally. However, a governor is not a delegate and is free to vote exactly as he or she thinks fit. This applies to parent governors, who should maintain close contact with other parents through the P.T.A. committees or the press, the teacher governors who cannot be mandated by the other school staff, and co-opted members. These three groups are clearly not restricted by an election manifesto, as are the political nominees.

Following the 1980 Education Act, one London borough reconstituted its maintained special school governing bodies as follows: 10 L.E.A. Governors; 1 Head Teacher (ex officio); 1 Teacher Governor; 2 Parent Governors; 1 Industry/Commerce/Trade Union Governor.

The Authority proposed that there should, in addition, be one governor representative of a voluntary association for the handicapped, preferably experienced in the needs of children for whom the schools were designed. These last posts, it must be said, have been difficult to recruit.

A survey by the National Association of Governors and Managers in 1975 found that only 3 out of 33 non-maintained schools used by one L.E.A. had parents on the governing boards. The large catchment area of most of these special schools makes it difficult to define the community they serve and, therefore, harder for the governors to form a link between the school and the community. Although Warnock (D.E.S. 1978) suggested that non-maintained special schools should have their own governing bodies, with at least one L.E.A. representative, we are far from this ideal situation at present.

An example of a governing body of an independent residential school for secondary maladjusted boys in the north west of England is given as follows: Educational Psychologist; Consultant Child Psychiatrist; Social Services Officer; Head Teacher; Local Cleric; General Practitioner; Wife of General Practitioner; Local Dignitary; Registrar. Even in this more enlightened independent school, which seeks to use the expertise of a range of professionals, there is no parent governor representative.

GOVERNORS' ROLES AND RESPONSIBILITIES

As has already been stated, each L.E.A. writes its own set of articles of government for ordinary and maintained special schools, prescribing what the governing bodies' functions are, although they must be approved by the Department of Education and Science.

Most articles, although recently revised and updated in many cases following the 1980 Act and Circular 4/81, are based on sections of the 1944 Act and the model articles presented at that time. Most articles expect governors to exercise general oversight of the conduct and curriculum of the school, subject to the proviso that the L.E.A. must determine the general character of the school and its place in the local educational system. In addition, most articles will stipulate the governors' responsibilities in the areas of finance, review of the school site and buildings, furniture and equipment, appointment and dismissal of teachers, and suspension of pupils.

In Governing Schools (Open University, 1981), the point is made that in practice the way that governing bodies of special schools interpret and carry out their duties may be different, in that they have to take into account the special needs of the pupils that they are responsible for. They will have roles different from the ordinary school in two key areas. Firstly, the selection of teaching staff; they will need to ensure that teachers are not only sensitive to children with special needs, but also that they are not too inexperienced or untrained to cope with the particular handicap. In addition, they should not be so concerned about the handicap that the educational aspirations for the children are set too low. In those schools where reintegration may be part of the educational process, e.g. maladjusted or delicate schools, governors need to ensure that staff appointed are committed to the integration principle.

Secondly, governors will have a role in helping the school to establish good community relations to reduce prejudice and misunderstandings about physical and mental handicap.

DIFFICULTIES IN THE EXECUTION OF THE ROLE OF GOVERNORS

The most extensive research on school governors was carried out by Bacon in Sheffield in 1976 and 1978, an Authority which introduced individual governing bodies to all schools long before the 1980 Act. Bacon identified a number of initial apprehensions in the early days of the new procedures.

(1) Initial worries by head teachers about possible interference by governors with the curriculum and internal school affairs. They saw their professional autonomy threatened.

(2) Politicians were worried about the widening of the representation of governing bodies, which they feared might subvert local education policy.

(3) Teacher governors in general were found to be reluctant to adopt a radical role which might serve to challenge the authority of their head teacher. Head teachers seemed to expect that a democratically elected member of their staff would remain publicly loyal to them and the policies they were pursuing. Head teachers felt threatened if teachers raised potentially difficult, delicate or embarrassing issues. As the teacher representative was usually concerned about his own career prospects and conditions of service, he was reluctant to be labelled as a trouble maker by pointing governing bodies to areas of concern. Another factor militating against teachers playing a radical role related to the fact that in any case of role tensions between manager and labour within a school, they were typically resolved by the governing body in favour of the head teacher.

(4) In most schools, parent governors lacked experience and detailed knowledge of current practice in schools, and even of the way that the L.E.A. committee procedures worked. This forced parents to look towards the head teacher for guidance on the policy of the school, rather than questioning its aims. Many parents were often not aware of, or were indifferent to having their interests represented through parent governors. This was reflected in the low turnout for parent governor elections. Few parents are probably aware that the National Regulations on Governors (Statutory Instrument 809) now oblige a school to make the governors' agenda and papers available to them on request.

Some parent governors felt that their child might be singled out if they raised difficult issues at a governors' meeting. Bacon posed the question as to whether parental representation was not simply an illusion of local participation in the decision making process.

(5) Co-opted governors tended to look to head teachers for advice and for help in initiating them into their duties and responsibilities associated with the office.

Bacon summarised his findings by suggesting that the head teachers' initial worries had been unfounded since the new governing bodies had, in fact, strengthened their managerial prerogative, while at the same time providing contact with groups previously unfamiliar to the school. Governors were being used as a shield from the community, or as a weapon against the L.E.A.

Having been assigned the role of lay people by the head teacher, governors were reluctant to look at wider issues such as the school curriculum, financial allocation and teaching methods. These roles were assigned by the head teacher to teachers as the highly trained professionals.

The bulk of time at governors' meetings was consequently spent discussing routine administrative matters and maintenance problems. The head teacher's report was frequently at the end of the agenda, and given and listened to in a perfunctory manner. It often contained bland and ritualistic accounts of the school's achievements during the last term. As Kogan and Van Der Eyken (1973) pointed out, unless governors were alert, they would end up with the situation of head teachers having the governors "in their pockets".

One might argue that these findings reflect a situation prior to the 1980 Education Act and that there is now an increased concern for accountability in education, as in other public spheres such as the health and social services. Fisher (1980), a parent governor, found that the majority of governors did not go to the school from one meeting to the next and, consequently, were unlikely to have any idea of the issues of concern. Dilley (1982), a second parent governor, suggested that the situation had changed little. He pointed out that his local councillors were often given two or more governorships as a reward for political service, with the inevitable result that they did not have the time to do their job as governors properly. He instanced the fact that they often had to leave halfway through a governing body meeting to meet a commitment at a council meeting.

Kelly (1982), a third parent governor, pointed out the considerable constraints on what can be achieved as a parent governor. Getting to know both the school at which one is a governor, and other schools, is seen as an essential but major undertaking. Meeting once a term, which is frequently the norm for this episodic body, was seen as too infrequent to produce a sense of continuity. The major problem identified by Kelly was the lack of opportunities given to governors to discuss, still less influence, important areas of school life, by head teachers who were unwilling to allow genuine consultation and debate.

Bayliss (1982) collated the views of twelve teacher governors. It was clear that the question of accountability was still a particularly tricky one, not least because the head is always present. It was gratifying to find that the teacher governor of a special school who was interviewed reported that her head teacher always showed her a draft of his report to the governors prior to the meeting, so that she could add any details.

Pring (1982), as a member of the Campaign for the Advancement of State Education (C.A.S.E.), an organisation which includes parents, teachers and political nominees to the governing bodies, expressed concern over the kinds of issues that appear on the agenda, the extent to which the governors are able to discuss them in an informal manner, and the difficulties or assistance that governors receive in fulfilling the responsibility and function as set out by the authority.

The most recent, but as yet unpublished, study on the role of governing bodies was carried out by Kogan, Johnson and Packwood at Brunel University Educational Studies Unit, with funds from the D.E.S. They used a case study approach and considered eight governing bodies in four L.E.A.s, including one senior special school for children with mild and severe learning difficulties in a shire county. The researchers attended governing body meetings over some fifteen months, visited the schools at other times and interviewed parents, L.E.A. officials and local interest groups.

Provisional findings suggest that the major issues appear to be the same for special school governing bodies as for ordinary schools. The role of governors is very much determined by how the L.E.A. sees their role and the relationship they can forge with professionals.

The L.E.A.'s influence is evidenced by how much they give governing bodies guidance, clerking (particularly by a senior officer), training and information. If they see the governing body as a community pressure group to which the school is accountable, then information provided in reports is likely to include general principles and to focus on the wider educational system. If they see the governing body acting as a pressure group on behalf of the school only, then information is more likely to focus on the school in question.

Teacher governors were seen by other staff as the trustees of their opinion and someone who could play a role in educating lay governors regarding certain key issues. Parent governors were found to be the most reluctant of all governors to fully take up their role, as they saw themselves as clients of the system. They were rarely in touch with the full extent of present opinion, having few links with P.T.A.s.

One finding of the study was that the role of the Chairman of the governing body is crucial. It is the Chairman who has the possibility of reshaping the way that the governing body works. One Chairman was able to initiate more structured reports about the principles of education through which the school worked. Other Chairmen indicated that their room for manoeuvre was limited by the need to maintain a good relationship with, and the trust of, the head teacher. This prevented them from being too critical.

In addition, there is such a diversity of interests and motives among the governors (political, public spirited, interested solely in the school, interested in education generally), resulting in many governors being more interested in what the school is doing on a day-to-day basis, rather than a concern for general issues.

Most governors were still found to look for leadership from the head teacher, and the bulk of the agenda was related to issues raised from the head teacher's report.

HOW GOVERNING BODIES CAN STRENGTHEN THEIR ROLE IN SPECIAL SCHOOLS

(1) Getting to know the school. School organisation, the timetable and teaching methods come to life when seen in the flesh. Governors can arrange individually with the head teacher to visit the school on an ordinary working day. This will lay the foundation for their contributions to decisions taken at the formal meetings. Attendance at school functions also helps to identify the degree of parental, staff and local community involvement in the school.

Governors can request an outline of the school aims, objectives, organisation, etc. This should include a list of staff, both teaching and non-teaching, and their responsibilities, size of teaching groups, arrangements for learning as well as copies of communications such as newsletters or a school magazine.

A useful list of information which governors of special schools need to know, and which ideally should be in the school booklet required under the 1980 Education Act, is presented by the N.A.G.M. (paper 5). It includes aspects such as special remedial measures used for physically handicapped pupils, the communication policy in schools which cater for pupils with language or speech disorders, the length of the school day and any limitations imposed on this by L.E.A. transport arrangements.

(2) Asking the right questions. Within a special school, in-depth questions need to be asked about the school's organisation and the way that it allows, as necessary, for appropriate medical and paramedical support during the school day; the curriculum balance, i.e. what is taught and how often, the methods of assessment for non-academic pupils; the role and qualifications of ancillary staff; the way the curriculum takes account of individual special needs; the equipment, particularly its availability, servicing and maintenance, and teaching resources; and in the light of the 1981 Education Act, the links with the community, particularly parents.

Questions about what the organisation is meant to accomplish, who decides how it is accomplished, the basis on which decisions are made and how the organisation is monitored and improved, will take the governor into the field of aims and objectives, values and beliefs, and evaluation.

Questions about methods of assessment will involve discussion on how the school monitors and assesses the progress of its pupils, the nature of its record keeping, the information contained in the records (e.g. educational, social, emotional and physical development), the accuracy of records and their confidentiality.

Governors of special schools, as a result of the 1981 Education Act, have one more inroad into discussion of the assessment and teaching procedures. Every child within a special school will have an annual review of his or her progress and governors can use this opportunity to probe current practices.

Unsatisfactory answers to questions about

the degree to which the school uses the external support services available - Health Authority (medical and paramedical), School Psychological Service, Social Services, peripatetic Advisory Teachers and Advisers - should prompt governors to set up a dialogue with those services. They may need to encourage the Health Authority to provide adequate support to the school, supply the teachers with relevant medical information of a non-confidential kind and ensure that the school personnel are aware of the medical implications of particular handicaps. They may need to ensure that social workers are familiar with the aims and objectives of the school to ensure parents are not given conflicting advice over the management of a child. They may need to press the education authority to ensure that adequate time and expertise is available to the school from its educational psychologists.

Questions about the system of discipline within the school, or the sort of pastoral system or pupil management programme that exists to deal with difficult pupils, raise issues related to playground and lunchtime supervision, punishment, and alternatives to supervision. Suspension is difficult in special schools and governors must try to ensure that satisfactory alternative arrangements are made.

Questions about home/school links and the degree to which the head teacher is committed to the use of the school building by the parents' organisation and community groups outside school hours, may move governors towards the role of forging greater links with the community and parents. Certainly the 1981 Education Act gives parents statutory rights in relation to the special needs of their children, and governors could use this as a way of increasing parental involvement in a school. While many special schools do make strenuous efforts to ensure that parents play a key role in the life of the school, others deliberately discourage parental involvement. Representatives from organisations such as Gateway Clubs and Handicapped Adventure Playgrounds may need to be encouraged to visit the school. Governors may need to foster the "parents as partners" concept by encouraging informal visits to the school by parents, the formation of P.T.A.s, school teach-ins, and information coffee mornings.

Questions need to be asked about the transport arrangements made by the L.E.A. with a view to ascertaining whether pupils spend long, tiring journeys on coaches before and after school. The governors can press the L.E.A. to review its arrangements in such cases.

Governors of pupils in residential schools should ask questions about the types of activities which occur at weekends and in the evenings. Are attempts made to encourage pupils to mix with the local community as far as possible in joining clubs, societies and organisations such as Scouts and Guides, and to provide opportunities for physical recreation? Are the rules and routines governing storage of possessions and privacy adequate? Are customs relating to ethnic minorities in matters of hair-style, earrings, etc. duly respected?

With the principle of integration enshrined in the 1981 Education Act, questions need to be asked about the policies of the school with regard to allowing the children to mix with non-handicapped children within ordinary schools.

Wragg and Partington (1980) point out that the head teacher and staff of the school have always had a fair degree of freedom to use their collective professional judgements in devising a curriculum for children. The ultimate responsibility for how children are taught has, therefore, rested with them.

However, it must be remembered that the responsibility for the curriculum is a legal responsibility and that governors have been called to account for their stewardship of the curriculum as in the Auld Enquiry on William Tyndale School. This may be the reason why D.E.S. Circular 6/81, The School Curriculum, urges a more active role for governors in bringing together the views of teachers, parents and the local community, and in the formulation of the school curriculum. To do this they must seek information, be consulted and give advice. Implicit here is the view that L.E.A.s and governors have not done enough to carry out their legal responsibility under the 1944 Act to secure a planned and coherent curriculum. The Brunel study certainly suggests that, far from having oversight of the curriculum, governors rarely discuss it.

Bennett and Gray (1983) argue strongly that the 1981 Circular revives the idea of a partnership between the L.E.A. and school governors, which will control curriculum policies and make substantial inroads into the jealously guarded preserves of the professional teacher. As a consequence, teachers will no longer be seen as expert practitioners able to take curriculum initiatives, but will become responsible to governing bodies not only for the ends to which they are working, i.e. what is taught, but also the means they employ to achieve those ends, e.g. resources used and methods of teaching. The local authority, in monitoring the implementation of the requirements of the governing body, is likely to place an increased emphasis on both self-evaluation of schools by their staff, and on the appraisal of schools and their staffs by L.E.A. Inspectors.

Searching questions need to be asked about the balance of the curriculum between a core of essential skills, particularly literacy and numeracy, and areas such as life-skills teaching, health education and social skills. If a particular change in the balance is contemplated, questions need to be asked about why such a change is envisaged, what the expected benefits will be, the cost of implementation and what areas of the curriculum might suffer as a result of proposed changes.

One important document to consider is an H.M.I.'s report on the school which is now an open document. Another might be a school self-evaluation programme which will require the governors to comment on it to the L.E.A. Both documents can provide the lever for discussion on a whole range of curricular issues, including the hidden curriculum.

(3) Studying the head teacher's report. The head teacher's report is the formal occasion at which the head gives an account of his or her stewardship and governors fulfil their duty of overseeing the conduct and curriculum of the school (Burgess and Sofer, 1978). If the head's report is an expression of his or her accountability to the governors for the day-to-day running of the school, governors should request more than a brief, dry record of the number of events that have taken place - visits and sport-

ing achievements.

The report should contain:

(a) Details of staff movements.
(b) Attendance of pupils and staff.
(c) Adequacy of buildings and their repair and maintenance.
(d) Spending of the school's capitation allowance, particularly on the purchase of new equipment.
(e) Results of standardised tests or examinations taken.
(f) Details of staff development.
(g) New curricular developments.
(h) Letting of school building outside normal school hours.
(i) Problem pupils.
(j) Admission of new pupils.
(k) Consideration and appraisal of the effects of the action by teachers' unions.

A report of this nature will allow an opportunity for discussion of issues such as staff turnover and whether they are due to chance factors or indicate fundamental problems. One possibility may be that inappropriate above-scale posts are being offered to teachers. Another may be a problem of communication between the head teacher and the staff.

Are there falling rolls? If so, is this a general decline or are there special factors within the catchment area, such as a factory closure? Figures on truancy or suspensions, particularly when compared with previous years, may lead to discussion on the pastoral system, the appropriateness of teaching, etc. When staff have been seconded to extend their expertise, governors need to know whether this has resulted in any changes within the school, such as school focused in-service training for other staff. Questions on the admission of pupils can raise fundamental issues such as the increase in the multiplicity of handicapped pupils into schools for children with severe learning difficulties, with a consequent need for a more favourable staffing allocation.

If the health and safety of the pupils are endangered by buildings, governors will need to exert strong pressure on the L.E.A. for the defects to be remedied. They can also play a key role with the school in seeking out educational needs in terms of minor works, such as adaptations or the need for, e.g. a mobile classroom. The skills of certain members of governing bodies can be useful in presenting a case to the L.E.A.

Questions about the distribution of capitation allowance will show to some extent the value that the head teacher places on different activities within a school and the priority given to new trends in special education, such as microcomputers. What proportion is spent in a school for children with severe learning difficulties on the "special care" department, as opposed to the rest of the school? What proportion on the non-examination pupils? Is there an inordinate amount of money spent in one area in a school for moderate learning difficulties, such as craft and design, because the head teacher is an ex-craft teacher? What is the process of consultation within the school that takes place before the capitation allowance is distributed?

(4) Preparing for interviews to appoint staff. The selection of teaching staff is one of the most important tasks that a governor has to perform, since any appointment could well affect the school for a very long time. Governors of special schools need to keep in mind, in making any appointment, the direction in which they and the L.E.A. want the school to develop, taking into account the strengths and weaknesses of the present team. Thorough discussion with the A.E.O. Special Education and the Adviser for Special Education should be a prerequisite for any appointment to the special school, if governors are to help ensure the quality and continuing effectiveness of the staff in the school.

(5) Suggesting agenda items for governors. Governors may suggest topics on which they would like the head teacher to report (I.L.E.A., 1979). The model guidelines for L.E.A.s (N.A.G.M., 1978) indicate that the governors' meetings belong to those governors. The agenda is theirs and they should not allow the initiative of deciding the agenda to slip away from them. Although the chairman of governors will decide the agenda in discussion with the head teacher, any governor has a right to place an item on the agenda by

contacting the chairman in good time. There should be no aspect of the school's functioning that a governor cannot enquire about.

(6) Keeping in close contact with the local community. As the pressure grows for increased accountability, the local community is likely to want governing bodies, whose interests they serve, to discuss fundamental issues related to the school and not just the marginal roles such bodies have been assigned in the past. Governing bodies have an obligation to respond to the expectations of the community. To do this they need to know the neighbourhood, promote links where they exist and mobilise resources for the school. Davies and Lyons (1981) argue that despite the overall statutory responsibilities of the L.E.A., the governing body may well become the prime focal point of accountability. To do this they will need to set up development plans at governing body level, outlining particular objectives over a given time period, such as three years, expressed in terms of expected achievements in key areas. This, they argue, would allow the governing body, as a separate entity from both the school and the L.E.A., the unique and important function of helping the school to become accountable to the community while developing professionally.

SOME WAYS IN WHICH GOVERNING BODIES AND SCHOOLS HAVE WORKED TOGETHER

One or two examples of schools known to the author where changes have been brought about by the joint efforts of governors and schools are presented.

(1) Working towards similar ends. Bailey and De Souza (1981) investigated, in one school for children with severe learning difficulties in north Devon, the extent to which parents, governors, teachers and other professionals concerned with the school had similar aims for the education of the children. All groups were asked to place eight aims in order of importance. The results are presented in Table A on page 113. The figures illustrate that for this school all groups in the sample were overwhelmingly in agreement about the most important aims. This state of affairs was due, in no

	B. Able to help self	C. Able to communicate	D. Able to socialise	A. Enjoys school activities	E. Able to occupy self	F. Develop fine and gross motor skills	G. Acquires basic skills in reading	H. Acquires basic skills in number
Overall Rank N = 68	1	2	3	4	5	6	7	8
Parents N = 43	1	2	3	4	5	7	6	8
Governors N = 4	2	1	3	4	5	8	6	7
Professional group Rank N = 21	1	2	3	4	5	6	7	8
Physiotherapists N = 2	3	4	1	2	5	6	6	8
Teachers N = 9	1	2	3	4	6	5	7	8
Advisers N = 2	2	2	1	6	5	4	6	8
Educators N = 2	1	2	3	5	4	6	7	8
Educational psychologists N = 2	3	1	1	4	5	6	7	8
Administrators N = 2	2	1	3	4	6	6	5	8

Table A. Rank Ordering of Means for Teaching Aims

small measure, to the school's efforts to involve these various groups in the children's education. The dialogue between parents, teachers, governors and professionals made all groups more sensitive to the needs of the pupils. This in turn led to a complete review of the whole school, its curriculum, teaching methods, in-service programme for parents etc., with the full support of staff, parents and governors alike.

(2) Supporting curriculum change. One school, following many years of stability but a degree of sterility in some areas of the curriculum with the appointment of a new head teacher and the support of its governors, was able to introduce necessary changes. The independent findings of an H.M.I. report allowed the school to move forward and broaden its curriculum without the sort of acrimony often present with a "new broom" syndrome.

(3) Using suspension positively. Packwood (1983) pointed out that L.E.A. officers expect governing bodies to act as school pressure groups and confirm that such pressure can bring results.

A school for children with severe learning difficulties had to exclude a pupil from its "care" department because of bizarre and dangerous behaviour. The school and its governors, together with the child's parents, made strong representations to the L.E.A. for additional welfare staff in order to cater adequately for this and similar pupils. The overtures were successful.

(4) Extending the horizons of a head teacher. Two governors from a school for delicate children were able, through briefing themselves in some depth, to persuade not only the rest of the governing body, but also a head teacher who was initially very opposed to the idea, to provide more outward-looking courses for senior pupils. The outcome was the involvement of the school in a M.S.C. funded project to develop curricular links for pupils with a local college.

SUMMARY

The Brunel study indicates that governors of special

schools face something of a dilemma. Unlike their ordinary school counterparts, they cannot focus on the educational product of the school, e.g. examination or reading test results. In consequence, oversight for many governors has frequently consisted of a residue of sympathy for the children and support for all that the staff are doing. There is thus a greater predisposition not to question the head teacher and the direction that the school is taking.

In addition, the study found no great awareness of the 1980 and 1981 Education Acts, nor of Warnock's comment:

> Those who work with children with Special Educational needs should regard themselves as having a crucial and developing role in a society which is now committed not merely to tending and caring for its handicapped members as a matter of charity, but to educating them as a matter of right and to developing their potential to the full. (D.E.S., 1978, 1.11)

As Bennett & Gray (1983) point out, the recent circulars and regulations from the D.E.S. require from governors a more active role and L.E.A.s will be expected to ensure that their governing bodies take on that role.

It is to be hoped that special school governors will grasp the nettle firmly and that teachers in special schools will view this involvement not in terms of a threat to their professional autonomy, but rather as a means of widening the professional support available to the school.

Chapter Eight

LINKS WITH OTHER PROFESSIONALS: THE HEAD AS A MULTIDISCIPLINARY TEAM MEMBER

by Vic Thomson

INTRODUCTION

The 1981 Education Act and the subsequent Circular 1/83 have as a major theme a multidisciplinary approach to working with children with special needs.

> By bringing together the skills, perceptions and insights of professionals in different disciplines, it should be possible to arrive at a more complete understanding. (Circular 1/83, 34)

The multidisciplinary theme of the Act was a statutory response to recommendations in two major and far reaching reports:

(1) The Court Report (D.H.S.S., 1976)

> It is the intermingling of different professional staff that maintains the join in the joint service. (14.41)

and (2) The Warnock Report (D.E.S., 1978)

> The development of close working relationships between professionals in the different services concerned with children and young people with special needs is central to many recommendations in this report. (16.1)

Each report was concerned with the promotion of existing good practice and both reports implied that there was improvement to be made in multidisciplinary relationships by all the professions. Tomlinson (1982) suggests that the history of special education is characterised by the very poor multidisciplinary relationships between all the professions concerned. Indeed, it might be argued that one of the special school head's most vital roles lies in improving these relationships.

WHO IS INVOLVED IN THE MULTIDISCIPLINARY APPROACH?

The growth and influence of the para-educational groups is stressed in the work of Baron (1981), Young (1979) and Tomlinson (1982). In a recent work on Educational Management, Paisey (1981) has observed that "a large number of auxiliary and related professions have developed in education during recent years" (p. 112). Education Welfare Officers, Psychiatric Social Workers, Speech Therapists, Occupational Therapists, Social Workers, Clinical and Educational Psychologists are some of the para-educational professionals who now visit and work in our schools. Each belongs to his own professional area with its particular aims, experiences, training and interests. Barton and Tomlinson (1981) even suggest that these professional groups have their own vested interests, areas of competence and a very real power over their clients. Several writers have tried to list the professional groups which work with children.

(1) The Court Report listed: Medical, Social, Psychological and Educational.

(2) Tomlinson (1982) listed: Medical, Psychological and Educational (pedagogic and administration).

(3) Barry and Tye (1972) listed: Parents, Governors, Local Education Authorities, Industry, Welfare Agencies and Education.

(4) Morgan and Hall (1982) simply divide the professionals into two categories:

   (a) The Internal (professional) Domain

   (b) The External (public) Domain

The head's role within a multidisciplinary approach was not defined within any of the lists, but would presumably be included within any group called "Education".

The special school head teacher's role in this type of approach has not been researched to any great extent, and barely a beginning has been made in studying the head or in looking at the various groups of non-teaching staff who work in or with the education service.

A SURVEY OF THE SPECIAL SCHOOL HEAD'S ROLE WITHIN THE MULTIDISCIPLINARY ENVIRONMENT

In a recent survey (Thomson, 1983), an attempt was made to identify and clarify the special school head's situation, particularly with regard to a multidisciplinary approach. Its objectives were:

(1) To identify the para-educational and educational groups with which the special school head interacts.

(2) To quantify the frequency of the interactions.

(3) To identify where the interactions took place, either in school or out of school.

The survey used seven categories to identify people with whom the head had professional contacts. The categories were:

(1) Medical: General Practitioners, Paediatricians, Consultants, Nurses, School Medical Officers, Physiotherapists, Speech Therapists, Health Visitors and any other employee of the area health authority.

(2) Psychological: Psychiatrists, Psychiatric Social Workers, Educational Psychologists, etc.

(3) L.E.A.: Anyone employed by an L.E.A. in either an administrative or advisory capacity.

(4) External Education: Anyone employed in a school, outside of the head's own school, a college or a university.

(5) Parents: including prospective parents.

(6) Social Services: Social Workers, Social Work Assistants, Educational Welfare Officers, Occupational Therapists and staff from Social Service hostels, Children's homes and Adult Training Centres.

(7) Own School: Teachers, Ancillaries, Kitchen Staff, Caretakers and Cleaners, Governors and Children.

An eighth category 'Others' was added for people not obviously fitting in the original seven categories.

Special school and primary heads were asked to complete a survey of their contacts over a number of set days. Each person the head interacted with during the survey was marked in the professional category most appropriate. The survey included the whole range of special schools from one county and also included a small group of primary schools.

The study indicated that all the heads surveyed, both special and primary, interacted with all eight of the categories. Within that overall effect there were a number of interesting variations:

(1) There was a difference in pattern between the special schools and the primary schools. All the primary schools had their own similar pattern which was different from the patterns of any of the special schools.

(2) The special schools displayed patterns of contact which appeared to be related to the category of the child (pre-1981 Education Act categories) being educated within the school, i.e. schools for children who had medical problems had a similarity in their pattern.

(3) Seventy per cent of the special school heads' contacts during the survey were with people who were not members of their own staffs. This seventy per cent of outside contacts was made up of (in rank order):

L.E.A.	16%
External Education	13%
Parents	12%
Others	12%
Medical	8%
Social Services	5%
Psychological	4%

From the returns in the survey the "Others" group could be replaced by being split into two separate categories:

(1) Voluntary Agencies

(2) Supplies, Contractor and Service Industries

The survey tried to identify where the contacts took place, i.e. contacts in school or out of school. The overall average for special school heads was eight per cent of contacts outside their own school: twice the average for primary school heads. Taking into account the travelling time which is obviously required for an outside contact, this factor of almost one-tenth of the head's contacts represents a substantial part of his or her work.

The survey would appear to confirm the view that the head is directly involved in a multidisciplinary framework. It also indicated no common framework surrounding each head, but showed that there is a certain similarity between schools whose pupils' special needs are similar.

The survey did not set out to find out the quality of the interactions, the nature of the initiator of the contact, or the frequency and type of interactions between other professional groups. All those topics will need to be researched in future to improve the information about a multidisciplinary approach.

WHY SHOULD THE HEAD BE INVOLVED IN THE MULTIDISCIPLINARY PROCESS?

(1) The traditional role of the head is as the representative of the school, the hub (Harling, 1981) around which the relationships with the environment are made and monitored.

(2) The unique common law situation in this country which puts the head in "Loco Parentis". Although not a statutory duty, this quasi custodial role is strongly supported in the education system not only as a guardian responsibility but as both a link with and spokesman for the family. This is a particularly important role for the head in special education, because as Barton and Tomlinson (1981) point out: "These children, adults and parents often have the least say and influence on a number of important decisions on what happens to them and are subject to the most pressure, persuasion and coercion sometimes quite overt, other times subtle, of any group in the educational system" (p. 18).

(3) The ethos of special education is one which sees everything which concerns the child's growth to maturity as coming within its influence.

(4) All the professionals have as a common basis of interest the child with special needs. The amount of child contact that these professionals

have varies, but it is the school which is the agency having most contact with the child and its needs. The school can present to any multidisciplinary situation the most objective, up-to-date and intimate information about the child and its needs.

(5) Recommendations which are made to meet the child's needs by the school or by other professions will have to be carried out either partially or in full by the school.

(6) Current legislation puts the responsibility of reviewing children firmly on the school (Circular 1/83, para. 55). Whilst statements are an important starting point they are a solitary exercise for each child who then has to be reviewed regularly. It will be the head's responsibility to collect and collate all the reports for the review which, while making an extra work load, will put the head right at the focus of the review process - a position of some influence.

These factors indicate that the head should be in a position to organise and manage the multidisciplinary situation and play a leading role in the process.

The extended role for the head is vital; without effective heads then the recommendations of the Reports and Act cannot be met (Bowers, 1980). The substantial network of contacts which appears to exist (Thomson, 1983) implies that the way to achieve the multidisciplinary recommendations is by increasing and improving communication and cooperation within that network. Ainscow et al (1978) warn that during this the role of the head will become more not less complex.

PROBLEMS IN THE MULTIDISCIPLINARY APPROACH

There are problems inherent in the multidisciplinary process which may well be responsible for the poor interprofessional relationship record of special education.

(1) The professional catchment areas (for instance Area Health Authority and L.E.A.) do not always exactly overlap, so the school is unable to work with one person from each of the professional areas. As a result, multidisciplinary teams will not always have the same composition and could conceivably be

different for every child in the school.

(2) The child may be involved with a range of people from within one professional area, e.g. General Practitioner, Health Visitor, Physiotherapist, Paediatrician, Surgeon.

(3) A wide range of opinions as to the child's needs can be valuable, but can lead to conflict (Bowers, 1980).

(4) The professional groups have different responses to information about their clients. The Warnock Report (D.E.S., 1978) noted the difficulties which hindered communication of information, particularly when the information was considered confidential.

IMPLICATIONS

There are management principles of which the head should be aware in considering the implications of a multidisciplinary approach:

(1) No situation is static, indeed change is endemic (Margulies and Raia, 1978).

(2) The concept of "Partial Equilibrium": that decisions are made in a constantly changing system and that the classical mistake is to think that any system is static. The head should be aware that having taken all things into account and looked as far ahead as possible, any decisions can and should only be temporary. Successes and failure will set new problems and the head can only expect decisions to last long enough - until the next decision is made.

(3) A systems view of the multidisciplinary approach suggests that the behaviour of any element within the system would affect all the other elements and that the system and its success depend not just on how well individual parts function but upon how those parts fit and work together.

(4) The head should realise that there is no single way to success in management; the head must bring his or her skills to bear on the

> given situation. There is no prescription, method or secret recipe that heads can find and use. No two situations are the same, therefore management has to be eclectic.

These management principles are particularly pertinent to the head in understanding the multidisciplinary situation and his reaction to it.

The implications of a multidisciplinary approach by the head must also consider the new legislation and the way in which it will be implemented. The 1981 Education Act is, in the way of English education law, a broad and enabling piece of legislation, not a coercive and prescriptive Act. This allows local educational authorities to take into account "local circumstances and existing patterns of provision" (Circular 1/83, 1.1) and, therefore, as has always been the case there will be no uniformity of implementation. Heads in different L.E.A.s will face different situations and approaches, all having led from the same piece of legislation.

The power within the special needs system will be moved towards education. This will mean the Local Education Authority but, as its agent, the head will be in a stronger if somewhat new position.

CONFLICT AND CHANGE

Each professional group will want to maintain its influence and interests during the changes after the Education Act. Professional conflicts of interest, anxiety over status and encroachment of areas of competence may well undermine any ideology of "smooth teamwork" towards which the Reports and Education Act aspired. There will be costs to a new working partnership "in terms of changing attitudes, organisational arrangements and practices" (Barton and Moody, 1981). This could be an uncomfortable experience, because, generally, previous experience and training will not have provided an adequate preparation for the new role. The change over will require effort, time, patience and persistence. Sutton (1981) suggests that the situation calls for either a tacit truce between often contradictory positions or for an overarching and universally accepted theory of pedagogy.

While there is this potential for conflict within the system there is also a strong vested interest against upsetting the "multidisciplinary apple cart" (Sutton, 1981) by all who ride on it because of the need to give mutual credence to each different professional contribution.

Tomlinson (1982) indicates that this cohesive factor may be generated because future conflicts are more likely to be with external forces rather than the interprofessional rivalry which has characterised special education. Both Tomlinson and Sutton feel the external pressures may be from central/local government in the giving/withholding of resources in seeking a cost effective service. The special education service has never had any real external accountability. This is probably because:

(1) There is effectively no examination system and, therefore, direct comparison is difficult.

(2) The esoteric nature of the system, with very few people outside it privy to things within it.

(3) The special education system crosses so many paymasters (D.H.S.S., D.E.S., etc.) and so many ideologies and practices.

(4) The sentimental side of public opinion is not in favour of pressure upon a service for the handicapped and thus helps to safeguard it.

The pressures upon the system to measure progress and communicate performance are greater than ever. This may promote cohesion with the system through resistance to external pressures. What may happen is that a rapidly changing special education system rationalised by integrating ideologies will continue to expand and become a more important part of the whole system. Therefore, the interests of the professional groups will be met by an increase in clientele, in work, and in their own areas of competence and expertise.

To enable this to happen, the roles of all participants would need to be clearly established. This would involve not only clarifying each professional role, but also that role within the multidisciplinary system. This is unlikely to occur at a national level or perhaps even at a regional level and would need to be settled locally, as far down perhaps as within individual school catchment areas. Without clear definitions it is more likely to result in interdisciplinary rivalry than cooperation. It must be remembered that cooperation requires interaction between roles.

THE HEAD'S INTERNAL SCHOOL ORGANISATION

If the head is to be as deeply involved in the multidisciplinary role as suggested, then his time available in school must be considerably reduced. The survey already cited indicated that on average only thirty per cent of the heads' contacts were with their own staff. In consequence the head must be confident that the internal organisation of the school is sound and capable of working well even though he or she is not in a position to manage and organise it on a daily basis. This means the head has to rely heavily on his or her staff; indeed, Bowers and Mayes (1982) have pointed out that there is in fact a greater degree of delegation in special schools than in primary schools.

The head is a major link with the external environment of the school, but he or she must continually question whether he or she is the only link or whether other staff would be more suited in some situations, e.g. if a psychologist wanted an up-to-date assessment of a child then the class teacher would be better placed than the head. The head must then take steps to put the professional in touch with the most appropriate member of staff.

The effectiveness of the internal organisation is central to the whole concept of a multidisciplinary approach. The head must give it a great deal of thought and preparation if he or she is to be comfortable in his or her multidisciplinary role.

THE HEAD'S EXTERNAL ORGANISATION

Working with a range of professionals over a wide catchment area means that communication is probably the most important factor. Circular 1/83 specifies that "there should also be clearly identified channels of communication" (para. 10). The actual channels of communication, or the means by which information is transmitted, are probably the smallest part of the problem in the special education system. What information is or is not communicated invariably causes the greatest problems. The question of confidentiality regularly arises and with a greater public access to records (1980 Education Act) and statements (1981 Education Act) the confidentiality could be a problem between professions, with some professionals being extremely reticent about access to their information.

The Warnock Report suggested that confidentiality should be a central point to the Codes of Practice:

> We therefore recommend that teacher associations, in consultation with local authorities associations and representatives of other professions, should draw up guidelines for teachers on the handling of confidential information as well as sharing of information with members of other professions. (16.5)

The very variance of the present responses to confidentiality makes it more not less difficult to operate a multidisciplinary approach within the special education system: "refusal to divulge information may be regarded as good practice within a profession, but be misunderstood or resented by another." (Welton, 1982, p. 277)

Case conferences will occur more often within the new statement and annual review system resulting from the 1981 Education Act than was previously the case. In the past, case conferences have tended to respond to crises rather than be regular. Such meetings served an immediate need but did not establish team work, common ideologies or understanding. It is only when the latter are established that decision-making will become more predictable.

Under the proposed review system the meetings may become regular but the membership of the conferences could vary considerably and it could be that a particular team could be infrequently convened. The formation of a permanently established multiprofessional group may be required above and beyond the conferences dealing with specific cases. This group could be based upon the school or at area level and involve senior personnel from each profession. Its role would be to improve and facilitate the interactions of the professional groups.

Welton (1982) suggests that this might aid in several ways:

(1) By raising the general sensitivity to the need for collaboration and joint action.

(2) Through the development of informal contacts between members of each profession and service.

(3) In the development of formal systems of co-ordination and communication as models for the practitioners.

The head will probably be in the unique position of being the only person common to all the case conferences and reviews about children in his or her school. The key for the head will be in being prepared. He or she will have two advantages in the new system to help him or her:

(1) All the information for review will have to pass through his or her hands and in some cases he or she may be the only professional who has seen all the paperwork before the review.

(2) Because the review will be based upon the work

> of the school, in which the head is instrumental, he or she will have control of the agenda.

We do not know enough about the structures which operate within case conferences, which evidence and which presentation of information is successful, which assumptions and attitudes of members tend to predominate and how the final conclusions are drawn. However, Squibb has speculated that "decisions reached will be influenced by factors extraneous to the case" (1981, p. 43).

The head may not always be in control of the multidisciplinary process, but by understanding the system, by planning and by effective action, he or she can influence the process. This will not, though, be achieved immediately, because effective multiprofessional work requires understanding and trust to be built up over a long period.

TRAINING OF HEAD TEACHERS

In the complexity of the multidisciplinary approach, we may ask, as Coulson (1976) has done, how adequate is the traditional, paternal concept of headship to meet the growing and increasingly complex needs? The head is unlikely to have acquired at least some of the necessary skills during his or her previous experience. Heads are usually appointed on teaching ability, yet the training of heads is becoming vital if they are to play their role in the special education system. The survey found that the majority of heads had (i) been a deputy head, and/or (ii) held a Diploma in Special Education. Both of these would have been weighted towards children and their special needs and neither would have met the Warnock Report's priorities for heads' training in (a) management and administrative skills; (b) interprofessional relationships.

Waters (1979) has argued that it is the second factor which is the most important, because however good his or her management techniques, if the head is lacking in the skills of relating to people then management will be an uphill task. The head in a multidisciplinary situation requires a very special sensitivity (Bowers, 1980).

JOINT TRAINING

The Warnock Report suggested that it would be appropriate for interprofessional training to be either:

(1) joint initial training leading to a dual qualification; or

(2) post qualification in-service courses.

Both types have a part to play in improving the multi-disciplinary process. Wedell and Roberts (1983) have observed that the mutlidisciplinary challenge cannot be met without further training of all concerned and point out that "there is little or no mention of them either in the Act or subsequent policy statements" (p. 8).

CONCLUSIONS

The importance of the multiprofessional approach is best summed up by the Court Report (D.H.S.S., 1976) which maintains that "to disentangle the strands is beyond any single expertise. Medical, Social and Psychological advice have therefore to be available if the child is to receive the best education that can be offered" (10.39). We must never lose sight of the fact that the multidisciplinary process is not about improving relationships; that is the enabling factor. It is ultimately about improving the service to children with special needs. The head in his or her privileged, if complicated, position within the multidisciplinary hierarchy is important, but not the only important person; perhaps he or she is best seen as just the first among equals. This theme is taken up more fully by Ian Galletley in Chapter Five.

The head, though, must be effective as a facilitator of work if we are to see the 1981 Education Act and the Reports implemented, as Bowers (1980) has pointed out. He or she cannot be expected to have all necessary knowledge at their individual disposal. Perhaps, as Anthony Jay (1980) in his consideration of work groups points out, we have always sought an ideal individual when what we ought to be looking for is the right team. In this instance the right multidisciplinary team.

Chapter Nine

PARENTS OF CHILDREN WITH MODERATE LEARNING DIFFICULTIES

by Mike Marra

> We have insisted through this report that the successful education of children with special needs is dependent on the full involvement of their parents, indeed unless parents are seen as equal partners in the educative process the purpose of our report will be frustrated. (Warnock Report, 9.1, 1978)

The Department of Education and Science has periodically stated the importance of involving parents in the education of their children (D.E.S., 1967; 1968; 1977; 1978). Equally, much has been written concerning close relationships between home and school enhancing children's educational progress (Halsey et al, 1961; Douglas, 1964). Numerous suggestions have been examined and postulated over recent years for involving parents (Craft et al, 1967; Donachy, 1976; Lynch and Pimlott, 1976; Cyster et al, 1979; Pugh, 1981). Inroads have been made with parents of severely learning disabled children by way of involving parents as partners in education (Mittler, 1979) and through parent workshops (Cunningham and Jeffree, 1971). Recently Mittler and McConachie (1983) have produced a comprehensive document relating to parents and mentally handicapped children. While contrasting styles of parental involvements have been reported by educationalists working with children with moderate learning difficulties (Ward, 1979; Barnes, 1979; Robinson, 1979), there is little reported on actual practices based on national or regional surveys. Hence, there is much uncertainty about what to do and how to start. In fact a recent report suggests that teachers are still reluctant to take parental involvement seriously (Smith, 1980).

THE SOCIAL DIVIDE

The social divide cannot be found to be greater than

between the parent of the child with moderate learning difficulties and the special school teacher. Teachers continually make value judgements on what is a relevant curriculum for the children in their care and some agreed consensus is maintained between parent and teacher for the average child in mainstream education. However, the predicament of parents of children with moderate learning difficulties is somewhat different. Children in larger families, which tend to be found among lower socio-economic groupings, are often at a disadvantage in spite of increased welfare provision. Also, 1 in 20 disadvantaged children have been said to fall within the old E.S.N.(M) category as opposed to 1 in 150 in ordinary children (Wedge and Prosser, 1973). Stein and Susser (1960), in their sample of young adults who had been ascertained as moderately educationally subnormal at school, also found that the fathers were mainly semi-skilled or casual workers or unemployed. Other studies have shown pupils attending special schools for children with moderate learning difficulties to be consistently generated from social classes IV and V (Chazan, 1964; Hunt, 1975; Marra, 1981). Here lies the overriding problem. The E.S.N.(M) "syndrome" has been described as a human pathological condition of polygenic origin (Ward, 1977), i.e. the combined effects of inherited below average ability and poor physical and social environment. The educational disadvantage experienced by these children is seen by others as being entirely attributable to social conditions.

> Children so labelled are seen as having an individual educational problem when, in fact, they are bearing the burden of all the ills of a technological era which grew out of history, urbanisation, economic greed, inadequate housing and education, poverty, unemployment, disease and social isolation. (Hunt, 1975, p. 28)

More recent writers have placed some of the blame for poor relations with the parents of subnormal children on the teaching profession itself.

> If a continuum of competence is envisaged along which professional people place the parents of the child with whom they deal, the parents of the subnormal children would probably be placed towards the end of the continuum. (Tomlinson, 1981, p. 248)

In the referral processes and the detached attitudes of

L.E.A. Admissions Sections, many of these parents tend to feel summoned. They bring their child to this place to which he or she is duly committed after a "mental test" and never pay another visit. Hence, parental attitudes about special school placement are steeped in deep-rooted misunderstandings of the handicapping condition. It is not surprising, therefore, that it becomes a personal problem of stigma and anxiety which they see as arising from their own inadequacy. Special schools tend to have larger catchment areas than ordinary schools, and the isolation of some parents from the school may be exacerbated by physical as well as psychological distance. The stigmatisation and isolation is further compounded by the lack of "understandable" information relating to their child's problems. In a recent survey, conducted by the writer, of 121 families, thirty per cent claimed not to have been told what their child's problem was. They were left to interpret the problem for themselves and the more novel responses included: "Seems to have a block", "You name it, she's got it", "Lazy mind - it just won't come out" and "He has a syndrome". Three-quarters of the families claimed to have been given no idea how long their child would attend the special school, or assumed that it would be until the statutory school leaving age.

Given this background of uncertainty, relationships between parents and teachers are bound to have potential for conflict and difficulty because teachers are the first people to care for a child for long periods outside the home. Given the geographical isolation of some families from the special school, relationships can become even more strained.

The parents of children with moderate learning difficulties are themselves seen as isolated and ostracised, apathetic and uninterested. However, there is little evidence to suggest any greater involvement with their previous neighbourhood school. The problems which parents encounter in getting into school to see staff are real. The difficulties do not necessarily arise from the school's side of the relationship, but in the day-to-day lives of parents. Theirs are practical difficulties of transport, family commitments, time, ill health, etc. Many parents find it difficult to organise themselves to visit school, and it is easy to put off a visit especially if they may be kept waiting or the meeting may be a strain. While many parents are socially and economically disadvantaged, they are not without feelings and are sensitive to the often uncompromising and patronising attitudes of teachers unfamiliar with the problems of their everyday existence.

PARTNERSHIP OR INVOLVEMENT?

We must remember that the cultural and social differences previously mentioned do not cease to exist after children have passed through the school foyer. Harmony needs to be established between home and school. Teachers need to be constantly aware that the ideals, values and relationships within the school may conflict with those of the home, and that the world assumed by teachers and school books may be unreal to some children. We must not lose sight of the fact that given an average school year, and a fourteen hour awakened day, children are in our custodial care for only thirteen per cent of the time. The family influence is far in excess of three times that time. Tomlinson (1981) states that social selection is involved when children with moderate learning difficulties are admitted to special schools, and further states that teachers, doctors and professionals do not select children from higher socio-economic groups to be ascertained E.S.N.(M). She goes on to say:

> It is logical given the existing power structures that professional people will not deem it necessary to consult or involve those they consider deficient, and it is problematic, given the paucity of research, how far the parents of ESN children are involved in the decision making processes about their children. (p. 250)

In a recent survey of some 369 children attending E.S.N.(M) day special schools, over one-third of the pupils had siblings attending or who had once attended special schools (Marra, 1981), and all too often children attending were second generation special school admissions. Therefore it is not difficult to understand that parental attitudes are greatly influenced by their own previous experiences or those of their children. In any professional relationship there is an assumption that the professional knows more than the client about certain aspects of the client's situation. If we are considering the concept of partnership, this places the teacher in a position of distinct and unfair advantage. In this situation parents are plainly at risk of being exploited (Ballard, 1975). There is much rhetoric on the subject of parents as partners, but much of this supersedes reality. Any partnership in education can take many forms, but it must be on a basis of equality in which each side has areas of knowledge and skill that it contributes to the joint task of working with the child (Mittler and Mittler, 1982), and must include a genuine, honest and sometimes embarrassing dialogue between the family and educationalist (Russell, 1978).

It is clear from the above that genuine partnership in the case of children with moderate learning difficulties may not be a practical proposition; the majority of parents would probably find themselves at best passive partners. For many of our parents the child is but a lesser problem for the family than some of their other burdens; indeed, sometimes a problem is solved by the child's attendance at special school. Given this fact, many of them regard and need to regard the teachers involved as people with special training in working with special needs children, they need to believe that their child is passing into the care of highly trained and skilled professional people. This was reflected in survey conducted by the writer (Marra, 1981) in which 70 of the 121 families said that they were relieved, pleased, thought it was in the child's best interest, or inevitable, when their child was admitted to a special school.

Parent involvement does not necessarily have to be active involvement. Indeed, it has been said that we must allow parents to choose not to be involved, if they so wish (Mittler, 1979). Active involvement educationally and socially may evolve naturally with some parents during the normal course of events (they may take the initiative and ask for homework), but some may wish not to be involved in detail in the day-to-day task of teaching their child. They may see it as too much of a commitment, possibly at the expense of other family members, and wish to spend their free time being "parents". They are not to be condemned for that.

As educators, however, we must encourage an interest in our parents in what is happening in school. Despite our overtures, parental involvement and interest may, often by necessity, come rather low on the list of priorities for some of our families. Nevertheless, they must be kept fully informed. For the parents of children with special needs there can never be too much information transmitted from school to home about what their child and his/her school is doing. It assures parents that we care about their child and we care that they are kept informed.

LINES OF CONTACT AND COMMUNICATION

It has been said (Mittler and Mittler, 1982):

> some schools have no system of communication between home and school; no visits by teachers to the home and only yearly formal visits by parents to the school. (p. 43)

This situation appeared to exist when the writer took up

his appointment at his present school. While partnership between teacher and parents can be seen as an ideal, a goal to which we should work, that of parental involvement is more of a realistic objective - at least in the short term. The pursuit of that objective of necessity involves communication. While good communication with parents is a fundamental objective of any school, in a special school, by the very nature of the problem, it should be of primary importance. The parents of children with moderate learning difficulties are notoriously elusive and, as has been stated earlier, geographically isolated. While geographical isolation is fact and cannot be changed, communication between home and school can be improved both in kind and frequency.

Communication with our parents usually takes the form of one of four main types: letter, verbal (messages carried by pupils either to the home or school), telephone and visit.

Letter communication is very convenient. However, it has a definite authoritative air. This is usually reinforced by the fact that most communication of this type relates to parental "failings" such as non-payment of dinner money, the child's non-attendance, etc. Its impersonality is buttressed by the restrictions imposed by length, syntax and the blandness of type. Verbal communication does introduce a personal element, even though conveyed by a third party, but again presents considerable problems. As educators we are well aware that the expressive language of children with moderate learning difficulties is often restricted and often governed by the lack of an adequately developed vocabulary and syntactic structures. Coupled with this is often the additional problem of the parents' inadequate expressive language function. It is obvious, therefore, that this method of communication can be the subject and vehicle of much misrepresentation contrary to what is intended. "Tell your mother/teacher ..." can often result in distortion implying personal criticism. By far the most convenient mode of communication for both parents and teachers alike is the telephone: it is immediate, personal to a degree and bridges the geographical divide. It is not the subject of misrepresentation and eliminates some of the impersonality of the letter, while maintaining a physical barrier behind which each party may take refuge if he/she so wishes - one can put the telephone down. In terms of the most effective and positive method of communication with parents, the home/school visit must take precedence. It provides one essential element which the others cannot: face to face interaction. Misquotation and misrepresentation are minimised and immediate issue can be taken by both sides on points raised. However, they require forbearance on the part of the teacher. We are the professionals and as such must be seen to be so.

On the writer's appointment to his present post it was decided to test the quality, kind and content of communications between home and school and vice versa. In an initial six-month period there were found to be four times as many personal letters sent home by class teachers compared with communication by the next most popular mode, the telephone. Each class teacher sent home an average of ten letters in that period. Class teachers averaged less than two home visits in that same six-month period, and the number of visits to teachers by parents was barely one per teacher in that same period.

Immediate concern needed to be directed towards the quality and content of communications between the two groups, i.e. parents and teachers. The lack of a policy on contacts had led to estrangement and sometimes alienation of parents from school and intolerance between teachers and parents. The result of this was that much contact tended to be of the authoritative (i.e. letter) kind and of a conflictual, non-constructive and sometimes negative nature. Home/school visits tended to arise as "crisis intervention" when often capitulation by one side or the other was the only way of resolving the problems. Intransigence by either party often resulted in a souring of relationships, and the "writing off" of one party by the other. Without a continuous and constructive dialogue between parents and teachers, the concept of parental involvement cannot be considered.

CHANGING ATTITUDES - THE DESENSITISATION OF RELATIONSHIPS BETWEEN TEACHERS AND PARENTS

In considering the desensitisation of relationships between parents and teachers, both standpoints need to be taken into account and it is for the two parties involved to convince themselves of what kind of parental involvement they want. The idiosyncrasies of both parents and staff need to be considered. Relationships between home and school may range from full cooperation of parents and teachers within the school on the one hand, to complete exclusion of parents on the other. The extent of the involvement will be related directly to the individual school, its geographical location, its population and physical structure and the personalities of staff and parents.

Parental involvement should commence on admission and hopefully grow and extend through a child's stay in a special school. This growth should be fed by an increase of information on each child's needs, offered to parents by teachers in honesty and without cynicism. Prior to special school admission, there will probably have been unwarranted stress on a child's negative aspects, inability or disability to an extent that parents may feel in a "no hope" situation. These feelings will have been nourished by well-meaning neighbours and relations who, on these occasions, appear to have knowledge of some child in exactly the same situation, with exactly the same problems, which evolves with age to colossal proportions. Against this background, parents whose children have been classified as having moderate learning difficulties, i.e. being "subnormal", have to be persuaded to allow their children to attend a special school. Parents ought to know exactly what is happening to their child, and many of the problems and misgivings would be minimised if parents were given an idea of what this meant in terms of the nature of the problem, its prognosis and amelioration. With problems of genetic and congenital origin this may be fine; but how does one approach and explain matters to the parent of a child whose difficulties are quite definitely of polygenic origin?

Much of the fear and distrust of parents could be eliminated if some groundwork was done prior to admission. In the survey conducted by the writer (Marra, 1981), 96 of the 121 families claimed that no one visited from the special school prior to admission, though some could remember visiting the special school themselves. Of those receiving a visit, no specific person was mentioned and most parents were informed of their child's problem by the referring head teacher. It should be implicit in any admission procedure that prior to admission the head teacher or delegated member of staff should visit the parent on "home ground". This should be followed as soon as possible with a visit by the parent and child to the special school. If the special school teacher has seen the child in situ in his/her present school then the dialogue will be far more relaxed and informative. The writer has yet to come across more than a handful of parental objections to admission if this procedure is adopted. However, expediency and the pedantic bureaucracy of administrative procedures often does not allow for this to materialise. The seeds of poor relationships are often sown by unsympathetic educational administrators prior to a child's admission.

As a head teacher of a special school, I feel an obligation actively to encourage staff to involve themselves with parents in home visiting as one of the professional responsibilities of teaching children with special needs. This, while an implicit role of the teacher in the writer's view, is not necessarily seen in this way by all special school teaching staff. They may quite rightly see their major function in ensuring the allocation of appropriate time to the structuring of programmes of work and the further development of expertise within the school. Much of this work cannot be conducted in school hours, and one must acknowledge the additional burden of parental involvement schemes. There may be the implication here that teaching staff should give time without reserve to this aspect of education. To live a balanced life is important to all staff. Some have personal problems and exacting family commitments, others may have the pressures of examinations, and all will have the need for fulfilment in their personal and social lives. Support of school affairs is of obvious importance to professional maturation and career structure. Parental involvement can be made inherent to any job specification but, of course, one cannot legislate for direct commitment beyond a person's own professional organisation's recommendation or beyond personal competence. Therefore, because of these and the other factors mentioned, the degree of participation in a parental involvement programme cannot be used as a direct index of interest or professional support. Nonetheless, all schools should ensure that they have a positive policy on parental involvement which forms an integral constituent of the school's ethos, and as such all staff should subscribe to its existence if not its active promotion.

Teachers themselves are a breed apart, able to wear at will the respective hats of both parents and teachers as the occasion demands. This detachment from the parental role appears to generate some of the misgivings of teachers to parents and their involvement. Often as teachers, acting in the heat of the moment, we make comments to children regarding their parents' responsibilities to which we ourselves would take exception as parents or individuals. An empathic approach, which is often seen as a condition of special school teaching, while making understanding of the parents' problems more feasible, does little for practical reality. Such platitudes as, "I can understand how they feel" and "I can see it from their point of view" have little meaning, given the fact that the problems of parents of special needs children do not tend to resolve themselves easily, nor do they directly affect our own personal lives.

In the desensitisation of relationships between parents and teachers, success is dependent on staff acceptance - an acceptance which acknowledges that in this situation it is the teachers who are the professionals and it is legitimate to expect them to take the major initiative. Highly subjective comment by teachers in the staffroom such as, "She's living with someone", or "They are no different" and "What more would you expect?" while not harming parent-teacher relationships directly do not help in the modification of staff attitudes or behaviour.

Through a series of meetings, staff can be directed and guided towards examining themselves critically in their approaches and judging the objectivity of recorded comments in reports, etc.

Much of staff opinion and comment of this nature can be based on unsubstantiated fact. Non-attendance at school functions and parents' evenings is stated as being due to lack of parental interest in the educative process. In the writer's survey (Marra, 1981), the problem was seen to be more one of a muddled frame of mind. Many of our parents are not the sort of people who, on receiving a letter from school, are accustomed to taking note of times and dates. Unsolicited open comment by staff in the classroom situation on such non-compliance with the teachers' middle-class expectations are transmitted in an appealing yet embellished way, to highly sensitive parents who take what is said as direct criticism. Teachers then in turn interpret this as some sort of personal criticism and back away from further involvement. Teachers need to be encouraged to utilise such a situation to positive advantage. A hostile and defensive parent confronted by a smiling and affable teacher may be more inclined to reciprocate a visit. It is difficult not to succumb to a person who insists on understanding your problem no matter how aggressive a stance you take with him or her. Aggression and defensiveness are often synonymous with our parents. They often feel the need to attack in order to stave off further criticism. Parents rarely remain aggressive if somehow genuine understanding is displayed by the teacher. In any interaction of this kind it is essential that the counsellor has a genuine, warm and positive regard for his or her client (Rogers, 1951).

I have found that teachers readily accuse parents of arrogantly criticising things which they know nothing about; they see them as unrealistic in their expectations of competence, particularly in literacy, without resort to the teachers' professional opinion. However, whatever their social class origins, children tend to conform to the expectations of teachers (McGreeney, 1969), and parental concern may on occasion not be without reason. Teachers need to acknowledge criticism levelled at them that "they know best" and be prepared at least to investigate comments more thoroughly in taking account of children's programmes of work. Relationships are improved when teachers involve parents directly, if they so wish, while ensuring at the same time that they furbish them with all the resources and information to participate and cooperate in the task, not just instruct them to "listen to him/her read". At the same time teachers should keep themselves well prepared for informed and articulate parents who have a legitimate right to ask two question: "What is/are my child's problem(s)?" and "What are you doing about it/them?"

HOME SCHOOL LIAISON: AN EXERCISE IN PUBLIC RELATIONS

If "partnership" is to remain our ideal it must involve the individual respect and recognition of the essential equality between parents and professionals. It must include a sharing of information, skills, feelings and decision making, and recognition of the individuality and uniqueness of each family's situation in dealing with a handicapped child (Mittler, 1982). How best can this sharing occur with children with moderate learning difficulties? It is this writer's opinion that this can be best achieved by "opening" the special school in all its aspects.

When speaking of "community education", Midwinter (1973) stated that it was a public relations exercise and should follow a logical sequence and progression. He qualified this by saying that progression should include publication, exposition, site improvement and involving parents in the process of education. In the case of the writer's school, this model was adopted but items two and three were reversed. In this section only "publication" and "site improvement" are considered.

The first objective was to increase the flow of information to parents by way of a "Newsletter". As at this stage staff were not convinced of the need for these elaborate measures, they had to come from the top both in the innovatory nature of the ideas and their execution. The usual circulars were bland and unattractive, often never finding their destination; even if they did arrive, they were sufficiently innocuous not to warrant attention. It was decided that the letters had to have visual impact, be concise and limited in content and sufficiently attractive to distinguish them from the usual school literature. They were intended to herald a new era of communication between school and home. Their printing was to be sufficiently novel to ensure that children would take them home to show their mums. These newsletters were supplemented tri-annually by a "News Magazine". This took the form of an eight-page booklet containing news stories, features, and articles and diary dates all arising from the solicited contributions of pupils. In addition, there was a centrefold "Kid's Page" and a cover designed by a pupil. Originals were used for the illustrations, but the text was typed. The whole was of a professional appearance. Some twelve months after the inception of both the newsletters and the magazine, over 100 parents (from 121) commented that they found them useful and informative. Most welcomed the children's contributions and many looked forward with anticipation to the next news magazine - perhaps it would contain a contribution by their child.

Running concurrently with this was a programme which involved the restructuring of display areas. All staff were co-opted to participate. Mounting and display techniques were discussed at staff meetings, providing assistance to the "non-arty" types. There was an immediate and noticeable improvement in the corridor areas and classrooms, with a comparable decrease in pupil defacement of displays. When there was defacement of a picture it was replaced without comment immediately. So the practice of defacement was eliminated completely. At the same time the local press were informed of feature events which were taking place in school, e.g. autumn fair, elderly citizens' Christmas party, spring bulb distribution, etc., and photographs duly appeared in the local and provincial press. Both parents and children expressed delight at this aspect. Now they could talk with neighbours and other children with pride of achievement.

After a period of twelve months the opportunity arose to create an above scale post with responsibility for home school liaison. The Home School Liaison Teacher (HSLT) and the head teacher then proceeded to visit each pupil's family or person with custodial care. Not being "crisis interventions", the visits served to cement the contact made by the publications. The appointment of a HSLT has subsequently added greatly to the amount of communication in both directions. It was never anticipated that the threshold of the home would be difficult to cross and in fact only one family declined a visit. However, the school threshold is not for most parents a natural crossing point, either to support the child or the school (Ward, 1979). The home visit allows parents and teachers to compare observations on attitudes and behaviour of pupils in the two separate yet interdependent settings and to make recommendations based on first-hand knowledge.

In this initial period each child received a school report of educational progress: the first in the school's history. These were very much appreciated by parents and formed a strong basis for positive discussion. The degree of appreciation for the reports was reflected in the return of over ninety per cent of acknowledgement slips. This compared favourably with an earlier exercise by McGreeney (1969) in an ordinary primary school in which a similar percentage of returns was made. This appeared to counter the criticism that many of our parents do not care. They do care if what is offered is relevant and meaningful. Home visiting also provides a clear base from which the HSLT can operate. It offers the possibility for an initiative with those families who never visit school at all. Indeed, it is in these instances where it is most valuable. It provides a vital link between disaffected families and school. Information can be delivered and the HSLT becomes a spokesperson for the parents and a resource of information to the class teacher who may not visit.

One consideration with home visiting and the role of the HSLT must be the cost effectiveness of the time taken in visiting. Other considerations need to be taken into account, such as who looks after the teacher's class while a home visit takes place in school time. While other class teachers remain unconvinced of the need, some evidence of return for this type of investment needs to be offered to others before they will be convinced that the exercise has a worthwhile function. One way of doing this is by the quick dissemination of information to the appropriate class teacher as soon as possible on return, in order that appropriate corresponding action may be instigated in the classroom situation. It has been postulated that if one teacher can be converted to good home-school practice, thirty pairs of parents and their children could benefit (Midwinter, 1973, p. 207). It is generally perceived that it would not be feasible for members of staff to take over home visiting effectively in the event of the HSLT ceasing to exist. This was found to be the case in the writer's present school prior to the establishment of such a post and policy on parental involvement. Pask (1981) found in her report on the work of the home school worker in the residential setting that some members of staff had reservations aside from logistics about visiting parents at home. Without a HSLT it has been found that either home-school visiting did not exist or became the responsibility of many individuals, some of whom would either not be able to make visits, or not want to visit. Evidence from the writer's present school suggested that visiting was at best patchy, often being restricted to certain classes of privileged parents and was questionable in its nature and validity.

In the selective encouragement of members of staff to engage in home visits, consideration must be given to the terms of reference of everyone involved. Care is needed in the visiting process not to usurp the position of another, otherwise there is the inherent danger that we may involve ourselves in issues which come within the terms of reference of other disciplines. Here we must consider the positions of the L.E.A. Officers, Head Teacher, Education Welfare Office, School Nurse, HSLT, Class Teacher, Social Worker, etc. Chance or careless remarks on a home visit are often seized upon, misinterpreted and misquoted, and may be utilised by parents in order to play one discipline off against the other.

Because of the personal and/or professional reservations of some staff about visiting parents, an unwritten system evolved in the early stages whereby an experienced and more confident member of staff befriended another for the purposes of the visit. This doubling of members appeared to offer no threat to parents, perhaps as there was for them a common factor in the visit - their child's efficient education.

The procedure now adopted in the writer's present school is as follows. If an educational problem or a problem with educational implications evolves with a child, the teacher directly involved is asked to discuss the problem in the first instance with the head teacher in order that a joint profile for discussion can be agreed upon. It was implied earlier that discussion with parents is best conducted by the teacher concerned; if the class teacher is unable to visit then the head teacher or the HSLT will visit. The outcome of any visit is then disseminated to the head teacher, HSLT or staff involved with that child in order to ensure that their positions are not prejudiced. The HSLT assumes overall responsibility for home visiting and parents can now expect at least one courtesy visit per year, supplemented as the need arises. A file card system is kept with the HSLT where dates and brief details of the visit are recorded. Expanded comments are transferred to the pupil's file at a later date. The file cards are kept in date order. A card goes to the back of the index following a visit, ensuring that those without visits are not neglected. This system ensures visits for all and makes everyone involved fully aware of all discussions and developments relating to the home visiting programme.

A PLACE OF THEIR OWN

Over sixty-five per cent of parents' responses in the writer's survey stated that they never or rarely visited school. Despite this, almost the same number reported that school had always made them welcome. In the same survey, eighty-four per cent of parental responses indicated a desire to be involved in school (with a quarter of this number qualifying their response with "if they wished to" or "had time") and half of them said that they personally would like to be involved in a parents' group. However, some of this positive assertion could probably be due to parental acquiescence. So why were they so disinclined to visit school?

Historically parents had always involved themselves to an enthusiastic degree in the school's social functions: autumn fairs, jumble sales and the like. Involving them educationally would be more problematic. Annual Parents'

Evenings only enticed a dozen or so parents to attend. Any educational undertones to our parental involvement programme would need to be carefully chosen in order to ensure that success was virtually guaranteed. It would be necessary for the scheme to reflect the parents' neighbourhood in the hope that parents would naturally and unselfconsciously become involved in it because it arose out of everyday life. Using school-based semi-structured afternoon group sessions, it had been shown that the effects could be beneficial (Widlake, 1980). This school base should provide that essential "natural social locus" which Midwinter (1972) claimed was so necessary in fostering home school relations and in attempting to involve parents in the educative process. Other school-based parental involvement programmes had highlighted stumbling blocks. Barnes (1979) found that parental response was likely to improve if what was on offer was worth coming for; while notifying parents sufficiently well in advance, they were still given continual reminders. Both Hunt (1975) and Pask (1981) pointed to the problems of time, family commitments and transport. On the question of transport, many teachers have been heard to accuse parents of opting out. "If they really wanted to come they would" is often the cry to be heard. This socially destructive verbiage in which parental attitudes are condemned and freely bandied about in the staffroom may be valid, but is counterproductive to what we wish to achieve. Parents need to be gently bullied into an involvement rather than be condemned.

The nettle grasped, parents were informed of the fortnightly parents' group meetings in a special newsletter. Experience had shown that parents became agitated when invited into school and then left dangling in the foyer because their arrival had come at an inopportune moment. For this reason a "parents' room" was made available. At future meetings they would be encouraged to make their way there freely, to that bit of school which at that time would be theirs. It would be the province of the parents where they would be free to ventilate their feelings and ideas. Over 100 of the 121 parents had recorded the fact that they felt that a teacher should be present at the group meetings in order to offer advice and help. For this reason the HSLT was made available at each meeting. The introductory letter invited all parents to visit the afternoon group. However, prior to each meeting a number of personal invitations were sent out to parents living in specific geographical areas and transportation into school in the school's mini-coach was offered. Transport was offered from a designated point in their immediate locality, to which they were returned. In the courtship of parents, additional incentives were offered in the parents' room: namely, tea and biscuits, a "good as new" wardrobe, leaflets on the various social benefits to which they might be entitled and literature on the recreational facilities in the different localities.

Parents were found to be attending the group meetings for a variety of reasons, varying from educational ones to a simple desire to get out of the house. Their individual motivations were in a way immaterial. The main fact was that they had come to school. In the course of those first four months, almost twenty-five per cent of parents visited these low key afternoon sessions. For these first early meetings nothing structured was offered, the essentiality being to create a comfortable atmosphere between parents and teachers in a school setting and to allow the group to establish its own identity. An earlier study by Marra (1982) had revealed that the strains and relationships in "stable" families with regard to parental aspirations for their children's futures were greater and of a different order to those of parents whose children's backgrounds could be described as of a more "unstable" nature (for a definition of these terms, see Marra (1982)).

Experience of evening meetings and parents' evenings had shown that these events tended to attract the more articulate and prosperous parents, and the school's "Friends" society consisted mainly of these parents. With the advent of the afternoon groups a polarisation of parents appeared to have evolved. Those parents attending the afternoon sessions were those who were more readily available during the day and from more socially and economically impoverished backgrounds. It appeared that the informality of the afternoon sessions suited their needs more than those of more affluent parents. Parents of the more socio-economically advantaged children were in the main those who over the years had satisfied themselves that their child's learning difficulties were of a medical or congenital origin; their children were "dyslexic" or their difficulties could be described by some other acceptable euphemism. The lack of corporate parental identity appeared to reveal itself in overt form for the first time. Parents saw themselves as being different not only in the nature of the child's problem, but also in their social and cultural values and life styles. When visiting speakers were invited to address the parents of the leavers' group they did meet together, but only for the purpose of listening to the speaker, not to share views or problems. If the alienation of either group was not to occur, then this problem would need to be given more detailed consideration in the future.

Issues needing resolution also evolved when a volunteer worker was introduced for the purpose of offering support to the project. Ward (1979) noted that the involvement of an intermediate worker can sometimes have a harmful effect on the relationship between teachers and parents particularly if their viewpoint is biased. If their role does not reflect the ethos of the school then their involvement can be counterproductive. Many of the initial problems revolved around the role of the volunteer as interpreted by the volunteer, and the teachers' interpretation of that role. Other problems related to basic philosophy.

Teachers are often quick to utilise any offer of classroom help. Experience has shown that when parents' groups were not in session, teachers had a desire to co-opt volunteers as classroom helpers. When the parents' group was in session there was a certain amount of jockeying for position in vying for parental approval. This problem was resolved by allowing the volunteer to participate in small group work with children which involved social training. Other time was spent helping to arrange recreational provision for children in out of school time. This approach appeared to comply with the volunteer worker's interpretation of role, and at the same time satisfy teaching staff. The other main problem closely linked with this was the difference in philosophical perspectives on the children's problems. The volunteer worker appeared to view their problems as only having sociological implications, and for the teacher it was educational. However, over a number of weeks each of the parties began to appreciate the position of the other, and the stance of each mellowed to produce a working relationship.

Within this school-based development, the class teacher's position needs to be considered. Implicit in the school's invitation to participate was the offer that parents could view the educational processes first hand. How would class teachers react to this? It was decided at this stage to introduce Midwinter's (1973) "exposition" stage. Staff were first of all asked to arrange specimen displays which involved children. It was felt that teachers would feel more comfortable in this situation and be less vulnerable. Displays in carol singing, physical education and modern dance were arranged to coincide with the parents' group meetings. This softening of boundaries made the parents' later incursions into the classroom less likely to be a point of potential breakdown as it was here that parental involvement educationally would be nurtured. It was envisaged that this grass-roots level of involvement would in time be the most productive. Dialogue, agenda and objectives would be within the parental compass and the setting here and in the group meeting sufficiently informative and elastic to invite spontaneous and productive ideas. Here the traditional barriers between parents and teachers would become less significant in the offer of an opportunity for improved relationships.

However, parental presence in the classroom is not without its problems. It can absorb time and energies too dearly needed for the children. In the classroom dialogue with parents, the amount of time spent in teacher-pupil interaction will be reduced according to the amount of time spent in discussion. Where such discussion proves to produce positive results in pupil attitudes and progress, such time may be considered as an investment. It has been reported that some twenty-five per cent of disadvantaged children with learning difficulties display unsettled behaviour patterns and a further twenty-five per cent can be described as maladjusted on the basis of social adjustment guides completed by class teachers (Chazan, 1964; Wedge and Prosser, 1973; Marra, 1981). Such a classroom climate requires skilled and sensitive management. The distractability factor is high. The entry of a parent into the classroom, particularly if the parent has some anxiety about a child, provides yet another problem for the teacher, and detracts from, if but briefly, the teacher's supervision. Conversely, there are times when the parent's presence in a meaningful context can have a salutary effect on the child.

FUTURE PROJECTIONS: TOWARDS PARENTAL INVOLVEMENT IN THE EDUCATIVE PROCESS

What has been described in this chapter reflects parental involvement in its infancy; the objective of educational involvement and the goal of partnership have yet to be reached. However, what have been described here are some of the principles for a possible partnership based on experience. Partnership may remain an ideal for quite a period of time to come, but the more practical possibilities are explored and reported, the more likelihood of its eventual outcome.

Transport is undoubtedly going to remain a problem in bridging the geographical divide but systematic home visiting has been shown to work and increases the possibility of a reciprocal visit by parents. The parents' group has obvious potential and will probably take over the role of the more pretentious "Friends" group. However, its efficient development will not depend so much on parental responses but on the internal management problems of staff cover and staff availability in the meeting of parental initiatives. Who looks after the shop while the teachers talk to customers? Volunteer help will always be a bonus despite the possibility of a philosophical impasse, but recruitment even in these days of economic recession remains difficult. However, this present recession has had an effect more in terms of the involvement of fathers in the programme; a number of them have been keen to participate as active classroom helpers in pottery, craft and physical education. This has done much to counter the view that only the mothers of younger children are willing to be actively engaged.

Over the past two years our parents have been coaxed, courted, cajoled and even "bullied" into attending functions, but in the end they will make up their own minds on the parameters of their involvement. Transport has been provided and parents' evenings have been held in their neighbourhood primary schools in attempts to elicit their attendance, but hopefully in times to come we will soon find ourselves in the position of weaning them off these incentives as they discover that the cake is attractive enough to eat without the icing. Parental involvement is about teachers and parents coming together with a shared interest - their child. The effectiveness of such programmes will be reflected in the benefits to the children and in the process there will be degrees of modification by both teachers and parents to the problems set before them and their attitudes to them.

My hopes for the future cannot be stated more succinctly than by an earlier writer on the subject:

> I hope that members of staff will be as ready to recognise the value of the many ultimate benefits to a school where the importance of parents' roles and attitudes is inherent in the school's philosophy. Strategies for such a change will inevitably vary according to the circumstances of the school. At best, there will always be setbacks; transition to such practices will never be wholly smooth and staffing ratios will be used as a challenging argument against time given to parents. But, in the end, the educative responsibility of home and school must be a joint enterprise (Ward, 1979, p. 20).

Chapter Ten

WORKING WITH PARENTS OF EMOTIONALLY DISTURBED CHILDREN

by Muriel Colley

THE CHILDREN

Parents are important people in Cavendish School, the London Borough of Ealing's day school for emotionally disturbed children of first to middle school age. The majority of the children who are referred to us have been aggressive, anti-social or anti-authority elsewhere. Many of our children feel themselves to have been rejected by most people, and some of them, being unable to succeed in any other way, have tried to become best at being "the worst" (and succeeded!). A good many of the pupils are suffering from the stresses caused by urban living described by Wolff (1973). Some of the children feel themselves to be uncontainable and this is frightening for them.

It is possible that their acts of violence stem from their panic states. Dockar-Drysdale (1971) has described the management of violence in disturbed children and her methods have been of help to staff at Cavendish School who at times have to contain such violence. Some of the children act in bizarre ways and cause problems of acceptance by the staff. Shields's (1962) description of some of his cases when he was working as a psychotherapist in a residential school are of help in putting some of this behaviour into an acceptable context. Some of the children see themselves as "mad". They have had no opportunity to express their feelings in any other way than aggressively and this has led to their referral to the school where, possibly for the first time in their lives, they are accepted as they are and offered help to change.

In contrast to other types of provision for children with special educational needs (where the handicap is visible and understandable instantly to the parents and the rest of the population), the provision required for emotionally disturbed children is elusive, intangible and not always quantifiable. In the case of other disabilities, there is clear evidence and no argument that help for these children is required.

The term "emotional disturbance" is not easily defined in immediately understandable terms and for many people it has no meaning, particularly in an educational - albeit caring - context. Indeed, there are many administrators and educationalists with power who still see the difficulty as something which requires punishment rather than help. Such people feel annoyed by behavioural disorders and feel that it is not necessary to have schools for emotionally disturbed children as there is really no such thing: rather that "emotional disturbance" is "naughtiness" or "delinquency" which ought to be dealt with by "discipline" which will make it go away. Discipline in this context usually means violence against the emotionally disturbed pupil because such pupils are regarded as trouble makers who need to be punished.

This attitude could probably account for the small number of day schools run by L.E.A.s for emotionally disturbed pupils and the larger number of boarding schools run by the private sector. Most of the research into methods of dealing with difficult children was carried out in the private sector in this country and a number of excellent books and papers on the subject have been written by people who have worked with such children and who pioneered the field which did not come into existence until after the Second World War (e.g. Wills, 1962). Until that time, children who had problems of a social and emotional nature were dealt with in psychiatric or mental institutions or stayed at home and did not receive any education as such in a local authority school.

It is important to note at this point three important factors influencing attitudes, and therefore provision, for this particular handicap:

(1) The first providers who recognised the problem were in the private sector and therefore the original research is in this sector.

(2) Provision was made in boarding schools which meant that the child was treated in isolation as a separate entity and not an integral part of the family in which the problem had its roots.

(3) It was not until day schools run by local authorities were started that the possibility of tackling the entire problem <u>as a family problem</u> came into existence.

Many of the boarding schools have social workers

and maintain links with the families. Indeed, some of the better boarding schools insist that there must be a social worker who is involved with the family doing ongoing work after the child has gone away from home. However, because of the distance between the school and the home, they do not have the opportunity for the close personal links that the day school has. Thus day schools are in the best possible position to do the maximum amount of work with families. This work should be considered to be of the greatest possible importance in the work of the school. The child is often only the tip of the iceberg. Underneath there are many problems which can only be resolved if the school understands and tries to provide as much help as possible.

Emotional disturbance is rooted within the family, sometimes back into many generations. This is why it is important - once the chance to deal with a disturbed child arises - for the school to work as hard as possible to break into the family rearing cycle so that the child will have a different set of values. It is only by the substitution of new attitudes and values that the next generation will have a chance of coping with social pressures.

PARENTS' POSITION AT THE INITIAL INTERVIEW

Many of the parents of children who are admitted as pupils to the school have been fighting a battle with the authorities to prevent the placement. Some of them have fought for several years, mostly by refusal to cooperate with agencies that have been trying to remove their child from the ordinary school and put him or her in a special school. The reason for the struggle is sometimes the reason for the child's referral in the first place. Often the parents have had bad experiences at their own school and dislike "education". The schools appear to be authoritarian and, as such, are to be avoided. One of the recurring symptoms that appears in the scholars is the anti-authority attitude that is prominent in the families. This, together with anti-social attitudes, makes it very difficult for any dialogue to develop between the parents and any organisation that might smack of being authoritarian. The other aspect of refusal to accept help is that an admission that "something is wrong" with a child who looks normal, usually has a reasonable intelligence even if under-functioning academically (which is frequently acceptable to the parents as they themselves did not flourish at their schools), and has no physical handicap, is an admission that "something is wrong" in the family itself.

Over the years, many of our pupils have been admitted at the point where the parents have had to give in because their child's behaviour has become so intolerable to the normal school system that he has been expelled or at least has been threatened with expulsion.

During the course of the referral, the following agencies will have been involved:

(1) The normal school. In many cases, schools will have been inviting the parents to school to meet the head and the teacher and these invitations will have been avoided in the hope that the problem will go away, the school will have given up, or the passage of time will bring a change of school and a fresh start.

(2) The psychologist. Having reached this stage, the parents still do not have to be involved. They only need to give their permission for a psychological test to take place at school. With luck, they hope, a test will be done and that will be the end of that.

(3) The child guidance clinic. If the psychological test indicates that there is emotional trouble, then the family will receive an invitation to discuss the problem with the social worker and later the psychiatrist. Here, once again, if the family refuses to be seen, or having been seen rejects the offer of help, then nothing can be done and the child continues to be a problem at school until there is a threat of expulsion.

THE EDUCATION AUTHORITY

At this point, the problem for the family has become acute and something has to be done for fear of legal action or for fear that their child will continue to remain at home causing trouble. In our Borough, there is a very charming, friendly and (more important for our families) neither pompous nor disdainful, representative of the Chief Education Officer who knows our school and she is usually able to persuade even the most difficult families at least to come and have a look at the school and make up their own minds.

THE FIRST VISIT

It is at this point that the family is almost defeated but, at the same time, it is a critical time for everyone, for it presents the first opportunity for the school to be seen as a caring, helpful, non-authoritarian institution where blame is not apportioned and is not even required, and that help in the way of coping with the child's violence or other anti-social activities as well as his education can be given. At the first visit the parents are often worried about what they now have to accept about their child's anti-social activities and they should be reassured that these activities will not be a problem to the school.

THE FIRST CONTACT

Usually, the first contact that any visitor to an establishment of any kind has is with the secretary. It is really helpful if the school secretary can be persuaded of the importance of her role as the first contact and maintaining ongoing contacts. This means that if she has a friendly and courteous approach to the people who ring in or who call, and if she finds chairs and offers coffee or other refreshment and smiles and is polite then this sets the scene for what is to follow.

THE SECOND CONTACT

The second contact is with the head and the social worker and always this should be a meeting where a friendly atmosphere is maintained. The parents are usually very defensive and tend to blame the authorities, their child's previous school, the Child Guidance Clinic and anyone who has had anything to do with getting them to this stage, but blame neither themselves nor their child. The head, at this point, should accept all the vituperation that will come out and all the denials. The aim, at this interview, is to keep things very calm and also to get the parents off the hook by pointing out that the school is not a school for dull children which most of them claim to believe, and indeed to indicate that on the contrary, dull children would be unable to cope with an environment which insists on the child accepting responsibility for his own behaviour and to be confronted verbally with it.

The second aim is to separate the child from the parents early in the interview in order to establish whether the child will be able to respond to the school environment. Indeed, the school has many facilities that maladjusted children enjoy, including a soft play environment, a learner swimming pool, a science and computer room, a very good woodwork room and an art room with pottery kiln and other exciting materials. Therefore, as early as possible, the head should take the child away from the parents to look at the school. The social worker will then invite the parents to his or her room to discuss what has gone on before the visit. By the time the head comes back with the child, who is usually insisting on being allowed to stay in the school, the social worker has established a kind of rapport with the parents. The social worker then takes them around the school and, at the end of this visit, there is no pressure on either the parents or the child to accept a place which is being offered, and they are sent away to make up their own minds and offered as much time as they require to 'phone in and either accept or refuse the offer. All of these strategies help to reassure parents and give them a chance of saving their faces. This allows the child to be freed from the blame which tends to show itself as soon as the parents relax and enables the head to make an evaluation of the pupil's suitability.

ONE PARENT OR TWO

If only one parent turns up for the initial interview, this may be an indication that there is marital disharmony in the case of a two parent family. If it is possible to persuade the visiting parent to defer accepting a place until the other parent has seen the school, this is a great advantage in working in the future. However, this is often impossible, however desirable, and sometimes it is necessary to take in a child whose father or mother has not seen the school. Then the work with the parents is more complicated, for the other parent will use the school as a rod with which to whip the partner who has "allowed" the child to come to a school for emotionally disturbed children. In several cases we have never met the other parent, and this situation bodes ill for the child. It may be necessary to refer him or her to boarding school as there is little help to be obtained from the home and the child will better be able to take care of him or herself if allowed to develop away from the poor environment of the family.

THE ROLE OF THE HEAD

The role of the head is crucial in working with the parents of emotionally disturbed chidren. This is because the parents, admittedly with exceptions, usually are themselves the victims of anti-authority and anti-social environments. They are unable to cope with bureaucracies. The head is a representative of a bureaucracy and, as such, is a bureaucrat. But the school is presented as a nurturing institution and therefore the head has to be seen as a caring, nurturing person. However, emotionally disturbed parents often have low self images just as their children do and therefore they need to be able to have a relationship with the most important person on the premises directly. Frequently they expect to see the chief of a large bureaucracy and take it personally if they have to see someone lower down the hierarchy; their feelings are hurt so they reject the whole establishment. In the case of a school for maladjusted children, this person has to be the head who is the representative of the Education Authority. The head must therefore be willing to expose him or herself liberally to the demands of people who feel humiliated by authority in order that they can reassure themselves that they are not "bad" people and that this authority figure respects them. This feeling has to be honest and real, otherwise it will have the reverse effect of what is intended. Emotionally disturbed people are highly sensitive and when they think someone is patronising them, they will rebuff and reject the help. This is a tightrope, for on the one hand it is necessary to carry out the duties of the Authority and to represent it, but on the other, it is necessary to assure the injured people that they are respected and cared for, or the therapy will not take place and the opportunity will be lost.

In the eyes of people who have had unsuccessful schooldays and who have left education as quickly as possible to get on with their life, a head teacher is a symbol of the power of authority and someone to be avoided as much as possible. A head teacher, having been appointed by a bureaucracy as powerful as an Education Authority with all that that implies in the minds of anti-authority people, is the representative of that bureaucracy with the power that it holds over people - the power to expel and the power to take legal action. Therefore the head's image in the minds of those people who have arrived against their wishes at the school is that of a force against those who are unsuccessful. Many of the parents themselves have suffered from poor nurturing and they know that they have failed both in their personal lives and in bringing up their children to a standard required by society. They are victims of poor family rearing patterns; they are suffering from low self image and depression arising from lack of success. If the head cannot with compassion put him or herself in the place of people who, through reasons for which they cannot be held responsible, are unable to attend open evenings or parents' functions because the memory of their own schooldays is so painful that any contact must be avoided, then the chance of working with these people must be forgotten. If the head can prove to the parents that their concept of power is wrong and that power can also be caring, then the possibility of progress exists. On the other hand, if the head is too humble and unassuming, the parents will reject him or her as being ineffectual. Therefore in order to make progress with the parents, it is necessary to show authority and power as well as humanity. By being linked to the bureaucracy, the head can be a mediator between it and the parents in the difficult task of assisting people who have been unable to manage their own emotions about society. No head can do this unaided. There has to be a team of people working in the school who are able to support the head and to demonstrate the function of the school as a place of assistance to parents as well as to the children.

THE ROLE OF THE PEOPLE WHO WORK IN THE SCHOOL

If the school is an open place where parents are welcome with or without an appointment, the staff of all kinds who work there must be prepared to find time when people arrive, even if they are busy, to talk to parents, show them their children's work and listen to their problems. If contact is made by telephone, and the parent is in a phone box, the recipient should take the number, for the problem may be important and money could run out in the middle of a critical conversation.

If the school welcomes ex-pupils, when teachers have moved on for promotion or for whatever reasons, there will continue to be expectations on the part of the ex-pupils, that they will be welcome even when it has been a long time since they were at school and nearly all the people they know have gone. Sometimes this can be very difficult for staff, as they have their commitments to the children on the roll at the present time and ex-pupils are frequently very demanding. Although there have been difficulties during the past ten years, the school has nevertheless been able to maintain its open, welcoming quality. This is a testimonial to the care of all the workers in the school and a tribute to their tolerance.

One of the bonuses of retaining a caring ethos is that some ex-pupils come back to help and this is a manifestation of the continuing effect of the pupil's first experiences of the school. It is very satisfying to find that as new teachers arrive to work here, they are able to replace in their attitudes the teachers who have left, thus maintaining the quality of the environment as a therapeutic community.

THE ROLE OF THE SOCIAL WORKERS IN THE SCHOOL

There are two half-time social workers in this school and having two people working with the families is a great advantage. There are some parents who only need the occasional visit and who are able to come along and take an active part in the work of the school. However, there are some parents who are in need of a great deal of help. Sometimes a social worker is involved in going to court, seeing the electricity company, organising help through the family doctor, attending case conferences with Child Guidance or Social Services and if there are a large number of problems, the work is very time consuming and painful. It is usually arranged that if experience has shown that a particular family will need maximum help, then the social workers take the heaviest burdens equally so that one is not too weighed down. The advantage of having two social workers is that the school receives the benefit of extra time, for both do more than a half-time job and therefore we get more for our money. A full-time social worker would be unable to do what the two half-time workers do.

The children who come here are emotionally damaged but physically and intellectually they are relatively unharmed; therefore the possibility of remission of the problem is quite high. Many of the parents are themselves emotionally disturbed and, as has been said earlier in this chapter, often the children who manage by their behaviour to get themselves referred here are victims of parental problems and sometimes are scapegoats of the family. When the children begin to relate well within the school and begin to make emotional progress, this may have repercussions within some of the families. Often the parents do not wish the child to get better as this would expose other areas within the family which are the real cause of the child's disturbance and many of them try to undo what is being done for the child by undermining the work or testing out the school in very demanding ways. In some cases, the parents are in need of mothering themselves. They are jealous of the care the children are given here and they themselves need enormous amounts of support so that the school can get on with the job of helping the children without too much interference.

It is here that the social workers fulfil the function of surrogate parents. They offer nurture to the parents in all kinds of ways. They are the people who know the children, the rest of the staff and the school ethos. They help to explain the methods and act as buffers between the parents and the children, the home and the school.

The social workers liaise with the psychiatric staff of this Borough which has four Child Guidance Clinics and they work with hospitals which are dealing with some of the children. They visit the Child Guidance Clinics and collect information on new children, then keep links with the psychiatric social workers, psychologists and psychiatrists to inform them of the child's progress or otherwise in the school. The social workers liaise with the Education Office when children are referred on and they help parents through the difficult process of weaning away from this school. On the practical side, they help with housing problems, holidays, clothing, hospital and dental appointments, help fill in forms and do the one hundred and one things that ordinarily functioning families can manage and which families under stress just cannot cope with.

The social workers keep the teaching staff in touch with any special difficulties that the families are going through in order to help the teachers tolerate the stresses that seriously troubled children bring with them daily to the school. The social workers are the key workers in the treatment of the families. A school for emotionally disturbed children without school based social work help is only able to make an extrinsic contribution to the problem.

WAYS OF WORKING WITH PARENTS

Types of Problem

Most of the families have had problems and conflicts over their marital situation and the majority of the children we have here are from split or one parent families and families where there is a mother and a stepfather or a mother and cohabitee. Quite often there are half brothers and sisters and there is sibling rivalry and scapegoating of the child who has finally come to be referred to the school.

Scapegoats

These children are treated quite badly, as most frequently the mother has rejected this member of the family for reasons which often have to do with her bad relationship with the father either when the child was a baby or later when there were other children. Sometimes the father has been violent and the child reminds the mother of him and therefore she cannot tolerate the child. Symptoms shown by these children are arson, stealing and drawing the attention of the police to themselves. Quite often, they make suicide attempts. It is usually the best policy when this happens for the school to insist on a referral to boarding school. The most common reaction is for the mother to insist on keeping the child at home, sometimes because she needs a scapegoat, while verbally assuring everyone that she would never "put away" her child; but it is important for the future well-being of the child for him to go away. Frequently, when the child is out of the family, a better relationship develops between the parent and the child. The process of finding a boarding school place often takes a long time and it is the job of both the school and the social worker to keep up the mother's morale and to accept that allowing her child to go is in his or her best interests.

THE CHILD ACTING OUT THROUGH FEELINGS OF GUILT

It is sometimes necessary to support the parent while negotiating a place at boarding school which will allow a "growing space" between child and parent. The need for this may arise from the mother's inability to let go and allow independence, or from the frictions created when the child feels dangerous and sees family problems as his or her own fault - a situation which can result from, say, the untimely death of a member of the family when the child had omnipotent feelings. Workers have to be prepared for action over a long preparatory period and also at crisis point.

School Refusal - a Family Problem

The school, succeeding in getting the child along, will become the "bad place" and the parent will try to undermine it. If possible, family therapy should be set up to help the school. Nearly all the school refusers referred to this school have presented the same family pattern. In one case, it was arranged that the head would pick up the child who was unable to get on to the school mini-bus. The mother who said she wanted the boy to get to school requested this help. She also arranged that if the boy would not go at the required time she would ring up and ask the head for help. She would take advice from no one else. This arrangement broke down because this mother, having asked for the boy to be picked up, would go to her part-time job, leaving the house keys with her son, preventing him from leaving as if he did so she would be locked out. The mother complained that the school was no good and to cover herself for her son's non-attendance, took him to her doctor who referred her to the psychiatric department of a children's hospital. The psychiatrist was of great help not only to the family but also to the school, for when the boy got into school every day after the father had been involved in getting him on to the mini-bus, the school social worker and the boy's teacher were invited along to the family therapy sessions. This case was a success, thanks to the recognition of the mother-father conflict and the intervention of the psychiatrist without whom the school would have failed.

Social Work Help Cases

In these cases, the family is usually at loggerheads with all the bureaucracies and is in trouble all round, mostly from an inability to cope with looking after money. There will be enormous rent arrears and sometimes a removal to sub-standard housing because of debts. The electricity bill will have been run up without any thought of payment and is now cut off, the gas likewise and the family is usually in despair. Once the child arrives at the school and the social worker makes a routine visit, it is often discovered that the cause of the child's difficulty is anxiety about all the problems of the family and often that particular child is the recipient of the mother's confidences. If the social worker is able to gain the confidence of the mother, the problems can be solved one by one. There is usually contact with the Social Security and arrangements made to have arrears in rent reduced gradually, also the debts for electricity and gas. Quite often the family will not have applied for free school meals even though they are entitled to them nor for clothing grants which they are also entitled to. The school social worker who is seen as a friend rather than as a figure of authority will be able to solve all these problems with the arrangement of the parent and things begin to improve all round. Gradually, the family gains confidence in its own ability to cope with these things on its own and in this case the social worker will be able to opt out gradually, only visiting occasionally to make sure that everything is all right. This is a straightforward case of a family mistrusting authority and having been unable to make its own arrangements, being helped by the school social worker. It should be noted that many of the families dealt with cannot even accept help from Social Services, as such help can only be obtained by going to the area office and this is too much of a compromise for some people.

Helping the Parents in the Management of their Children's Behaviour

In some cases where the family is able to have good contacts with the school and is willing to participate with the teaching staff in the management of behaviour, it is possible to make contracts between the family, the school and the pupil for the eradication of highly anti-social behaviour. This involves the use of punishment and the help of the parent. The punishment is a day off school. All the pupils who attend this school enjoy the activities that they participate in and dislike holidays and days off school. Therefore, when some form of very bad anti-social behaviour is shown, if it is possible to get the family to agree to having the child at home the day after the behaviour has taken place no matter how much the child pleads nor how well he or she behaves after the event, then the behaviour quickly diminishes. In order to do this, the treatment has to be completely consistent and always carried out.

In one case, a girl pupil used to have frightening hysterical temper tantrums and it was not possible to find out what sparked them off. During these, she would scream, bite, scratch, kick and punch. This behaviour was very destructive for her and not very pleasant for the staff who received injuries. After some time and a lot of discussion, it became obvious that only punishment would work with this girl. Her mother and father were called in and they agreed that they would help in the way they were asked. At first the girl was excluded at least twice a week for a day, but as the weeks went by and she realised that the treatment never varied and if she had a violent temper tantrum then she would be at home the next day, the attacks diminished and after about three months she had no temper tantrums at all. It was possible for this girl to go back into the ordinary school system. At the time when she was going through her difficult behaviour, it seemed that the only place for her was a psychiatric unit. This is a case where the parents' cooperation is of the greatest help to the school.

Parents who will not come to the School

In other cases where the parents are hostile to the school and do not want to come in, it is useful to write reports on the behaviour of the children. If this can be done in such a way that the parents have to reply to the reports, then it is possible to set up a little dialogue. These are very difficult cases as they do not admit that there is anything wrong with their child. They do not believe in the system and they believe that with punishment the child will be normal again. However, even a little scribble of a note or the occasional telephone call is important as it means that all links have not been severed even if the going is really hard.

A SPECIFIC CASE HISTORY

Occasionally we see members of a family who are in difficulty partly because of their own marital and personal problems but specifically because of some traumatic happening which has upset one of the children (usually the one who is being referred to the school). The child is taking the responsibility for the trouble, or in the absence of knowledge, is blaming himself for the problem. Below is a case which was dealt with some years ago in the following manner.

A nearby borough requested an interview for a family consisting of a mother, her son and her second husband (the boy's stepfather). The boy was eight years old and was in a unit for disturbed children in the borough which had no special school, and he was proving so disruptive that the unit was unable to contain him. In fact, he was succeeding in disrupting almost the entire junior school. They arrived for the interview and the mother was obviously pregnant. The stepfather seemed to be kind and caring. There was a history of violence in the first marriage and a series of separations, the child having lived with relatives from time to time during earlier troubles. The present problem was that the school could no longer tolerate this child; it was considered appropriate for the boy to remain at home at least until after the arrival of the new baby and we were being asked to take the responsibility. The mother was desperate as was the neighbouring borough and it was felt appropriate to take him. He was an active child and although he was far from his own home, he was not averse to running away from the school and having to be searched for by the police. He seemed to be trying to disrupt even our school. He enjoyed the facilities but he was hardly able to stop to take a breath and he put a great strain on our resources. His history was as follows:

At the age of six years, he had been picked up by a friendly policeman when he had been discovered throwing bricks at the windows of a newly built but only partially occupied block of flats. The policeman took him home to his mother and gave her a lift down to the local Child Guidance Clinic where he was interviewed and he had been seen from time to time since then. It was felt then that he should continue in his infants' school which was able to cope with him. When it came to the time to move into the junior school, he was referred to the unit where he was reasonably contained. Although he was never an easy pupil, he became totally impossible when his mother became pregnant and he had done a good deal of damage to the school before he was referred to us. With a pupil like this, it was necessary to see the mother frequently in order to discuss her child's behaviour with her, and it was during these sessions that the information came out that when he was five years old, having been an only child, his mother had become pregnant and she had had a child just as the boy was starting school. He was very jealous and was often caught at the pram or the cot squeezing the baby's neck or slapping its face or trying to hurt it. This made his mother very angry with him and she rejected him verbally and compared him unfavourably with the baby. The little boy's anger was overwhelming and he said to her that he wished the baby would die. It was very sad that the baby did die (it was a cot death). After the baby's death, the child was so violent and uncontrollable that the mother did not know what to do with him. It was during this period that he was found by the policeman and taken to the Child Guidance Clinic. The mother had been counselled by the psychiatric social worker at the Clinic and she seemed to be able to accept help. She knew how important it was to keep her son at home until the new baby was born. She was willing to do anything to help her child as she realised that by her rejection she had caused the little boy to wish the baby dead, and she understood that the actual death was so damaging for the boy as he really believed that he had somehow killed the baby and his subsequent actions were avoidance techniques to help him forget his pain and guilt.

Joint councils were frequently held and we all did our best to work together to keep this boy. His behaviour became more and more outrageous the nearer the time came for the birth. When a baby girl was safely delivered we all heaved a sigh of relief. A girl was no threat to this child and it was a very healthy baby so he was able to relate with it. He was so glad that he set the school field on fire. After a few more weeks, the term ended and he went off quite happily to his boarding school. We were all very happy to see him go. It was doubtful whether we would have been able to cope with him much longer. Although it was a poor placement for the child, being only temporary, and although it had a very bad effect on the school, in the circumstances it had been thought that the function of the school would be to support this family as much as possible through its problems.

SUMMARY

This school has always considered that it is of vital importance to work with the parents to give them as much access to the school as they can cope with and to encourage them to take an active part in seeing what their children are doing at school. It is now statutory that this shall be done and the new legislation should, if anything, make it easier for schools to work with parents provided the parents trust the school. It is, though, vital that those in leadership roles should place great emphasis in this aspect of our work.

We work mainly with the mothers and with a tiny

minority of fathers who are supporting psychiatrically ill, delinquent or violent mothers. The school population is and always has been predominantly male. The problem lies apparently mainly in the inability of some girls to be able to mother adequately when they grow up. This is because they have been shown no satisfactory model on which to base their behaviour: they are hidden "carriers" of maladjustment. Yet the school population does not include these girls. Therefore, although we are helping alleviate the resultant problems, we are not really breaking into the cycle that creates them. Until there are better ways of ascertaining female maladjustment then the fundamental problem remains virtually untouched. This is a question that needs to be answered. What are the symptoms of maladjustment in young girls? If we could answer that and make provision for their needs, the problems would be reduced more cost effectively and more quickly.

SECTION 3

– STAFF DEVELOPMENT

Chapter Eleven

POWER AND CONFLICT: FACTS OF LIFE

by Tony Bowers

This chapter will look at two terms which, for many people, have pejorative connotations. It is somehow bad to seek the first or to experience the second. It is argued, however, that neither of these phenomena will go away if we ignore them: they inevitably exist within any organisational setting. Moreover, in their own ways both are utilisable for the development of the school and for the benefit of the clients which it serves.

THE NATURE OF POWER

One of the characteristics of leadership is that leaders exercise power. Essentially, "power" refers to the ability to influence the opinions and behaviour of others. It would, though, be too simplistic to suggest that power, defined in this way, solely rests in the hands of leaders. Everybody, potentially at least, has power. Often this is unrelated to formal status: a Scale 1 teacher or a classroom assistant may have considerable ability in one way or another to influence events in a school; a member of staff in the education office, whose clerical grade may be very low, may still be in a position to withhold or to allocate resources; an assistant caretaker may, by giving or withdrawing cooperation, be in a position to allow or prevent evening and weekend activities in a school.

A major distinction between formal and informal power has been made by Etzione (1961), who discusses the difference between position power and personal power. Individuals who rely upon their position in a school or in the educational system (head teacher, adviser, education officer and so on) to induce others to perform their jobs in a particular way are using position power. Those who derive their power from their followers are considered to have personal power. In practice, a large number of people in management positions use both; the ratio of one to the other, however, will vary.

The concepts of position and personal power relate quite easily to French and Raven's (1960) five sources of power, the first three falling within the positional bracket, the last two being more heavily personally orientated. For these authors, a leader's source of influence - and those of anybody else - can be categorised in the following ways:

(1) Legitimate power, or the acceptance by others of their obligation to acknowledge a leader's influence. We tend to be socialised from very early on to see some job titles as carrying authority; the very labels "head teacher", "inspector", "teacher-in-charge", etc. confer varying degrees of legitimate power on their possessors.

(2) Reward power, which stems from the number and extent of positive outcomes that a leader can produce for those that he or she seeks to influence. In practice, within the maintained education sector, these are often not very plentiful. Salary scales are laid down nationally and the ability to promote to higher scales is a limited one. Heads may use the prospect of career advancement, achieved by means of their support in confidential references, as a potential reward. It is only too possible, though, for such rewards to slide into category 3 below, and to become phrased as "If you don't, I won't ..." A good leader will examine the ways in which staff can be rewarded within their school and will be aware that the nature of these will vary with individual likes and expectations.

(3) Coercive power, the obverse of the last category, stems from staff expectations that unpleasant events will follow if they do not comply with the aims of a potential leader. Again, the formal coercive potential for those in leadership positions in schools is, perhaps fortunately, relatively low. In only the most serious cases can threat of disciplinary procedures provide a coercion; however, when a head or senior staff member controls such minor resources as duty rotas or stock, it may occur. Actually, far more coercive power is often possessed by subordinate staff members in schools, which can be exercised through not attending meetings, unexpected absence, and similar strategies of noncompli-

ance.

(4) Referent power is based on people's identification with a potential leader and with what he or she stands for or symbolises. The ideals and values of the leader coincide with or are adapted by those with whom they work. Potentially, this is a very potent form of power.

(5) Expert power is held when a potential leader has particular expertise or knowledge in some area which is significant and relevant to the task in hand. Because of its situational specificity, expert power is a shifting commodity. In a case conference, for example, particular specialisms may have their contributions to make. When the relevance of a specialist knowledge is accepted, their recommendations are likely to be given considerable weight by other members. Such power, however, may only last while the relevance of that specialism is acknowledged. There are times when heads and senior staff, and some L.E.A. officials, may try to gain more expert power than their expertise justifies: the "know-it-all syndrome"; it is important that those in managerial positions should be aware of the use of expert power and of when to give it up.

The mix of these sources, and indeed the presence or absence of any of them, will not depend solely upon the individual but may vary according to those with whom they interact and with circumstances. However, within a school it is often quite easy to relate the prevailing climate of satisfaction or dissatisfaction, openness or suspicion, cooperativeness or hostility, to the predominant reliance of leaders upon particular power sources.

POWER-ORIENTED BEHAVIOUR

In an analysis of managers' tendencies to employ behaviour directed towards "developing or using relationships in which other people are to some degree willing to defer to one's wishes" (p. 27), Kotter (1978) has argued that a great deal of working time and energy is normally engaged in establishing and maintaining influence. The extent of this engagement is determined by what he called "job-related dependence" (p. 28), and can be as great as eighty per cent.

There is, of course, a tendency for the amount of

dependence in a job to be related to the responsibility inherent in it. The class teacher whose sole function lies within the walls of the classroom will be dependent upon fewer other people than will a head of department or team leader who must attempt - in a variety of ways - to gain consent and cooperation from others. A head teacher of any school has a considerable number of dependencies. Areas of dependence will include his or her teaching staff, who can give or withhold their cooperation in a wide variety of ways; caretaking and cleaning staff who, in different ways, may do the same; parents, whose support for the school will influence the nature and number of its intake; staff at the education office, who can expedite or delay the easy running of the school in such areas as, say, the replacement of teachers or the repair of buildings. These are obvious dependencies. More subtle ones will also exist, with the local press for instance, and with the police.

Frequently, special schools are smaller than mainstream schools in terms of pupil numbers and often are smaller in terms of their Group size and the number of middle and senior management posts which they are able to offer. If Brennan's (1981) predictions are correct, many will become smaller still. However, from a management standpoint, they frequently involve a large number of areas of job-related dependence; with greater diversifications of role, it is highly probable that this number will increase still further. Interestingly, the author notes that some L.E.A.s, while encouraging the resource role of special schools through the allowance of notional fractions of attendance on the school roll for pupils supported outside the school, will not give credit for them in arriving at the Group size of the school. Such a policy is likely to damage the management structure of such innovative schools at the very time when their diffusion of resources causes even greater power-dependence upon forces in their environment.

Kotter's (1978) principle that "the larger the number of job-related dependencies, the more time and energy the managerial incumbent tends to put into power-oriented behavior to cope with those dependencies" (p. 30) has particular significance to special schools which are actively engaged in creating a role within the community rather than simply operating behind their walls. A head's dependencies represent his or her Achilles' heel: they are the spots where the manager is vulnerable, where a lack of cooperation from others - for just or unjust reasons - can affect the achievement of job-related objectives.

A comparison between the dependencies inherent in two school management jobs, that of a typical primary school and that of a special school familiar to the author, until recently known as a school for physically handicapped children, is shown below (Figures 7 and 8).

This model demonstrates the extent of the special school head's dependencies in one particular instance. In addition to the increased number of power-dependencies, levels of dependencies common to both schools are in some instances higher in the special school. Whereas the local primary school is the automatic choice of most parents, parents of potential pupils of the special school must be convinced that it will best meet their child's needs; they must also remain convinced that subsequent decisions, relating to provision either within the special school or within other settings resourced or supported by that school, are appropriate. Since many of the school's physical resources and staffing ratios will be subject to greater discretion than will those of the primary school, dependency on L.E.A. administrative staff, in particular the assistant education officer for special education, is increased.

Similarly, dependencies upon referring and placement agencies, in particular the assistant education officer for special education, local educational psychologists and school medical officers of health, are very high. Without influencing their conviction of the appropriateness of the school's resources, numbers will fall. The school has a nursery, and relies also on referrals from health visitors and local general practitioners. Beyond this, the complexity of organisation and staffing indicated in Figure 8 dictates the extent to which the head teacher is power-dependent.

For managerial jobs with few dependencies, a leader can be relatively unskilled at power-orientated behaviour, or unwilling to engage in it, and still be quite successful. Where a manager has a large number of dependencies, Kotter (1978) argues that it is virtually impossible for him or her to be successful without engaging in power-oriented behaviour. The alternative to such an engagement is to reduce the number of power-dependencies; to do so, though, is likely to reduce the effectiveness of an organisation such as a special school. In our example, it would be possible, say, to reduce dependence upon therapists working in the school and the associated dependence upon their line managers within the Area Health Authority. To do so, though, would inevitably lead to a less comprehensive functioning of the school and thus either threaten the organisation or lead to increased dependencies in other areas.

Power-oriented behaviour, then, is necessary both for organisational maintenance and for the achievement of a school's objectives. We may hear heads label such activity as "a waste of time" or as "silly politics", usually when their job calls for more power-oriented behaviour than

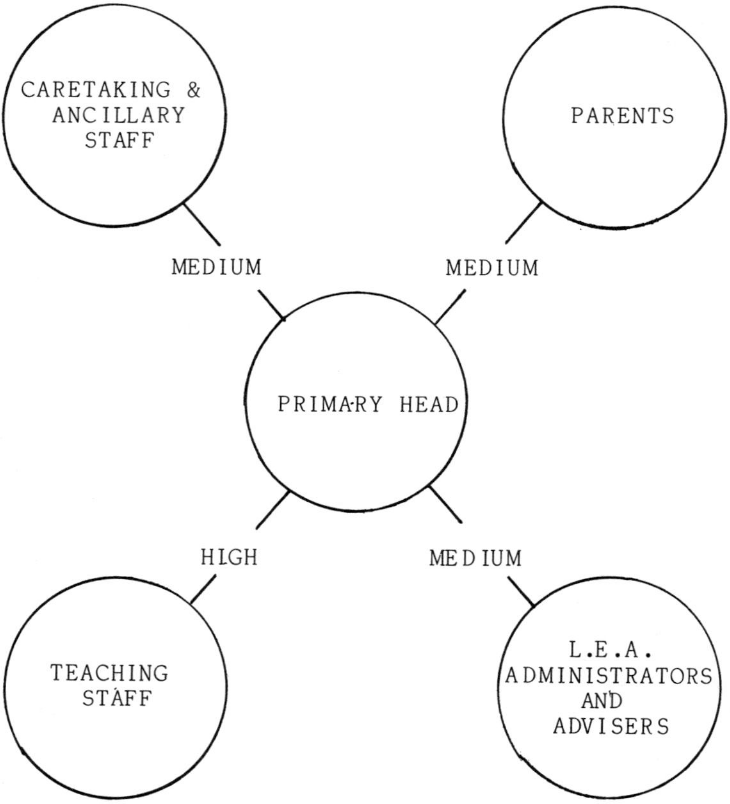

Figure 7: Typical Primary School Power Dependency Model

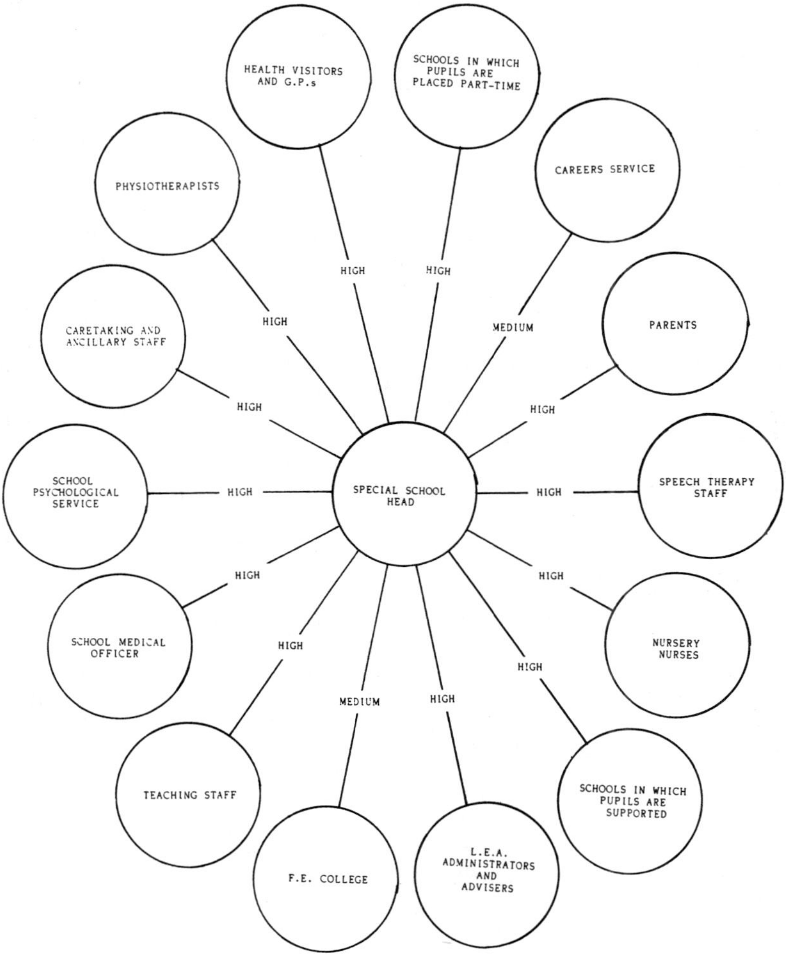

Figure 8: Special School Power Dependency Model

they can offer. As a result their schools at best "tick over". Unfortunately it is not enough, under the circumstances prevailing within our special educational system, for a head to be a competent teacher. One head teacher, rejecting the need to spend most of his time in "trivial" contact with agencies outside the school, resolved to set a good example to his staff by teaching most of his time. He did this well; his school is now closed.

CONFLICT DEFINED

When we look at any human system, whether it be a family, group of friends, football team or, in the context of this chapter, a school, we will see differences in the components within that system. These differences arise because the components within the system can never be perfectly integrated, because they are changing and reacting to change, or because outside disturbances occur. For example, a school has teachers with different outlooks and expectations, different ways of teaching, of keeping discipline, different likes and dislikes. Staff go on courses and come back with new ideas; rolls fall and some staff feel threatened and so endeavour to justify their indispensability. All these will lead to varying degrees of tension within the system. When tensions gang up and become more or less sharply opposed along the lines of two or more components, then this is conflict.

No living system exists without tension and conflict: they are, as Chin (1976) has pointed out, "in" any system. Often the idea of conflict is abhorred and even denied by those working in organisations; the head teacher who says "We're always just one big happy family", is probably indulging in wish-fulfilment at best, or demonstrating a total lack of perception of the way that the system of which he or she is a part operates.

The special school offers an arena for potential conflict which is more extensive than that of many mainstream schools simply because of the extent of many such schools' dependence upon external agencies: the special school and its environment create a large number of intersystem boundaries, and each one of these increases the probability of tension within the system.

When individuals work together, the potential for conflict is increased when their perspectives and objectives differ. The special school may well have within it not only teachers but a large body of classroom assistants and N.N.E.B.-trained nursery nurses, together with one or more members of other professions who work all or a large proportion of the time within that school. Depending upon the nature of needs within the school, nurses, speech therapists, physiotherapists, occupational therapists, art therapists, music therapists, movement therapists or psychotherapists may all work with children on the school premises. Their priorities may or may not be the same as those of teachers, their view of the curriculum may differ from that prevailing within the school. Other professionals, visiting though not working in the school, may well attempt to influence the activity of the school - to use power - and thus potentially place themselves in conflict with others in the school. Educational psychologists, medical officers of health, advisers and education officers are among those who represent environmental systems whose objectives may at times be in conflict with those of the school and which can create strains within the school system which themselves lead to secondary conflict.

COPING WITH CONFLICT

The ability to cope successfully with conflict is one of the most important skills that a manager can acquire. Almost invariably, though, conflict-management skills are learned without formal education or guidance; conflict-management style will usually emerge from using others' behaviours as models. If those models are good and the situations one encounters are similar to those in which the style has been effective, then success will probably result. If not, one may learn an effective style too late.

Thomas (1976) has looked at conflict in relation to two dimensions: assertiveness, or satisfying one's own concerns, and cooperativeness, the extent to which the individual attempts to satisfy the other's concerns. These two dimensions define five distinct styles for coping with conflict. Given the very large potential range of conflict situations that anyone in a leadership position within special education may encounter, it provides a useful model upon which to base coping strategies.

(1) Competition. The most assertive and least cooperative people use the competitive style. To achieve the desired result - namely winning - the competitor uses whatever power is available to him or her. If the stakes are high enough, a very competitive person's use of power may well be limited only by some greater external power such as a senior member of a local education authority or even the law.

The belligerent, aggressive or domineering leader is one who probably uses win/lose competitive strategies most of the time. Often they will win, though others' resentment at being forced into such a situation will tend to have negative consequences in terms of reduced interaction and potential hostility. One of the problems with competitive conflict management styles is that if two parties actively use it, they "stake in" so much that neither can afford to lose. Pik (1981) has presented an interesting analysis of teacher-pupil conflict which has many applications in other settings.

Those who use a competitive approach all the time are likely to be seen as hard-liners, however much they may attempt cosmetic adjustments to their strategy. Below is an extract from a letter recently sent by a special school head teacher to a member of his staff with whom he was in conflict. The use of disciplinary procedures and the break-down in interpersonal communication implicit in the document indicate that, despite the apparently collaborative surface intention, a competitive conflict management style prevails. Somebody at this stage has to gain a major advantage over the other.

Dear Madam,

This letter is to formally record that a meeting was held this morning at which you were informed that I am sufficiently concerned about certain aspects of your conduct as a Teacher as to intend to invoke Stage I of the Education Service Disciplinary Procedures. You were given the opportunity to have present at this meeting a member of Staff of your choice and you requested that Mr. X a member of a Teachers' Association be present, I was happy to comply with this request. Mr. Y, Deputy Head, was also present.

When a copy of the Disciplinary Procedures was handed to you you asked me what the purpose of instigating these procedures was. I explained to you that the purpose of these procedures is to formalise the continuing help and support which you will be given to assist you to improve your performance in those aspects of your professional behaviour which are causing concern, and which will be specifically identified at the next stage of this procedure. You asked me if what I wanted you to do was to leave the School - to "give in your notice". I replied that this was not the intention of invoking the procedures and that you must be responsible for your own decisions in this respect.

The meeting ended abruptly when you remarked that you were not intending "to listen to any more of this rubbish" and left the room.

Yours faithfully,

Whether aware of it at the time or not, this head teacher has staked a great deal into the conflict. The room for accepting any cooperative relationships with this staff member appears to have been almost entirely removed; a straight win/lose alternative is available.

(2) Collaboration. This involves the maximum use of both cooperation and assertion, since the aim is to meet the needs and concerns of both parties. Collaboration involves (a) acknowledging that there is a conflict; (b) identifying and acknowledging one another's needs; (c) identifying alternative resolutions; and (d) selecting an alternative that meets the needs, concerns and goals of each party. Obviously, a collaborative approach appears to be one that makes most sense and leads to the most acceptable solutions for all concerned. When time is short, where there are poor interpersonal relationships between individuals, or where values differ substantially, it may not be a viable alternative, however. In a recent article, Karp (1983) has endeavoured to attach the creative elements of collaboration to the potentially destructive components of competition. This will be looked at later.

(3) Avoidance. In contrast to the last approach, avoidance is characterised by both uncooperative and unassertive behaviour. It involves evading the issue and withdrawing from discussion. In the short term, it may provide a way of allowing a potentially fraught clash to cool down. As a permanent strategy, it has negative implications for all concerned. The teacher who doesn't attend curriculum planning meetings because of an earlier disagreement over methods is not going to have any commitment to the decisions which will still be made without him or her. Additionally, avoidance over a particu-

lar issue is likely to spread out into general avoidance, making satisfying or productive interpersonal relationships between the parties virtually impossible to sustain. Essentially it is a dishonest strategy, since it seeks to smother the issues which led to its use.

(4) Accommodation. This is characterised by cooperative and unassertive behaviour. It basically means placing the other's needs and concerns over one's own. If one party is not as concerned as the other about the outcome, it is probably a good strategy, since it may lead to good will and cooperative relationships. As a general strategy, though, it can lead to being seen as easily swayed and irresolute.

(5) Compromise. Here moderate amounts of cooperativeness and assertiveness are required. The compromiser expects partial fulfilment of his or her own needs, concerns and goals. More issues are confronted than would be if avoidance were used, but less than when collaboration occurs. In terms of honesty, it is midway between the two. However, although the solution to a compromise is mutually acceptable, it only partially satisfies each person's needs. Thus it is probably less potentially satisfying than the results of either collaboration or competition.

It is arguable that an effective leader should have all of these strategies at his or her disposal. What we often see, though, is an individual who becomes locked into one - or at best two - of these. Another approach, briefly mentioned earlier, is that advocated by Karp (1983). Arguing that the most valuable skill needed to handle conflict is not the ability to get along well with others but the ability to fight them well, he has laid the ground rules for what he terms "creative fighting".

His assumption is that conflict can be potentially productive, in that it can lead to new understandings and new solutions, provided that certain ground-rules are observed in the competitive process. For a more detailed account of the processes which he outlines, the reader is referred to Karp's (1983) article. However, in brief he recommends that anyone attempting to use a competitive style creatively should:

(1) Establish the legitimacy of fighting. Essentially, the norm within the school should be that it is all right to disagree openly; that conflict can

strengthen rather than weaken relationships. Without creative conflict management, Karp argues, "personal relationships deteriorate and become characterised by spite, sniping, silent vows of vengeance, sulking, self-pity, and complaints about being misunderstood" (p. 217).

(2) Deal with one issue at a time. Don't bring up unresolved arguments from the past; don't open "old wounds". Focus on the point in contention only.

(3) Avoid reacting to unintentional remarks. Establish a norm that when unexpected or unintentional remarks are made, they must be clarified and confirmed, or else disregarded.

(4) Avoid resolutions that come too soon or too easily. If a conflict ends prematurely, there will be unfinished elements that won't go away; though temporarily repressed they will manifest themselves later.

(5) Avoid cornering an opponent. If the opportunity to demonstrate that you are "right" and to devastate an opponent arises - resist it.

(6) Agree to disagree. Both parties should acknowledge that each has a right to the viewpoints that they adopt. Equally, though, they should make clear all the positive, productive aspects of their working relationship, including common values and past successes.

(7) Focus on what is wanted rather than why it is wanted. Almost all conflicts occur because the participants want different things. It is therefore essential to establish what each party wants and how objectives differ; it is equally important not to spend time and energy in exploring why each person wants what he or she wants.

(8) Maintain a sense of humour. The conflict may be taken seriously, but participants should not take themselves equally seriously.

An approach such as that outlined involves confrontation. The term has negative and aggressive connotations; really, though, it refers simply to facing up to disputes. Research by Lawrence and Lorsch (1967) concluded that the most successful organisations, in terms of their results, used more confrontation. Easy answers, then, such as forcing a compromise through the use of position power or denying that conflict exists, are less likely to yield useful results.

IN CONCLUSION

It is important for those in leadership roles in special education to recognise that while conflict is inevitable within any setting, the potential for disagreement and discord is high when those with differing professional perspectives work together. This chapter has looked briefly at some of the issues involved in conflict management; more detailed consideration of the necessary skills - beyond the scope of this book - is provided in manuals such as that of Bolton (1979). Given those skills, we would not expect to see such confused and unhappy questions as those of a teacher in a special school which appeared in Special Education in September 1980. Having observed the disharmony between head and staff, this teacher goes on:

> Throughout it all it is the children who suffer. They sense the tension and may find it difficult to concentrate and work hard. They also receive less than the best from teachers who are emotionally preoccupied ... What solution is there for teachers who find themselves caught in this situation? Should they continue to be vociferous in staff meetings about the need for more teacher involvement in school policy, should they shut up and put up with it or should they seek employment elsewhere? (p. 15)

A word of warning, though, is needed. Conflict is relatively easy to create unintentionally as an act of mismanagement. Effective conflict management skills may at times be useful, however, in increasing tensions and conflict in order to facilitate creativity and change. A marked lack of conflict may at times point to smugness and rigidity within a school. Chapter Three, concerned with the psychology of change, lists some of the characteristics of innovators, and these are themselves likely to generate some tension. Skilfully used, conflict within a staff over such issues as teaching methods or the contribution which parents can make to the educational process, may lead to problem-solving activities. By bringing conflicting interests together to solve those problems, improvements in the functioning of the school may well result. This theme is reflected in Vic Thomson's chapter in this book, while some practical implications are considered in the final chapter.

Chapter Twelve

SPECIAL NEEDS AND SCHOOL-FOCUSED IN-SERVICE EDUCATION

by Vivien Casteel

For the last fifteen years, the special school in which I work has had a commitment to continuing the professional development of its staff members both within and outside the school. Having benefited from the policy myself, both as a staff member and latterly as head teacher, and having seen others do so, I am convinced that taking responsibility for encouraging teachers to continue to learn, and providing an environment which encourages them to do so, is an important function of the head teacher.

What follows is a statement of what I believe are the advantages of school-focused in-service education and training (INSET) and an explanation of the ways and means whereby in-service needs which arise in a special school can be met, as well as some of the difficulties which arise.

WHY SCHOOL-FOCUSED INSET?

We want constantly to improve the quality of the teaching in our schools so that we provide a better education for the pupils for whom we are responsible. How can this upgrading most effectively be achieved? One particularly effective means is school-focused in-service education. By this I mean firstly that overall organisation and direction of the professional development programme is the responsibility of the head and staff of the school. Secondly, the provision is aimed at meeting identified individual and school needs, rather than relying passively on onuses provided by outside agencies. I do not suggest that each school must provide for all its needs on its own premises or rely exclusively on its own personnel. Quite apart from the fact that individual special schools are just too small for this to be possible, the insularity which such an approach would foster is not at all desirable.

Further discussion appears in Morant (1981). Since the head and staff are the people who best know what their unique circumstances require at any point, school-focused INSET will always offer advantages which an externally directed approach cannot.

Traditionally, however, further in-service education and training has largely been the responsibility of outside course providers, such as universities and colleges of higher education, and we have encouraged teachers to attend in the hope that their classroom practice would be improved on their return. But at this time, it seems, economies (or at least current governmental policies) are making a necessity of the virtues of the school-focused approach.

The need for INSET in some form is well established. The James Committee (D.E.S., 1972) recommended that by 1981, three per cent of the full-time teaching force should at any point in time be seconded for full time INSET. The Warnock Committee (D.E.S., 1978) drew particular attention to the urgent need to help all serving teachers to become competent in dealing with children with special needs. Cutbacks in educational budgets, however, have prevented these targets being reached. Many L.E.A.s no longer offer full-time secondments. Some short course provision has been made by local teachers' centres, L.E.A. advisory services and professional bodies such as the National Council for Special Education, but this in itself is not enough to meet teachers' demands. Meanwhile, head teachers can no longer rely on staff changes to provide needed expertise, as opportunities for teacher movement are contracting. To counteract the current difficulties, heads and teachers should be prepared to identify and themselves provide some of the further professional development they need to cope with the increasing demands being put upon them. In doing so they will not be entering wholly uncharted territory; already the isolated way in which the special education service has developed has meant that, because their teachers were rarely encouraged to join local provision for mainstream teachers, special schools have often been obliged to take responsibility for the positive development of their own teachers who are having difficulty coping with the special problems presented by their pupils.

ESTABLISHING A PATTERN

The organisational systems which a school builds up are a most effective means for facing teachers with uncomfortable questions about their practice and so creating an awareness of the need for professional development.

A teacher, confronted by a record-keeping system which shows that a child has, for instance, made no progress in acquiring a sight vocabulary, despite having the necessary pre-reading skills, cannot avoid questioning his choice of objectives and his choice of method. Thus is created the opportunity to extend that teacher's skills. Just as records can reveal specific teacher/pupil difficulties, curriculum development processes can highlight broader inadequacies in the school's performance.

The INSET programme at Colnbrook School was initiated in just such a way in 1968. Teachers were asked to record what they had done within their class group (with respect to six aspects of child development - reading, number, creative development, physical development, social and emotional development and language). The headings alone asked certain questions of the staff. Before long, teachers started to compare notes and wanted to respond in a more standardised form that made information easier to share. From teachers' real needs a system of individualised record-keeping developed with individual assessments and suggested teaching responses being made on a regular basis. The gentle discipline imposed by such a system could not help but make teachers face difficult questions, at their own level, about their ability to meet their pupils' needs.

The problems revealed by this record-keeping led rapidly to the start of formalised school-based INSET. Weekly staff meetings were devoted to aspects of professional development. In the first place the aims of these were not very ambitious; simply awareness of certain issues, consideration of which was appropriate for teachers of children with special needs - for example, the effect of various physical handicapping conditions, the role of the child and family psychiatric service, a demonstration of a standardised test used by a psychologist, the use of an audio-visual aid, or teacher-devised reading materials to supplement the woefully inadequate and inappropriate published resources of the late 60s and early 70s.

Teachers were expected to attend these meetings and usually did so. The relevance of them soon encouraged even reluctant participants. As teachers were class- and not subject-based it was assumed that they should be interested in all areas of children's development. Subsequent applicants for appointments at the school were told clearly of the commitment expected of them to meetings outside school hours. It was a time of rapid expansion, so new staff members could help to shift the climate of opinion.

The next major step was taken in 1970, when a teacher within the school was given a post of responsibility for in-service education, because the prescriptive approach to meeting pupils' needs was revealing teachers' difficulties which had to be responded to at short notice. The job outline written at the time said that the post involved:

> the organisation of the weekly professional development meetings, ensuring, firstly, that teachers know about and are encouraged to attend courses which might interest them and, secondly, that participants report back to the rest of the staff; the organisation of a staff reference library of books and periodicals; organisation of staff visits to other schools; the support of new members of staff.

Widespread staff perception of the benefits of these activities within the school gradually lifted the general level of professionalism, and consequently raised the expectations of further progress in this direction on the part of both current and new members of staff. Both the record-keeping system and the post of responsibility for school-focused INSET have continued to evolve over the intervening years.

The record-keeping system has moved through a period of teacher-devised assessment inventories combined with a small amount of standardised testing to monitor levels of achievement, to a curriculum-related recording system. Subsequently this was expanded to its current form - prospective weekly records of individual objectives chosen from the curriculum coupled with cumulative curriculum record files and detailed annual reports for parents. Each small change has resulted from the whole staff group evaluating and attempting to improve upon that which had gone before. Responsibility for in-service training has changed hands on two occasions to meet changes in school circumstances. After the promotion of the original post holder in 1976, the deputy head at that time co-ordinated the curriculum development work which had just started.

This curriculum development process initially involved the whole staff group discussing and documenting overall aims and objectives for the school, next mapping out "areas of experience" which would be offered to the children, and then setting out detailed steps by which to achieve the aims within each area. The study of theory and practice, conceptual thinking and carefully structured progress involved in curriculum development confer upon it a parallel role in staff individual professional development and the improvement of the team function (Stenhouse, 1975). Indeed, the process provided almost the entire Colnbrook INSET programme for a period of nearly four years.

Once the process of curriculum development was fully established as a constant component of the school's programme, and hence as a continuing generator of INSET requirements, the need for one teacher taking full responsibility for INSET in its wider forms again became apparent. This role is now undertaken by a member of the senior management team (on a Scale 3(S) post) who, in addition to having the tasks already outlined, is wholly or partly responsible for:

(1) Co-ordinating the school induction policy.

(2) Organising multidisciplinary pupil reviews and assessments.

(3) Arranging INSET for teachers in local mainstream schools whose staff wish to improve their skills in working with pupils with special needs. (This latter programme, developed with a grant from the Schools Council Programme Two, involved helping teachers clearly to identify their needs and devising ways of meeting them either by loan of resources or by regular support from a teacher with particular expertise.)

I am fully convinced that a really good practising classroom teacher is particularly well equipped to support other teachers in improving their classroom skills. Both advisers and, to a certain extent, head teachers may be perceived to have lost sight of classroom realities and hence credibility in the eyes of those they wish to support. There are other reasons why a head teacher may not be the best person to support their own class teachers; for instance the head's power over promotion prospects may make teachers reluctant to disclose their own inadequacies. Warwick (1975) discusses this issue more fully.

MAINTAINING DEMAND

It is difficult after a fairly lengthy period of evolution to identify those elements within a school which continue to underline the need for INSET, but I think that the following "systems" are important.

Curriculum Development and Evaluation

One of the great joys of working in special schools has been the autonomy enjoyed in attempting to make the curriculum as relevant as possible to pupils' needs. Such autonomy demands responsibility and it is important that the school should have a policy for the development, implementation and review of its curriculum, in both its formal timetabled aspects and also in the climate of relationships, attitudes, styles of behaviour and general quality of life established in the school.

These important aspects will need consideration by some school self-assessment procedure such as that devised by the I.L.E.A. Inspectorate (1977) in their document Keeping the School under Review. A working group of special school head teachers in my own Authority has devised similar guidelines for local use, and I understand that similar activities are occurring in other L.E.A.s.

The curriculum development in our school is now the mainstay of the school-focused INSET programme. The regular pattern of three-yearly review of each defined area of experience within the curriculum keeps this momentum going. Because of its importance, one approach to the head's role in curriculum planning has been fully dealt with in Chapter Two.

Participatory Planning

The head teacher has a great deal of influence over the opportunities presented for information sharing and participation in decision-making in schools. Generally, I believe, the more information staff members have, the better their decisions are likely to be. Similarly, the more opportunity they have to be made aware of and to discuss all of the information relating to a particular educational issue, the more likely consensus among the staff becomes. At best, the likelihood of commitment to a contemplated change will be increased; at worst, there will be an understanding of the reasons for the decisions.

Allocation of Posts of Responsibility

At Colnbrook, most Scale 2(S) posts are allocated to co-ordinators of curriculum areas. The job specifications ask that co-ordinators keep abreast of developments in methods and resources, lead the curriculum reviews in their area, help with the induction of new teachers and monitor practice both in the classroom and through the recording system.

PLANNING INSET PROVISION

Having established, as it were, the case for school-focused INSET, the first practical task is to identify particular individual, group and whole school strengths and weaknesses. Since the effectiveness of the approach adopted will be the major factor in determining both the relevance of INSET provision and the motivation of those participating, the factors influencing this effectiveness warrant consideration.

Individuals

The help that will benefit each staff member will depend upon his or her aptitude, expectations and stage of career. Although this chapter is concerned mainly with continuing education for teachers, we should not forget that the same considerations apply to all the other personnel, from caretakers to ancillary staff.

Ancillary Staff Members

Ancillary staff in special schools, at least in my experience, tend to give the lie to the adage that "you get what you pay for". Their quality far exceeds their monetary reward. In addition to being offered an induction programme into the systems of the school, many will welcome opportunities for job enrichment by taking on responsibility for some aspect of the school's functioning, such as first aid, maintenance of audio-visual aids, the road safety programme or driving the mini-bus.

The school may be able to fund attendance at courses run by voluntary bodies such as the St. John's Ambulance Brigade, or a local motoring school. Some L.E.A.s run courses specifically for clerical assistants or for classroom assistants working with children with special needs.

Teachers

The head teacher can formally help teachers to discuss those professional strengths and weaknesses which their responses to the school's systems have highlighted. One such technique is the industrial model of "appraisal interviewing". This means that teachers are offered individual interviews on an annual (or possibly termly) basis to discuss their work within the school, their career development and consequent INSET needs.

The interview involves looking in some detail at whether the objectives jointly set at the last interview have been attained, and a discussion of the difficulties encountered on the way; the setting of objectives for the coming period in relation to their present responsibilities; and anticipated needs for support or education and action required from both parties. It is important that the head teacher should also take the opportunity in this interview to receive some feedback on his or her own performance in supporting colleagues. Appraisal is a two-way process.

We have been using the appraisal interview technique for the last two years. The existence of this formal system has disciplined meetings with staff members

APPRAISAL INTERVIEW

NAME: DATE: 20.1.83

CLASS: Infants POST OF RESPONSIBILITY: Curriculum Co-ordinator Physical Education

OBJECTIVES:

1. To institute a system with P.E. staff so that the objectives of each term's activities for each group are more clearly defined and a way of recording that lessons are aimed at objectives.
2. To compile a draft of 'Games' component of P.E. curriculum, reporting back to full staff meeting in May.
3. Await publication of L.E.A. guidelines for DANCE; use them to help P.E. staff look at all objectives in this area.
4. Prepare Teachers' file for P.E. teachers containing curriculum guides, county published guidelines, safety booklet. Duplicate copy in staffroom.
5. Review storage (equipment) for possible inclusion in 1983/4 financial year.

PROBLEMS:

1. Swimming curriculum: not fully used in lower school or when pupils go for voluntary help at local secondary school.
2. Showers: new curtains and soap required.
3. System of children bringing P.E. kit on Mondays is slipping. Not all class teachers are actually checking, leading to problems later in week.

ANY INSET NEEDS:

1. All P.E. staff are taking part in F.P.S. Dance/Movement Course finishing Summer 1983.
3. Need to include 'safety' course for all teachers who supervise swimming (Summer Term INSET?).
3. Only 2 teachers with R.L.S.S. qualifications, both of whom may leave, interested teachers (2/3?) need opportunities for qualification.

PERSONAL:

1. Would like to extend skills in nursery education, as would like eventually to work with nursery/pre-school children with special needs.
2. Would like to develop skills at advising other adults (either parents/ teachers) for mainstream liaison work or advisory work with parents of nursery pre-school children.

ACTION REQUIRED:

1. Arrange Nursery exchange (H/T to discuss with Nursery-Special Needs Advisers).
2. Discuss possibility of interpersonal skills course run by L.E.A. with adviser.
3. Head Teacher to discuss showers (cleanliness) with caretaker, arrange purchase of soap dishes and regular supply of soap (P.E. vote). Order shower curtains through equipment officer (approach Friends of the school for payment).
4. Next staff meeting: remind staff to check P.E. equipment. Send letter home before half-term.
5. ------ to organise files.
6. Head Teacher to organise space for INSET meetings in Summer Term.

Signed ....H/T

.........................T

Figure 9: Example Appraisal Interview Form

and aided my memory at subsequent appraisals (Figure 9). The next step in establishing the system would be to give teachers a copy of the form for their agreement that it represents a summary of the discussion and agreed action. Interviews such as this allow opportunities to marry the personal development of staff members with the school's planned development.

On a recent educational exchange with the Canadian province of Nova Scotia, I had the opportunity to see their system of annual teacher appraisal. School principals there have a responsibility to write annual supervision reports on each of their staff members, to discuss the report with them and send a copy to the administrative officers. A senior administrative officer interviews the head teacher in a similar way. Most teachers I questioned liked the system of getting formal feedback and knowing what others identified as their difficulties.

I favour this as a beneficial in-school exercise which exists in a climate of trust and professional integrity, rather than a system which has the overtones of an authoritarian inspection. It might be possible for head teachers who feel they would like similar feedback at their own level to invite other colleagues from different L.E.A.s to make their comments on different aspects of their school.

Teachers - Career Progress

Needs presented by teachers also change in relation to their career stage. Warwick (1975) has identified seven stages of teachers' careers which give rise to needs for different types of professional development:

Warwick's Stages	Characteristic INSET Needs
1. Student Teachers	Experience of school settings.
2. Probationary Teachers	Development of classroom management skills.
3. First 5 years (1S)	More and varied responsibilities.
4. Promotion Ladder (2 & 3S)	Major school responsibility. Group leadership skills. Further professional study.
5. Deputy Head Teachers and Senior Staff	Organisational responsibility. Management skills, e.g. interviewing techniques. Advisory work.

6.	Head Teachers	Further study. Management skills.
7.	Approaching Retirement	Preparation for leisure and time management.

Groups within the School

Most special school staffs are made up of a number of functional groups:

(1) Departmental groups composed of all the staff working in whatever divisions the school organises such as Lower, Middle and Senior Departments.

(2) Curriculum working groups composed of all staff members working in one particular curricular area such as Mathematics.

(3) Management groups composed of all members of staff working at a particular level such as Heads of Departments or Curriculum Co-ordinators

(4) Special groups such as an Arts Festival Planning Group or, in our school, the Mainstream Support Group - made up of all the teachers who support colleagues in local mainstream schools.

Individual staff members may well be involved in a number of such groups, each of which will have development needs related to their particular task and their ability to work as a team. The means for identifying and meeting their needs are similar to those for the whole school group. They do need, however, the opportunity regularly to share the results of their work with the whole staff body.

School Needs

In the 1980s schools are being called upon, to a perhaps unparalleled extent, to respond rapidly to the changing educational scene. The head and teachers benefit from working out together a strategy for planning how to effect change in their school.

The following planning stages need to be included if change is to be successful:

(1) A thorough assessment of the base from which change is being attempted.

(2) A clear statement of the desired or required objectives.

(3) A plan for achieving these, including a timetable, a suggested work allocation and INSET requirements if necessary.

(4) An assessment of progress and outcomes.

A real example may help in illustrating this process, which tends to be iterative, the next change being based upon the outcome of the previous one. During the 1981-2 academic year, the senior school staff at Colnbrook were not satisfied by the way in which we had followed the secondary school model of widening our curriculum on a subject basis to teach Physical Sciences, Biological Sciences, Humanities and Moral Education. They agreed that these areas of experience should be included but felt that there would be advantages to the children in an integrated studies approach, cooperatively taught by all the teachers concerned.

However, no senior school staff member had any experience of this approach. A lecturer at the local college of higher education supplied appropriate background reading, much of which pointed out the difficulties in succeeding with this approach. Our own reservations, in the light of our investigations, centred on whether it would or would not be possible to achieve a reasonable balance between all the areas of experience and whether it would be possible to provide enough "enquiry" learning. Nevertheless, the advantages if the approach were successful seemed to outweigh the disadvantages. Therefore, a timetable was drawn up for devising the course.

(1) The aims and objectives of the course would be suggested by the whole staff group.

(2) The teachers involved would plan the units of the course in outline during the summer vacation.

(3) Any other teachers interested were welcome to attend (and did!). This outline planning would consider balance between the different areas of experience; pupil groupings for different parts of the course (mixed ability, male/female etc.); materials and methods to be used.

(4) Detailed lesson planning, teacher preparation and pupil assessment was to be carried out at weekly meetings during the term time.

(5) No further training was considered necessary at that stage.

Progress was to be assessed at the weekly meetings, when the previous sessions would be evaluated and modifications made to the units to inform future teaching. The overall balance would be reviewed at the end of each of the two years of the course. Pupils' opinions would also be considered.

During the last year, the senior school staff group have devoted at least seventy-five per cent of their group meeting time to the development of this course, and their close teamwork has produced the first year of a really exciting multi-media course. Obviously, while so much of their attention has been focused on this, other equally deserving developments have had to wait.

Without full consideration of all stages of the change process, a small school is likely to try to take on more changes than it can successfully cope with at one time. In our school, we choose annually to involve all staff members in identifying and arguing over our priorities for development and related training. We spend quite a lot of time on this phase, typing it in with an overview of our work during the preceding year. I believe that if staff members are fully involved at this stage, their commitment to next year's whole school in-service programme is likely to be secured. The teacher with responsibility for in-service education then co-ordinates the detailed programme planning.

PROVISION

The means at a school's disposal for achieving training aims can be selected from a surprisingly wide range of possibilities, both in school and external to it. These can be variously combined, if so wished.

In School

(1) Staff working parties drawing on their own resources (e.g. to make materials to support the Maths curriculum).

(2) School based mini-courses (e.g. use of V.C.R.s) run by an outside expert.

(3) Microteaching (e.g. examining classroom practice; pupil counselling techniques).

(4) Lectures (e.g. information about a new test).

(5) Action research (e.g. structured classroom observation).

(6) Self-teaching packages which can be used by school staff (e.g. some O.U. courses).

External

(1) Visits to examples of good practice (innovatory work in craft, design and technology).

(2) Attendance at courses either within or outside school hours.

(3) Guided reading (literature surveys on areas of interest).

(4) Attendance at exhibitions (Reading Books for Reluctant Readers).

(5) Involvement on L.E.A. working parties to draw on experience gained in similar institutions (Science Curriculum Working Party).

(6) Teacher exchanges (in-depth experience of another teaching situation. We had a recent one day per week exchange of one of our infant teachers with a nursery school teacher).

(7) Research (a lecturer acting as external curriculum evaluator, using a case study approach).

To demonstrate the value of this range of options, I list some of the programmes which we have tackled at Colnbrook over the last three years, with varying degrees of success, together with the related training provisions we have been able to make.

(1) Revising the record-keeping and review system to support the demands of the 1981 Education Act, involving reviewing appropriate literature and setting up working parties.

(2) Establishing links with mainstream schools in our area to determine to what extent we could act as a "resource centre" for meeting special educational needs (D.E.S., 1978). Involving support from an outside agent in the form of the Schools Council and action-research. This has revealed a need for skills in working with

adults, to which the L.E.A. is responding by providing a course in interactional skills.

(3) Providing a new course for 16–19 year olds to meet demands for further education, as no suitable local provision was available, involving visits to schools and colleges.

(4) Investigating the use of micro-computers in special education involving research, a school-based mini-course run by an outside expert and involvement in an L.E.A. working party.

(5) Curriculum development, as already detailed.

(6) Developing closer working relationships with parents - involving staff working groups and the acquisition of counselling skills by all staff members. We were unable to find anyone to run a school-based course. Three staff members attended separate courses but because of the experiential nature of their learning they have not really been able to share this with the rest of the staff group.

A major benefit that can be derived secondarily from releasing individual staff members to study for advanced qualifications, is the focusing of their research on areas relevant to the school. Thus the Maths Co-ordinator wrote up a study of the curriculum development work he led in school, which involved a complete re-write of the Maths curriculum and associated recording system and cataloguing the supporting resources. The Communication Skills Co-ordinator similarly used her work on the language curriculum and another is currently working with children using the Turtle robot with our micro-computer and observing the part that it plays in fostering language development.

EVALUATION

Because of pressure to move on rapidly to the next development awaiting attention, this is the stage of the change process which is most often badly handled (Henderson, 1981). Very few teachers have any training in evaluation techniques; nonetheless they do need to look at how far they have been successful in their attempts at change. How they intend to do this should be discussed as part of the initial planning. It may be enough to build in some discussion sessions to look at problems after a new or revised area of the curriculum has run for a year. It may require quantitiative assessment to see if one method of teaching spelling in fact leads to more effective learning than the previous method. Effective in-school evaluation is probably a direct result of a school climate which has fostered discussion amongst staff members characterised by its openness and level of professional integrity. The head really has to lead by example in showing that there is nothing to lose by reflecting publicly on ways in which they themselves could have done things better, and encouraging such considerations by others. If this approach is regularly adopted in relation to minor changes, it becomes easier to use it in major evaluation exercises as well.

DIFFICULTIES

Even in a school where a pattern of in-service education is well established and which really does try to respond to genuine needs, there are continuing problems.

(1) Lack of time. All the activities I have discussed involve the investment of a large amount of individual time. In some ways the more active the staff members are on external courses, professional organisations etc., the more difficult it becomes to find times for productive meetings. We try to settle on one night in each week when all staff members will be involved in school, but this pattern is inevitably interrupted by teachers' centre courses or educational visits. Departments and working groups also try to schedule their meetings well in advance. Even at the beginning of a term, these commitments can make the school's diary look frighteningly full.

I have never been convinced that the end of a tiring working day is the most productive time for meetings. Teachers sharing this view have occasionally chosen to work together on Saturdays or during their holiday times because they feel that they achieve more in the same amount of time. This level of commitment is itself testimony to the extent to which they value their own development work, in helping them to do their job better. Teaching contracts in certain other countries extend their teachers' working days to include a number of days for their in-service education (in parts of Canada, for example, ten days are added). Such a development would, I feel sure, be welcomed by school management in this country as it would then be possible to plan in the expectation that all staff members would attend.

(2) Staff changes. Staff movement, particularly the promotion of enthusiastic and talented teachers, often means significant setbacks in areas of a school's development, e.g. a teacher with curricular responsibility for early language development is promoted before the new scheme has been implemented. Such disruptions can be alleviated by trying to have more than one person involved in all stages of change. In special schools, teachers usually take on more than one role such as teaching of two subjects (e.g. Craft and P.E.). It can be impossible to find similar combinations. Foresight on the part of the head, in making sure that there is never only one person involved in any subject area, can prevent some problems of this nature arising.

(3) Varying staff abilities. Different staff members have different levels of energy, of competence and indeed of interest in their work. For the sake of the children's education, the head must take responsibility for motivating and supporting all of them. As demands are being put upon schools to become more open and accountable institutions, the varying abilities of staff members are becoming more visible, and the head's need to compensate for weaknesses is correspondingly emphasised.

Motivation for each teacher will be different. Some are intrinsically motivated; others require extrinsic stimulus such as interest or praise; in some cases adopting a role to take account of individual ability, or helping teachers to set realistic professional goals for themselves in which their success is ensured, will help maintain a high level of effort.

I have often found it uncomfortable to respond to the individual expectations that staff members have of the role of the head, and consequently to behave differently and give varying amounts of attention to individual teachers. I now accept that you need a repertoire of interactive styles: "different strokes for different folks".

The motivation of the whole staff group can be adversely affected by badly planned or indeed over-ambitious INSET. Attempting innovation without sufficient staff consensus can also affect motivation. In our school we purchased a micro-computer three years ago, having convinced the L.E.A. and the parents that we would make full use of it; however, I did not spend sufficient time discussing with the staff the contribution that a computer could make across the curriculum, in teacher support and in administration. Teachers were not really convinced that it was a good use of school funds and it has taken a long time to begin to overcome the resistance caused by lack of preparation. Even this change occurred inadvertently when the time the computer could save in a burdensome administrative procedure was recognised by all teachers and their interest aroused.

Individuals have different levels of tolerance to stress. Innovation, insecurity, ambiguity and accountability all have different effects on individual teachers. Increased anxiety levels, while initially improving performance, produce diminishing returns after a while. Head teachers need to be aware of signs of stress in their colleagues, and indeed in themselves, and to develop techniques for dealing with them.

(4) External curriculum constraints. If they are to attempt to facilitate integration, special schools need to try to make the curriculum they offer as compatible as possible with that offered by mainstream schools. There are two obvious problems with this. The first is that special schools have links with a large number of mainstream schools and cannot even attempt to achieve curriculum compatibility with all of them. The second is that often the mainstream curriculum offered to pupils with special needs, particularly at secondary level, really is neither appropriate nor balanced and if special schools attempt to parallel it they may be forced to move away from the better aspects of special schooling. Dealing with these issues presents a need for in-service education which is shared by both mainstream and special schools.

(5) Multidisciplinary demands. Special school teachers have more direct involvement with members of other professions such as psychologists, doctors and social workers than do their mainstream counterparts. Successful contact requires that special school teachers learn to be sensitive to the different frames of reference of these other professions and skilled enough at case conference participation and report writing to make sure that their educational input commands respect. These considerations are expanded upon in Vic Thomson's chapter in this book.

(6) Restrictive systems. There is a danger in relying too heavily upon the organisational systems of a school to promote staff development. They can in fact be so inflexible that they prevent rather than promote individual development, e.g. by allowing a teacher no choice about the route through the curriculum for each child, or no choice in appropriate methods.

Devising a system which attains the optimum balance of flexibly supportive and structured elements is a task which must command the head teacher's closest attention. It is by no means easy. Not to do so will gainsay the school's claims to make individualised responses to the varied special needs presented by their pupils.

(7) Isolation. Special schools in the past were often educationally isolated. They were encouraged to see themselves as separate and specialised. Consequently it could be difficult to mobilise external support for INSET activities. It was understandable that an indifferent specialist adviser might not put helping the development of a curriculum for a very small number of pupils very high on his priority list. Special schools must work hard at developing and maintaining links with the advisory service and with mainstream schools to ensure that their needs are considered in the planning of INSET programmes.

(8) Financial constraints. All-round cutbacks in finance for education have inevitably affected INSET. The means for meeting individual needs have been limited by lack of full-time secondment in some L.E.A.s and by the closing of

residential centres. Teachers may no longer be able to get to an appropriate course. Although these changes have given an impetus to school-focused INSET, they have also limited the ways in which schools can get information. Similarly, lack of money has meant that a school such as ours is no longer able to keep its professional library up to date.

(9) External direction of issues. Increasingly, centralised control is removing some of the autonomy previously enjoyed by schools. Recently they have had to respond to the 1980 Publication of Information Act, and 6/81 Curriculum Circular and the 1981 Education Act and Regulations for its implementation. Such demands often do not fit in with the perception the staff have of their own needs and may interrupt the programmes that schools have worked hard to devise.

THE OUTLOOK

Notwithstanding these difficulties, the virtues of continuing the professional development of all staff members in any one school remain. It seems to me that practice bears out the theoretical advantages of a school-focused approach in achieving this objective. I believe these virtues include the following:

(1) Improved individual staff capabilities and thus improved school performance.

(2) Help in the motivation of teachers throughout their careers, hence maintaining a high level of involvement, and encouraging innovation born out of sound classroom practice.

(3) Improvement of overall ability to manage change.

Most important, to my mind, is the likelihood that teachers still learning themselves will be better teachers per se, as well as retaining the flexibility needed to respond to the dynamic processes of our post-inductional social evolution.

Chapter Thirteen

DEVELOPING EFFECTIVE TEAMS

by Richard Knight and Tony Bowers

WHAT IS A TEAM?

"Team" is an overworked term in many schools. In special education we hear it used in relation to "interdisciplinary teams", "support teams", "advisory teams", "curriculum development teams" and so on. In a lot of cases, though, they are simply what Payne (1982) has described as work groups. For him, a work group is of a lower order than a team; it exists whenever "people are brought into relationships with one another by virtue of the fact that they work together" (p. 5). Only when tasks or responsibilities are shared and the act of working together enhances the work that is done can a team be said to have formed.

Woodcock (1979), in a work devoted to improving team development, has identified the symptoms of bad teamwork. For him, a lack of adequate team formation, or indeed the absence of any true team activity, is characterised first by a lack of commitment and motivation; grumbling and retaliation are usual behaviours, and in a school context might be evidenced in private "moan" sessions in corridors, lavatories or in the staff car park, or in the silence which descends on the staff room when a senior staff member enters. Unhealthy competition, which may take various forms such as back-biting, influencing pupils to the detriment of a colleague, or keeping teaching resources within a classroom or department, is also an indicator of poor teamwork. The quality of meetings is another: if people look forward to the regular staff or group meetings, then teamwork is probably well developed; if they dread them, it is certainly not. The degree to which people help one another is also a sign of the extent to which a team has developed. As a rough rule of thumb, on going into a school, the expressions on the faces of staff - and in some cases of pupils - can be a good indicator of teamwork; if an effective team exists, then work will be an exciting and enjoyable place, and people's faces will reflect it.

Creating a team rather than accepting that an aggregation of individuals work together in a school or, if it is larger, in some or all of its departments, is a vital task of management. It is not surprising that the term "team" is used a lot; what is disappointing is that not all head teachers give much attention to creating what Francis and Young (1979) have described as "an energetic group of people who are committed to achieving common objectives, who work well together and enjoy doing so, and who produce high quality results" (p. 8). Indeed, the authors are familiar with some heads who take a pride in their "divide and rule" strategies. This chapter is not directed at them, other than to ask them to question what they are doing and for what purpose. It is, though, addressed to those whose values embrace the above definition and who see effective teamwork as of prime importance - the development of the service that they have to offer to children, their parents and the community.

LEADERSHIP STYLES

There is little doubt that the style of management exercised by key figures such as the head and deputy head of the school, and by others with responsibility for team functioning, will have an influence upon the development of the team. Unfortunately, it is not easy to identify a "right" style for all the different situations that may be found in a special educational setting.

A popular view of leadership behaviour is that it can be characterised either by concern for the task in hand or concern for relationships with colleagues and subordinates, or by behaviour corresponding to some intermediate stage between these extremes. The first is someone who tells others what to do, while the second shares responsibilities by involving others in planning and carrying out the task. Clearly, the "teller" is using an authoritarian style, based on the Theory X (McGregor, 1960) assumption that people are innately lazy and unreliable; the leader who shares responsibilities is using a democratic style based on the Theory Y assumption that people can be basically self-directed and creative at work if properly motivated. The second style has an immediate attraction, of course, to anyone planning team involvement. However, it should be remembered that simply sharing responsibility without sharing the power to take decisions - and make mistakes - is unlikely to motivate or to be seen for long as democratic. It is important to distinguish, too, between leaders who are democratic in style, giving their followers considerable freedom in their work, and those who are even further along the authoritarian-democratic continuum. Unfortunately, some special school heads have been there, demonstrating a laissez-faire style in which staff members can do whatever they want to do, no policies or procedures are established and no one attempts to influence anyone else.

The dichotomy between task-orientation and relationship orientation appears to be a somewhat false one: the two are not necessarily mutually exclusive. It has, though, been adopted by Fiedler (1967) and more recently examined by him in relation to educational management (Fiedler, 1979). Arguing that there is no "best" style, he has looked at the effectiveness of particular styles in relation to the particular situations in which a leader finds him- or herself. This situation can be plotted in three dimensions which correspond to the leader's personal relations with staff members, the degree to which the team's task has a clearly defined structure, and the power and authority that the leader's position provides. The most favourable situation for a head teacher or other staff member in a leadership role is one in which they are well-liked by group members, have a powerful position and are directing a well-defined job. An example might be a popular deputy head directing a group of classroom assistants in making visual display cards to accompany prepared audio-tapes. On the other hand, the most unfavourable situation for a leader is one in which he or she is disliked, has little position power and faces an unstructured task, such as an unpopular holder of a Scale 2(S) post endeavouring to co-ordinate language activities across the curriculum.

Having developed this model for classifying group situations, Fiedler (1967) has attempted to determine whether a task-oriented or a relationship-oriented style is most effective for any of the situations which may be encountered by a manager. Briefly, he has concluded that task-oriented (or autocratic) leaders tend to perform best in group situations that are either very favourable or very unfavourable; relationship-oriented (or democratic) leaders, on the other hand, tend to perform best when conditions are somewhere in between these extremes.

In an analysis of the effectiveness of educational management training, Sergiovanni (1979) has contended that it is difficult for a leader to shift between styles to suit the situation which he or she encounters. As an alternative, people with particular styles should be chosen after carefully looking at the situations that they are likely to face. The problem here, of course, is that situations themselves change: people leave, attitudes alter, working conditions become harder or easier. An appropriate style may quickly become inappropriate. What seems to be needed, if we accept the situational view, is the development of a greater degree of flexibility in using team leaders. Obviously, a large school provides greater opportunities for this, in that particular individuals can be chosen for a particular job and then moved on to another. In one special school in which one of the authors worked, particularly bad relationships had developed between the head of the Nursery department and other staff. The department head was paid on a low-scale post (low position power) and was unsure of what was expected of her (unstructured task). A more senior staff member, whose style was essentially authoritarian, took over to good effect, but quickly developed specific objectives for each child (high structure), paving the way for a Scale 3(S) staff member (medium position power) with a more democratic style to take over responsibility for the Nursery.

Rather than looking at one dimension of style, it is possible, as Stogdill (1974) does, to see concern for people and concern for the task in hand being complementary attributes. In other words, a team leader can care about getting the job done and also care about the welfare and satisfaction of the people with whom he or she works. Bowers and Mayes (1982) examined these two dimensions - "structure" and "consideration" - of leadership style in head and deputy head teachers in special schools and primary schools. Task orientation was not as pronounced in primary school leaders as it was in heads and deputies of special schools, perhaps reflecting the greater emphasis on behavioural objectives to which the latter have been exposed in recent years. What was of particular interest, though, was that significant differences between heads and deputies were found in the two types of schools. Whereas primary heads were more people-centred than their deputies, the reverse was true in special schools: deputies were higher. Similarly, special school deputies were more task-oriented than their heads, whereas primary heads exceeded their deputies on this dimension. Blake and Mouton (1978) view growth on similar dimensions as indicative of enhanced managerial skill; it is encouraging, therefore, to see the potential for effective team development which was possessed by the special school deputies in this sample. It is not suggested that these were innate qualities: one explanation is that the organisational demands of special schools (for an elaboration of these, see Chapter Eleven) render a greater degree of delegation of responsibility to deputies both possible and necessary.

TEAM BUILDING WITHIN A MULTIDISCIPLINARY SETTING

Work in special education should involve high levels of collaboration: collaboration with colleagues within the school setting, and collaboration with the many professionals coming into the school from other schools, other agencies or other services. Often, though, the school environment dictates an individualistic pattern of work where members of the staff team operate independently, carrying out their work in their own way in their own classroom or unit. Indeed, in teams where work is carried out individually, it is essential that high levels of planning are undertaken in order to allow the specialist pattern of work to operate, and to enable staff to be mutually supportive. Collaboration implies that individuals are committed to work within a team and share their skills with other members and other agencies. Each gives up some autonomy and self interest in the belief that the goals of the team are important and of course personally satisfying and rewarding. After all, teams exist in order to undertake tasks and without a task no team has a basis for existence.

As was noted at the start of this chapter, it is the team "atmosphere" which encourages people to work with each other with optimum activity and success in an enjoyable and relatively open way. There is often either an identifiable "good atmosphere" in a school or a "bad atmosphere". This atmosphere may well be the result of a combination of individuals' "personalities" and the physical environment; as such it can be modified. A crude summary of Herzberg's (1966) work suggests that what makes people happy at work is what they do; what makes people unhappy at work is the environment or situation in which they do it. It is relevant, in considering the need for team development, to ask: Are there symptoms of frustration present? Is there a lack of inspiration and motivation? Are there high levels of disharmony and frustration? Is there a lack of openness? Is a presence of unhealthy competition evident? Are staff actually looking depressed? Are meetings looked forward to or avoided? Is there trust and confidence in the senior staff? Does the school welcome outside assistance from other professionals such as advisers and psychologists, or is it defensive in its response to them?

Team building is in part about achieving a balance between conflicting interests. Essentially, the balance is achieved through bargaining and negotiation in which two or more parties agree to change their behaviour in exchange for some desired change on the part of the other. This process is not complete until any agreement can be written down in terms which include the agreed changes in practice/behaviour and make clear what each party is expected to alter in return. It is important to ensure that in negotiating for change, any hint of a win/lose situation should be avoided. Successful negotiation results in a win/win outcome.

NEGOTIATION FOR CHANGE

In a culture that seems to stress winning, it is no wonder that competitive behaviour persists where it is not appropriate. In so many staff meetings, members interrupt each other to introduce their own ideas; proposals are made which other members do not acknowledge; members support one programme against proponents of another. They are acting as competing individuals in a win/lose contest rather than a collaborative group.

Moreover, the win/lose contest may also be present within the institution in other ways. One department may strive for dominance over another, or there may be animosity between professional interest groups, such as care staff and teaching staff; time is diverted from the main issues requiring attention; sensitivity is decreased or destroyed, deadlocks are created; defensiveness and provocation result. Decisions and agreements result in a reduction of uncertainty for individuals, and also in a reduction of anxiety and ambiguity for the school's structure itself.

SETTING ABOUT IMPROVING TEAM WORK

Anyone in a leadership position must ask three initial questions:

(1) Do I think better team work will help us to work more effectively?

(2) Knowing that this will mean facing buried issues, am I prepared to try?

(3) Am I willing to spend time starting to work on these issues?

If the answer to any of these questions is "No", there is no point in looking deeper. If all the answers are "Yes", it is necessary to understand that teams go through a number of stages before they begin to work efficiently. The process involved in achieving efficient working is lengthy and entails dealing with many issues. Four main stages have been identified by Woodcock and Francis

(1981), during each of which clear characteristics will be exhibited. These four stages, although in some ways oversimplified, aid in the understanding of where a group is in the developmental process and the direction in which it needs to move.

STAGES IN TEAM DEVELOPMENT

(1) Unclear Objectives

In this stage people may talk together socially, but they do not work as a unified team. Staff tend not really to know each other or care greatly for one another. If mistakes are made, they are covered up. Outside "threats", such as parents' criticisms, are met with defensiveness. There is no common view of what needs to be done or how to approach doing what needs to be done.

(2) Increased openness

Here the group is organised and has a leader to pull the strings. "Taboo" subjects - for example, accepting parents in class - begin to be discussed, but one person is the mainstay of the group and he or she makes the decisions. Others may play limited parts, but look to the leader to make decisions and co-ordinate effort. Things are coming to life and the team is becoming potentially more effective. However, the group remains heavily dependent upon the leader and can only give a small amount of energy to unified working.

(3) Improved relationships

Here the team is untidy. They have tried the formal way of working (stage 2) but found it did not meet their needs, and as such the group is attempting to go deeper into the problems of working together and sorting out issues of personal relationships, principles and methods of operating, and factors surrounding cooperation. It involves honesty: honesty about each staff member's expectations of others and about their feelings in given situations; it also involves starting to share both physical resources such as equipment and materials and personal resources such as attention and time. This is an intermediate phase leading to the mature team.

(4) The mature team

Here leadership is decided by the needs of the situation rather than protocol. Teamwork is dependent on shared leadership - different individuals will lead at different times as appropriate. People talk about fundamental issues and openly express what is really on their minds. There is a commitment to group goals and commitment to joint problem solving. A good example of this movement towards the mature team within an educational environment is provided by David Weingast (1980); the mode of corporate involvement which he provides has many applications within the multi-perspective environment of the special school. The mature team realises it is part of a wider organisation and that continued success depends on continued development and collaboration at all levels, both internal and external to the organisation. This has clear implications for the special school which attempts to create links with mainstream schools and to work cooperatively with other agencies. Above all, the team is happy and work is a rewarding place to be and happiness is conducive to achievement.

Each one of the issues blocking mature group functioning has a great deal to do with communication. Poor communication is the result of a deeper malaise and cannot be fundamentally improved without treating the causes.

PLANNING THE WAY FORWARD

Issues now have to be identified, discussed, agreed upon, implications considered, a way forward agreed (plus time scale), and decisions made on how progress will be evaluated.

Consider the situation of the long-serving member of staff and the newly appointed deputy, who are having frequent disagreements over the work that was allocated by the latter to the former. The long-serving member of staff has insufficient knowledge of modern teaching methods and causes unnecessary problems by failing to follow priorities and targets as requested. The two air their dissatisfaction with one another's performance but no significant change occurs.

Consider the young teacher who complains of too close supervision by his department head; the teacher argues that his department head intervenes to change the way he has organised work for particular children and checks up with insulting frequency to see whether he is carrying out the department head's instructions. The young teacher is actively trying to obtain a post in another school because he feels he cannot do meaningful and creative work with so much interference from above. On the other hand the department head argues that the young teacher does promising work with the children but is secretive, unwilling to heed advice, and deviates from agreements they thought they had reached about how work should be carried out. The department head feels he has to spend far too much time checking up on the young teacher and is wondering whether his otherwise promising work is worth the trouble required to manage him.

Consider the situation when a new head teacher is appointed and is attempting to develop practice within a school which remains rooted in the past; where children are encouraged to be dependent rather than independent; where customs and traditions determine much of the school's activity. A third of the staff group are behind the new head, yet the other two-thirds pay only lip service to his requests for change and use every possible opportunity to subvert the head's wishes.

Consider the situation where an external agency - say, the Social Services Department or the Schools Psychological Service - is failing to keep its part in an agreement following a case conference on a particularly difficult child which leaves everyone in the school feeling angry with the lack of cooperation.

The following appear to be inherent in these four examples:

(1) No common agreement of approach.

(2) No accommodation of differences.

(3) No sharing/exploring of differing values.

(4) Group members may have personal objectives which have not been disclosed to the group.

(5) Limited collaboration.

(6) Varying levels of commitment.

(7) Subversion.

(8) Objectives not explicit.

OVERCOMING OBSTACLES

It is easy to talk of generating a climate of open and honest communication, trust and commitment; it is another matter to attempt to achieve these qualities. Without a lead from the top, it is unlikely that they can be approached. It has to be established in as clear a way as possible that they are the norms of behaviour within the team; in other words, they become part of "the way we do things around here".

The paths leading toward the creation of an effective team climate will vary according to circumstances. It is important to point out, though, that all will involve the dedication of time and energy and, in facing potentially uncomfortable issues, may not seem the easiest available option. Formal "team development" activities, so often presented in manuals (e.g. Woodcock, 1979; Francis and Young, 1979), are not always necessary. Provided that a leader can show by his or her words and deeds that a climate such as that described is desirable and helpful, and is prepared to give "space" to resolve issues as they occur, such avenues as a case conference, curriculum planning meeting or discussion of how to raise funds can be potent in developing effective teams.

Some important areas to bear in mind are:

(1) When reaching a decision on any topic, has agreement really been reached by everyone, or is there only an assumption that others agree? Focusing upon this in relation to special education team decisions, Ysseldyke et al (1982) have pointed out that effective decisions, in terms of their outcomes, involve consensus. Here every group member, however high or low their formal status, shows an understanding of the decision, has an opportunity to express feelings about the decision and publicly commits him or herself to carrying out the decision for a trial period.

(2) How clearly defined are the group's goals? Confusion regarding goals may lead to inefficient expenditure of time and energy, to members being at cross-purposes, and to frustration and conflict. Schwartz et al (1976) have described a sequence of goal-related activities that contribute to team effectiveness: (a) discussion of goals in specific terms that are understood by every member; (b) the team specifies a method of evaluating progress towards its goals; (c) the team modifies its behaviour on the basis of evaluating progress.

(3) How can we ensure that feedback is provided openly and positively? Giving and receiving feedback is a core element of effective team-building. So often, individuals define their job, their purpose and others' behaviour in terms that they can understand but which exclude the viewpoint of anyone else. By opening ourselves to feedback (information relating to the effects our behaviour has on others that we work with), we start to see ourselves as another team member might do. This can sometimes be an

uncomfortable experience; however, change in people and in working groups is never energised from complacency and comfort.

A team leader can assist in modelling appropriate provision of feedback - showing how to do it in a non-threatening way - and receiving it from others without reacting defensively. Ground-rules for feedback include: (a) asking for clarification and specific examples when given feedback; (b) listening to feedback rather than acting as though persecuted or reacting persecutingly; (c) "owning" what one says, through the use of the pronoun "I"; (d) focusing upon behaviour - what a person does - rather than personality - what a person is.

FACILITATING TEAMBUILDING

A procedure used by one of the authors in starting to enhance team development is briefly outlined below. The term "facilitator" refers to anyone who sets out to assist the group's growth by observing some of the points set out in the earlier section. This person may be a member of the team or in some cases may be an outside "consultant": a person brought in to assist in overcoming early blocks to the team's development. Such a role is common in industry and in other areas of the helping professions, but is not frequently seen as necessary within education. It is perhaps something to which professionals who link closely with schools, such as advisers and educational psychologists, should address the development of their own skills.

(1) A facilitator discusses the goals of the activity and gives a brief overview of the design.

(2) Team members pair off by selecting a person with whom they have not talked recently.

(3) The pairs interview each other on the topic "What problem situations should we work on in this team building session?" Interviews to last for five minutes each. No notes are to be taken (in order to increase listening skills). Interviewers to report back to the group members what their interviewee said.

(4) The facilitator lists problems (in members' own words). Each interviewee then "corrects the record" by adding things left out or by

adjusting any misrepresentations. (During this phase team members may respond only by asking questions for clarification.)

(5) The lists of problems are posted on the wall, duplicates are combined and then items given numbers.

(6) Each team member selects by number the three problems he believes are most important.

(7) The facilitator posts a new list of items with the highest frequency in the tally.

(8) Each participant is instructed to rank-order the problems/situations in terms of which is the most important.

(9) The facilitator tallies the ranks.

(10) The facilitator posts the final agenda on the wall and leads a discussion of reactions and asks for feedback.

The group will now move into the second stage of the agreed programme, which might include more interpersonal activity exercise, assignments, projects, courses and so on.

TO THE FACILITATOR

A major facet of team building is to help people discover their own potential and what they actually experience - whatever that experience may be. Some people's perceptions will seem strange and surprising; any judgement or scorn is a condemnation of the process and will not encourage openness. The facilitator must be able to stop judgement by others whether it is verbal or non-verbal. What our experience in team-building activities has repeatedly shown is that people are more capable, more intelligent, stronger and more able than either they and others believe. One of the aims of the facilitator is to keep people's attention focused on the goals and try to eliminate anything which interferes with this and respond sensitively to what is happening to people and between people.

It is helpful to bear in mind the personal elements that affect all relationships. These may be to do with the attitudes, prejudices, values and beliefs, and all the irrational elements that people bring into their relationships and incorporate in their positional roles. Some people may seem to be more supportive simply because of their cheerfulness, good nature, tolerance, patience, friendliness and possession of other valued qualities. Others may be seemingly consistently unsupportive because of their unreliability, avoidance of responsibility, intolerance and sheer inability to listen and attend to others' expressed needs. What has to be looked at is how people can make better use of the resources that they carry within themselves and become more aware of the impact their behaviour has on others. These issues should form an essential part not only of the basic team-building programme, but also of training for supervisory and managerial roles.

OPEN COMMUNICATION

The goal of open communication, which is at the root of good management, is hard to achieve. Nevertheless, the team-building process is a most effective way of approaching the resolution of "blockages" within any organisation and can change beliefs and attitudes of those involved. To aim to bypass the "rules" which have regulated an individual's communication style of a lifetime and instantly to establish open communication is unreasonable, especially as for the majority of us open communication is a new experience; it may take many weeks or months to overcome the fear of being misunderstood, judged, disliked, ostracised, and so on - all of which help determine our original defences and behavioural facade. The risks must be matched against the prospective gains. If these gains fail to materialise, the motivation to change will disappear; yet without open communication and involvement, learning and moving forward both as an individual and an organisation is virtually impossible. Open communication implies that anyone, including the senior manager, can be questioned regarding his or her statements and actions. This freedom to question anyone is mandatory if a school or any other organisation is to survive and grow.

In any attempt at open communication between team members, it is necessary to be aware of the subtle - and often unconscious - strategies that individuals are using to maintain old ways of relating and to prevent constructive growth within the team. One way into such an understanding is to look for the psychological games (Berne, 1964) which occur as part of an individual's struggle for control and which reflect his or her need to reinforce an established theory of life. Looking recently at the application of Transactional Analysis to special needs teams, Sewell (1982) has seen it as a valuable medium for allowing groups of staff to develop more open and trusting relationships among themselves.

A sample of the games which may be encountered, described in the terminology of Transactional Analysis, is provided below. The list is by no means exhaustive; there are many more.

(1) Kick me. Some people set themselves up to fail and to be criticised, for instance by not doing something they are expected to do. The self-styled "victim" is consequently rebuked or reprimanded and goes away to lick his or her wounds, feeling justified in maintaining a negative view of others, particularly those in authority roles.

(2) If it weren't for you ... Individual failure is excused as being outside the person's control. For example, "If it weren't for you wanting me to learn about microcomputers, I could spend more time on my record-keeping." The perception of unfair treatment justifies the person in feeling not responsible for the results which they achieve or fail to achieve.

(3) Yes, but ... Using this strategy, an individual appears reasonable but is, in fact, closed to suggestions. The response to any change goes something like, "I'd like to try this, but ..." with a seemingly acceptable reason for inactivity being provided.

(4) Blemish. This is a way of feeling good by demonstrating that others are less valuable. At school, the game may be played by anyone who sets out to destroy any suggestion for action by picking on a minor blemish and ignoring overall virtues which it possesses. Picking up and emphasising a spelling mistake in a case report, or an inaccurate reference in a curriculum document, are examples of blemishes.

(5) Let me help you. In this, the payoff for the individual derives from feeling more helpful, caring or self-denying than another. Sometimes there is considerable competition to see which person can show the most of these qualities.

(6) Wooden leg. Here a particular characteristic – accent, background, specificity of training, or

just plain "nervousness" - is used as a way of saying "With my problem I can't be expected to do well at this."

(7) Now I've got you, you son of a bitch. By finding an excuse to make others suffer, some people satisfy a need in themselves. Those who play this particular game often show considerable skill in waiting for a potential victim to make a mistake - even misleading them into making the mistake - and then pounce.

(8) I've got too much to do. In this game, a staff member will take on large amounts of extra work, spend almost every working hour in teaching, marking, preparing, writing up, attending meetings, and so on. Finally, by proving to themselves that they cannot cope, they receive a payoff of depression and self-justified non-contribution.

Although these and other games underlie many of the interactions between people, for a team to function really effectively there must be a high value placed upon authentic relationships. It is important that games of this nature should be recognised for what they are and purged from the currency of interactions. It should be remembered that they can be major distractors, since on the surface they are never about the real issues which underlie the presenting behaviours. An authentic team deals with real issues.

IN CONCLUSION

With an increasing emphasis being placed upon collaborative work, often between members of differing professional backgrounds with varying expectations about the importance of outcomes - for instance, between whether "education" or "treatment" are of greater significance - teambuilding must be a vital managerial concern within special education. Vic Thomson's chapter in this book serves further to reinforce this assertion.

It was pointed out at the start of this chapter that "team" is a word which is often used lightly. To create a truly cohesive, soundly functioning team requires a lot more than putting people together; it needs commitment and energy and requires of anyone in a leadership role the ability to look searchingly at their own style of relating to others and at the ways in which that style may be meeting their own needs rather than assisting their would-be team to grow. In short, teambuilding is a demanding and testing activity. Its results, though, in terms of harmonious working, cooperation, adaptability, problem-solving skills and commitment to decisions will eventually more than justify the attention it has received. We have found, both in courses and in consultancy work with schools, that it is eminently possible for people to change their ways of working; so often, though, we hear those in leadership positions despair of altering others' approaches or attitudes. It can be done, but not if it is seen as a one-way process; the starting point has to be that leader's own style and view of his or her own role as a manager. Through this understanding, the task of changing a work group into a team - of combining individual energies into corporate synergy - can most effectively begin.

REFERENCES

AINSCOW, M., BOND, J., GARDNER, J. and TWEDDLE, D.A. (1978) A new role for the special school. Special Education: Forward Trends 5, 1, 15-16.

AINSCOW, M. and TWEDDLE, D.A. (1979) Preventing Classroom Failure: An Objectives Approach. Chichester: Wiley.

AINSCOW, M. and TWEDDLE, D.A. (1981) The objectives approach: a progress report. In Taylor, R. (ed.) Ways and Means 2. Basingstoke: Globe.

BACON, W. (1976) School governors in Sheffield. Trend 2, 33-37.

BACON, W. (1978) Public Accountability and the Schooling System. London: Harper & Row.

BAILEY, T. and DE SOUZA, D. (1981) What do parents, governors and professionals consider to be the most important aims for children with severe learning difficulties? Apex, Journal of the British Institute of Mental Handicap 8, 130-131.

BALLARD, R. (1975) Special parents - special relations.- Special Education: Forward Trends 2, 3, 10-12.

BARNES, R. (1979) Bridging the thirty mile gap. Special Education: Forward Trends 6, 4, 21-22.

BARNSLEY SPECIAL EDUCATION TEAM (1981) A team approach to disruption. Special Education: Forward Trends 8, 1, 8-10.

BARON, G. (1981) Research in educational administration in Britain. In Barton, L. and Tomlinson, S. (eds.) Special Education: Policy, Practices and Social Issues. London: Harper & Row.

BARRY, C.H. and TYE, F. (1972) Running a School. London: Temple Smith.

BARTON, L. and MOODY, S. (1981) The value of parents to the E.S.N.(S) school: an examination. In Barton, L. and Tomlinson, S. (eds.) Special Education: Policy, Practices and Social Issues. London: Harper & Row.

BARTON, L. and TOMLINSON, S. (eds.) (1981) Special Education: Policy, Practices and Social Issues. London:

Harper & Row.
BAYLISS, S. (1982) Plain speaking - or status quo? Times Educational Supplement, 15.10.82, 23.
BENNETT, N. and GRAY, L. (1983) Governing bodies and the curriculum. School Organisation 3, 7-13.
BENNIS, W.G. (1972) The sociology of institutions or who sank the yellow submarine? Psychology Today, November, 112-120.
BERNE, E. (1964) Games People Play. New York: Grove.
BLAKE, R.R. and MOUTON, J.S. (1978) The New Managerial Grid. Houston: Gulf.
BOLTON, R. (1979) People Skills. Englewood Cliffs: Prentice-Hall.
BOOTH, T. (1982) Westhall School for children with learning difficulties. In Booth, T. and Statham, J. (eds.) (1982) The Nature of Special Education. London: Croom Helm.
BOOTH, T. and STATHAM, J. (eds.) (1982) The Nature of Special Education. London: Croom Helm.
BOWERS, A.J. (1980) Training teachers as managers. Special Education: Forward Trends 7, 4, 31-33.
BOWERS, A.J. and MAYES, J.K. (1982) Patterns of leadership in primary and special schools. Educational Research 24, 140-141.
BRENNAN, W.K. (1979) Curricular Needs of Slow Learners. London: Evans/Methuen.
BRENNAN, W.K. (1982) Changing Special Education. Milton Keynes: Open University.
BURGESS, T. and SOFER, A. (1978) The School Governors' and Managers' Handbook and Training Guide. London: Kogan Page.
BURNHAM, P.S. (1968) The deputy head. In Allen, B. (ed.) Headship in the 1970s. Oxford: Blackwell.
BURNS, T. and STALKER, G. (1966) The Management of Innovation. London: Tavistock.
CAMERON, M. (1983) The special school: rhetoric or reality? In Bowers, A.J. (ed.) Conference proceedings: "The Place of the Special School". Cambridge: Cambridge Institute of Education.
CHAZAN, M. (1964) The incidence and nature of maladjustment among children in schools for E.S.N. British Journal of Educational Psychology 34, 292-304.
CHIN, R. (1976) The utility of system models and developmental models for practitioners. In Bennis, W.G., Benne, K.D., Chin, R. and Corey, K.E. (eds.) The Planning of Change (3rd edition). New York: Holt, Rinehart & Winston.
COOK, J.M.E. and LEFFINGWELL, R.J. (1982) Stressors and remediation techniques for special educators. Exceptional Children 49, 54-59.
COULSON, A.A. (1976) The role of the primary head. In

Peters, R.S. The Role of the Head. London: Routledge & Kegan Paul.
COULSON, A.A. (1980) The role of the primary head. In Bush, T., Slatter, R., Goodey, J. and Riches, C. (eds.) Approaches to School Management. London: Harper & Row.
CRAFT, M., RAYNOR, J. and COHEN, J. (1967) Linking Home and School. London: Longman.
CUNNINGHAM, C.C. and JEFFREE, D.M. (1971) Working with Parents - Developing a Workshop Course for Parents of Young Mentally Handicapped Children. Manchester: National Society for Mentally Handicapped Children.
CUNNINGHAM, C.C. and JEFFREE, D.M. (1975) The organisation and structure of workshops for parents of mentally handicapped children. Bulletin of British Psychological Society 28, 405-411.
CUNNINGHAM, W.G. (1982) Teacher burnout: stylish fad or profound problem? Planning and Changing 12, 219-244.
CYSTER, R., CLIFT, P.S. and BATTLE, S. (1979) Parental Involvement in Primary Schools. London: N.F.E.R.
DALIN, P. (1978) Limits to Educational Change. London: Macmillan.
DAVIES, J.L. and LYONS, G. (1981) School governing bodies as agents of quality control. Educational Administration 9, 2, 28-43.
D.E.S. (1967) Children and their Primary Schools (The Plowden Report). London: H.M.S.O.
D.E.S. (1968) Teacher Parent Relations in Primary Schools. London: H.M.S.O.
D.E.S. (1972) Teacher Education and Training (The James Report). London: H.M.S.O.
D.E.S. (1977) The New Partnership for our Schools (The Taylor Report). London: H.M.S.O.
D.E.S. (1978) Special Educational Needs (The Warnock Report). London: H.M.S.O.
D.E.S. (1978a) Primary Education in England. London: H.M.S.O.
DESSENT, T. (1983) Who is responsible for children with special needs? In Booth, T. and Potts, P. (eds.) Integrating Special Education. Oxford: Blackwell.
D.H.S.S. (1976) Fit for the Future (The Court Report). London: H.M.S.O.
DILLEY, M. (1982) School governor - a personal view. What Next 1, 2, 7-8.
DOCKAR-DRYSDALE, B. (1971) The Management of Violence in Disturbed Children. London: Longman.
DONACHY, W. (1976) Parent participation in pre-school education. British Journal of Educational Psychology 46, 31-39.
DOUGLAS, J.W.B. (1964) The Home and the School. London: McGibbon & Kee.
DUFFEY, J.B. and FEDNER, M.L. (1978) Educational

diagnosis with instructional use. Exceptional Children 44, 246-251.
ETZIONE, A. (1961) A Comparative Analysis of Complex Organisations on Power, Involvement and their Correlates. New York: Free Press.
FIEDLER, F.E. (1967) A Theory of Leadership Effectiveness. New York: McGraw Hill.
FIEDLER, F.E. (1979) Responses to Sergiovanni. Educational Leadership 36, 394-396.
FISHER, D. (1980) ... if you ignore them long enough, they'll go away. Where 161, 30-31.
FRANCIS, D. and YOUNG, D. (1979) Improving Work Groups. San Diego: University Associates.
FRENCH, J.R.P. and RAVEN, B. (1960) The bases of social power. In Cartwright, D. and Zander, A.F. (eds.) Group Dynamics (2nd edition). Evanston, Illinois: Row, Peterson.
GEORGIADES, N.J. and PHILLIMORE, L. (1975) The myth of the hero-innovator and alternative strategies for organisational change. In Kiernan, C. and Woodford, F.P. (eds.) Behaviour Modification for the Severely Retarded. Amsterdam: Associated Scientific.
GROSS, N., GIAQUINTA, J.B. and BERNSTEIN, M. (1971) Implementing Organisational Innovations. New York: Harper & Row.
HALLMARK, N. and DESSENT, T. (1982) A special education service centre. Special Education: Forward Trends 9, 1, 6-8.
HALLMARK, N. (1983) A support service to primary schools. In Booth, T. and Potts, P. (eds.) Integrating Special Education. Oxford: Blackwell.
HALSEY, A.H., FLOUD, J. and ANDERSON, C.A. (1961) Education, Economy and Society. New York: Free Press.
HARLING, P. (1981) The primary head, how powerful is he? The Head 1, 6, 20-21.
HAVELOCK, R.G. (1970) A Guide to Innovation in Education. Michigan: University of Michigan.
HEGARTY, S. and POCKLINGTON, K. (1982) Integration in Action. Windsor: N.F.E.R./Nelson.
HENDERSON, E.S. (1978) The Evaluation of In-Service Teacher Training. London: Croom Helm.
HENDERSON, E.S. (1981) Evaluation, the missing link. In Donoughue, C. (ed.) In-service: The Teacher and the School. London: Kogan Page for the Open University.
HERSEY, P. and BLANCHARD, K.H. (1977) Management of Organizational Behavior: Utilising Human Resources (3rd edition). Englewood Cliffs: Prentice-Hall.
HERZBERG, F. (1966) Work and the Nature of Man. New York: World.
HUNT, S. (1975) Parents of the E.S.N. Manchester: National Elfrida Rathbone Society.
INNER LONDON EDUCATION AUTHORITY (1977) Keeping the

School Under Review. London: I.L.E.A.
INNER LONDON EDUCATION AUTHORITY (1979) School Governors Handbook. London: I.L.E.A.
JAY, A. (1980) Nobody's perfect - but a team can be. Observer Magazine, 20th April, 26-32.
KARP, H.B. (1983) The art of creative fighting. In Goodstein, L.D. and Pfeiffer, J.W. (eds.) The 1983 Annual for Facilitators, Trainers, and Consultants. San Diego: University Associates.
KELLEY, D. and CONNER, D.R. (1979) The emotional cycle of change. In Jones, J.E. and Pfeiffer, J.W. (eds.) The 1979 Annual Handbook for Group Facilitators. La Jolla, California: University Associates.
KELLY, C. (1982) Too important to leave to professionals. Times Educational Supplement, 15th October, 24.
KIRTON, M.J. (1977) Kirton Adaption-Innovation Inventory. Windsor: N.F.E.R.
KLEIN, D. (1976) Some notes on the dynamics of resistance to change: the defender role. In Bennis, W.G., Benne, K.D., Chin, R. and Corey, K.E. (eds.) The Planning of Change (3rd edition). New York: Holt, Rinehart & Winston.
KOGAN, M. and VAN DER EYKEN, W. (1973) County Hall: the Role of the Chief Education Officer. Harmondsworth: Penguin.
KOTTER, J.P. (1978) Power, success and organisational effectiveness. Organizational Dynamics 6, 26-40.
KYRIACOU, C. and SUTCLIFFE, J. (1978) Teacher stress: prevalence, sources and symptoms. British Journal of Educational Psychology 48, 299-306.
LAST, J. (1983) Call out the flying squad. Times Educational Supplement. 4th March, 23.
LAWRENCE, P.R. and LORSCH, J.W. (1967) Organization and Environment: Managing Differentiation and Integration. Boston: Harvard Business School.
LYNCH, J. and PIMLOTT, J. (1976) Teachers and Parents. London: Macmillan.
MACDONALD-ROSS, M. (1975) Behavioural objectives: a critical review. In Open University, Curriculum Design and Development Course Team, Curriculum Design. London: Croom Helm for the Open University.
MCGREENEY, P. (1969) Parents are Welcome. London: Longman.
MCGREGOR, D. (1960) The Human Side of Enterprise. New York: McGraw Hill.
MARGULIES, N. and RAIA, A.P. (1978) Conceptual Foundations of Organisational Development. New York: McGraw Hill.
MARRA, M.E. (1981) The incidence and nature of secondary handicaps among children in day ESN(M) special schools. Remedial Education 16, 89-94.
MARRA, M.E. (1982) How are you doing now? - a follow up

study of 48 ex-pupils of an ESN(M) day special school. Remedial Education 17, 115-118.
MASLACH, C. (1976) Burned-out. Human Behavior 5, 76-83.
MATTINGLY, M.A. (1977) Sources of stress and burn-out in professional child care work. Child Care Quarterly 6, 127-137.
MATTINGLY, M.A. (1979) Stress in work with children. Children in Contemporary Society 12, 21-24.
MATTINGLY, M.A. (1981) Occupational stress for group care personnel. In Ainsworth, F. and Fulcher, L.C. (eds.) Group Care for Children. London: Tavistock.
MAUND, D.J., POUNTNEY, G., SCRIVENER, T. and WARD, C. (1982) Management in the Primary School. Coventry: Coventry L.E.A.
MAYO, E. (1945) The Social Problems of an Industrial Civilization. New York: Macmillan.
MIDWINTER, E. (1972) Social Environment and the Urban School. London: Ward Lock.
MIDWINTER, E. (1973) Community education in the urban school. In Raynor, J. (ed.) Communities and the Young. London: Routledge & Kegan Paul.
MITTLER, P. (1979) Patterns of partnership between parents and professionals. Parents Voice 29, 2.
MITTLER, P. and MITTLER, H. (1982) Partnership with Parents. Warwick: National Council for Special Education.
MITTLER, P. and MCCONACHIE, H. (eds.) (1983) Parents, Professionals and Mentally Handicapped People: Approaches to Partnership. London: Croom Helm.
MORANT, R. (1981) In-service Education within the School. London: Unwin.
MORGAN, C. and HALL, V. (1982) What is the job of the secondary school head? Report, December 1982, 10-13.
MORRISH, I. (1976) Aspects of Educational Change. London: Unwin.
NATIONAL ASSOCIATION OF GOVERNORS AND MANAGERS (1975) School Governors and Managers: Some Facts and Figures. London: N.A.G.M.
NATIONAL ASSOCIATION OF GOVERNORS AND MANAGERS (1978) The Government of Special Schools. London: N.A.G.M.
NATIONAL UNION OF TEACHERS (1982) Teacher Governors. London: N.U.T.
NIAS, J. (1980) Leadership styles and job satisfaction in primary schools. In Bush, T., Slatter, R., Goodey, J. and Riches, C. (eds.) Approaches to School Management. London: Harper & Row.
OPEN UNIVERSITY. GOVERNING SCHOOLS COURSE TEAM (1981) Governing Schools. Milton Keynes: Open University Press.
OPPENHEIMER, R. (1955) Prospects in the arts and sciences. Perspectives U.S.A. 2, 10-11.
PACKWOOD, T. (1983) Helping the amateurs in a professional world. Education, 29 July, 86-87.

PAISEY, A. (1981) Organisation and Management in Schools: Perspectives for Practising Teachers. Harlow: Longman.
PASK, E. (1981) The Home School Worker at Town Thorns School. Coventry: Community Education Development Centre.
PAYNE, M. (1982) Working in Teams. London: Macmillan.
PETER, M. (1981) Editorial. Special Education: Forward Trends 8, 4, 5.
PIK, R. (1981) Confrontation and teacher support systems. In Gillham, B. (ed.) Problem Behaviour in the Secondary School. London: Croom Helm.
POSTER, C.D. (1976) School Decision Making: Educational Management in Secondary Schools. London: Heinemann.
PRING, R. (1982) Myths and manipulation. Times Educational Supplement, 15th October, 24.
PUGH, G. (1981) Parents as Partners. London: National Children's Bureau.
REE, H. (1968) The changed role of the head. In Allen, B. (ed.) Headship in the 1970s. Oxford: Blackwell.
RHINE, W.R. (1981) Making Schools More Effective. New York: Academic Press.
ROBINSON, W. (1979) How can we involve parents? Special Education: Forward Trends 16, 2, 13-15.
ROGERS, C. (1951) Client Centred Therapy: Its Current Practice, Implications and Theory. London: Constable.
ROSE, G. and MARSHALL, T.F. (1976) Counselling and School Social Work: an experimental study. London: Wiley.
RUSSELL, P. (1978) Warnock and after - a parent's view. Special Education: Forward Trends 5, 3, 29.
RUTTER, M., MAUGHAN, B., MORTIMORE, P. and OUSTON, J. (1979) Fifteen Thousand Hours. London: Open Books.
SADLER, P.J. (1975) Leadership style, confidence in management and job satisfaction. In Open University. Management in Education Course Team. Management in Education. London: Ward Lock.
SALLIS, J. (1979) School governors - partnership in practice. London: A.C.E.
SALLIS, J. (1981) A new framework for school governors. Where 171, 8-11.
SALVIA, J. and YSSELDYKE, J.E. (1978) Assessment in Special and Remedial Education. Boston: Houghton Mifflin.
SCHON, D.A. (1967) Technology and Change. New York: Delacorte.
SCHWARTZ, M., SMITH, N. and SCHMUCK, R. (1976) The Development of Educational Teams. Eugene, Oregon: Center for Educational Policy and Management.
SERGIOVANNI, T.S. (1979) Is leadership the next great train robbery? Educational Leadership 36, 388-394.
SEWELL, G. (1982) Reshaping Remedial Education. London: Croom Helm.
SHAW, S.F., BENSKY, J.M. and DIXON, B. (1981) Stress and Burnout: A Primer for Special Education and Special

Services Personnel. Washington: ERIC.
SHIELDS, R.W. (1962) A Cure for Delinquents. London: Heinemann.
SMITH, T. (1980) Parents and Pre-School. London: Grant McIntyre.
SPANOIL, L. and CAPUTO, G.G. (1979) Professional Burnout: a Personal Survival Kit. Lexington, Massachusetts: Human Services Associates.
SQUIBB, P. (1981) A theoretical structuralist approach to special education. In Barton, L. and Tomlinson, S. (eds.) Special Education: Policy, Practices and Social Issues. London: Harper & Row.
STEIN, A. and SUSSER, M. (1960) Families of dull children. Part II: Identifying family types and sub-cultures. Journal of Mental Science 106, 1290-1303.
STENHOUSE, L. (1975) An Introduction to Curriculum Research and Development. London: Heinemann.
STOGDILL, R.M. (1974) Handbook of Leadership. New York: Free Press.
SUTTON, A. (1981) The social role of educational psychology in the definition of educational sub-normality. In Barton, L. and Tomlinson, S. (eds.) Special Education: Policy, Practices and Social Issues. London: Harper & Row.
THOMAS, K.W. (1976) Conflict and conflict management. In Dunnette, M.D. (ed.) Handbook of Industrial and Organisational Psychology, Vol. II. Chicago: Rand McNally.
THOMPSON, D. and JONES, C. (1974) Towards integration. Special Education: Forward Trends 1, 1, 29-31.
THOMSON, V.J. (1983) A survey of the inter-professional aspects of the head's tasks in a special school. Unpublished M.Ed. Thesis, Bulmershe College of Higher Education.
TOMLINSON, S. (1981) Educational Subnormality: a Study in Decision Making. London: Routledge and Kegan Paul.
TOMLINSON, S. (1982) A Sociology of Special Education. London: Routledge & Kegan Paul.
TURNER, P. (1979) Three heads respond to Warnock. Special Education: Forward Trends 6, 3, 19.
WARD, C. (1977) The Bradford Grange Project: Headteachers Report. Unpublished.
WARD, C. (1979) Who involves whom? Special Education: Forward Trends 5, 6, 19-20.
WARWICK, D. (1975) School-Based In-Service Education. Edinburgh: Oliver & Boyd.
WATERS, D. (1979) Management and Headship in the Primary School. London: Ward Lock.
WEDELL, K. (1981) Concepts of special educational needs. Education Today, 31, 3-9.
WEDELL, K. and ROBERTS, J. (1983) Special education and research - a recent survey. Special Education: Forward Trends Research Supplement 9, 3, 19-24.

WEDGE, P. and PROSSER, H. (1973) Born to Fail. London: Arrow.
WEINGAST, D. (1980) Shared leadership: "The damn thing works". Educational Leadership 37, 502-505.
WELTON, J. (1982) Schools in a welfare network. Child: Care, Health and Development 8, 271-282.
WELTON, J., WEDELL, K. and VORHAUS, G. (1982) Meeting Special Educational Needs: The 1981 Act and Its Implications. London: Institute of Education.
WIDLAKE, P. (1980) Parents, Teachers and Social Workers in the Bradford Grange Project 1973-79. Unpublished.
WILLS, D. (1962) Throw Away Thy Rod. London: Gollancz.
WILSON, M.D. (1981) The Curriculum in Special Schools. London: Schools Council.
WOLFF, S. (1973) Children Under Stress. Harmondsworth: Pelican Books.
WOODCOCK, M. (1979) Team Development Manual. Farnborough: Gower.
WOODCOCK, M. and FRANCIS, D. (1981) Organisation Development Through Teambuilding. Farnborough: Gower.
WRAGG, E.C. and PARTINGTON, J.A. (1980) A Handbook for School Governors. London: Methuen.
YOUNG, P. (1979) What a headteacher needs to know. Special Education: Forward Trends 6, 4, 10-12.
YSSELDYKE, J.E., ALGOZZINE, B. and MITCHELL, J. (1982) Special education team decision making: an analysis of current practice. Personnel and Guidance Journal, 60, 308-313.

SUBJECT INDEX

accommodation 176
accountability 2, 98, 112, 124, 196
adapters 43
advisers 31, 33, 41, 90-92, 111, 173, 184, 203, 208
ancillary staff 54, 61, 106, 118, 172, 186
appraisal 186-188
assessment 7, 8, 14, 16, 19, 24-26, 37, 38, 41, 77, 106, 125, 182, 189, 191, 194
avoidance 175, 176, 211

boarding schools - see residential schools
burnout 49, 50

caretakers 118, 165, 168, 186
Castle School 86
categories 7, 8, 10, 19
Cavendish School 148
change 3, 26, 40-50, 76, 78, 80, 84, 114, 123, 124, 178, 185, 189, 191, 198, 203, 204, 208, 211
charisma 23, 80
collaboration 10, 17, 45, 46, 47, 48, 126, 175, 203, 207, 213
Colnbrook School 182-185, 190, 192
communication 44, 45, 60, 64, 124, 132-135, 206, 207, 211-213
community 3, 11, 25, 41, 56, 59, 60, 98, 100, 105, 107, 108, 139, 143, 200
competition 173-175, 204
compromise 176
computers 45, 111, 193, 196, 212

conflict 4, 26, 43, 48, 54, 56, 75, 78, 91, 95, 122-124, 132, 135, 159, 165, 172-179, 203, 208
confrontation 176-178
consultation 3, 30, 52, 53, 124
co-ordination 3, 55, 56
counselling 12, 57-59, 63, 193
Court Report 116, 117, 128
credibility 52, 65, 90, 184
criterion-referenced tests 26
curriculum 3, 4, 9, 10, 12-17, 19, 21-39, 40, 43, 65-67, 76, 78, 86, 94, 95, 97, 101-103, 106, 108-110, 114, 130, 175, 182-185, 189, 192-197, 201, 212

decisions 24, 35, 36, 51-54, 63, 67, 69, 71-78, 200, 205, 214
delegation 3, 51-53, 58, 124
delicate schools 101, 114
dependency 167-171, 188
deputy head(s) 44, 51, 52, 75, 77, 127, 183, 201, 202
discipline 107, 149, 159, 160, 174

Education Act, 1944 1, 7, 98, 100, 108
Education Act, 1970 1, 54
Education Act, 1980 99-101, 106, 115, 125
Education Act, 1981 1, 8, 9, 40, 56, 58, 67, 106, 107, 115, 116, 123, 125, 128, 198
education welfare officers 117, 141
educational psychologists 117, 141
emotion 68, 69, 205
emotional disturbance - see maladjustment
evaluation 23, 24, 32, 37-39, 48, 89, 184, 185, 193, 194, 207

feedback 50, 89, 188, 208, 209

gatekeepers 28
governors 3, 4, 98-114, 117, 118

head teacher's role 3, 21-39, 52-67, 77, 78, 81, 117, 124, 125, 128, 153-155,

	162, 178, 180, 185, 194-196, 200, 201, 213, 214
health services	11, 107, 118, 121, 161, 197
hearing impaired	7, 14
Heltwate School	85-87
hierarchy	67, 68, 71, 74, 154
innovation	21, 27, 28, 32, 34, 43, 44, 46, 49, 63, 66, 73. 78, 91, 94, 168, 192, 195, 197
innovators	34, 41, 43, 45, 53, 63-66
in-service education	4, 18, 21, 31, 41, 45, 46, 58, 60-62, 85, 87, 92, 181-199
integration	6, 9, 12, 16, 60, 84, 101, 108, 196
interviewing (parent)	152, 153, 161
interviewing (staff)	62, 186-188, 208-209
James Report	181
job description	33
job satisfaction - see satisfaction	
job specification	185
language disorders	106
leader behaviour	2, 200
leadership	3, 4, 21, 28, 50, 52, 67, 78, 95, 105, 162, 164, 173. 178, 188, 201, 213
leadership style	28, 30, 42, 53, 55, 173, 200-202, 213
literacy skills	14, 108
Longford School	86
maladjustment	12, 13, 15, 16, 85, 100, 101, 146, 148-163
management style - see leadership style	
meetings	35, 75, 98, 105, 126, 166, 175, 186, 194, 199, 203, 204
microteaching	191
moderate learning difficulties	13, 17, 54, 85, 129-147
morale	44, 46-48
motivation	27, 52, 54, 62, 63. 84, 105, 195, 196, 198-200, 203, 210
negotiation	70, 74, 92. 203, 204, 209

objectives 14, 24-26, 36-39, 44, 61, 67, 70, 71, 73. 74, 105, 134, 145, 169, 176, 183, 186, 189, 198, 200, 202, 205, 207

parents 4, 42, 46, 56-59, 88, 89, 100, 102, 104, 105, 107, 108, 112, 117-119, 129-147, 148, 149-163, 168, 192, 200, 205
physical disability 8, 13, 17, 25, 53, 87, 106, 156, 168, 169. 182
physiotherapists 118, 122, 173
Portage scheme 85, 86
power 53, 68, 73, 123, 154, 155, 165-170, 184, 200, 201
problem-solving 22, 55, 206, 210, 214

record-keeping 42, 182, 183, 212
reinforcement 35
residential schools 11, 12, 16, 19, 50, 100, 108, 141, 149, 162, 198, 204
resisters 27, 28, 34, 47-49, 196
resource centre 3, 8, 10, 16-18, 41, 83-97
resources 65, 85-88, 124, 182, 199, 205, 211
review - curriculum 185
review - pupil 32, 33, 36, 58, 106, 126, 184

satisfaction 30, 49, 167, 206
secretary 152
self esteem 48, 154
sensory disabilities 13, 17, 53, 87
severe learning difficulties 12, 14, 54, 87, 88, 114
social services 16, 100, 118, 119, 156, 207
social skills 14, 109
social workers 117, 141, 150, 153, 156, 157, 197
specific learning difficulties 12
special care 111, 114
speech therapists 31, 117, 118, 172, 173
staff council 54, 55, 72-78
staff development 61-63, 110, 180-197
staff recruitment and selection 43, 52, 53
statements 8, 11, 14, 106, 125, 126
stress 26, 49-50, 73, 80, 148, 196

support services 63, 91, 93, 199
Sweden 15
systems approach 122, 172

Taylor Report 99
task analysis 16, 36
team 4, 54, 56, 116-128, 155, 168, 189, 199, 200, 203, 204, 213
team development 50, 191, 199-214
therapy 7, 8, 11, 148, 158
time, use of 51, 52, 58, 62, 85, 141, 194, 195, 204, 208
training - see in-service education
Transactional Analysis 211-213

visual handicap 14
voluntary workers 60, 145, 146

Warnock Report 1, 2, 7, 8, 13, 16, 22, 61, 67, 82, 99. 100, 115, 116, 125, 129, 181
William Tyndale School 74, 108